SCOTLAND
UNDER MORTON
1572–80

SCOTLAND
UNDER MORTON
1572–80

George R. Hewitt

JOHN DONALD PUBLISHERS LTD
EDINBURGH

The publishers acknowledge the financial assistance of the
Scottish Arts Council in the publication of this volume.

ISBN 0 85976 0774

Filmset by R D Composition Ltd., Glasgow.
Printed by Bell & Bain Ltd., Glasgow.

Acknowledgements

I SHOULD like to thank Dr. Ian Cowan of the Scottish History Department, Glasgow University, for all his assistance. This book owes a great deal to his perceptive criticism and unfailing encouragement when he supervised my original thesis. My thanks are also due to the following: Dr. Ian Donnachie of the Open University for providing such excellent maps; Dr. James Kirk of the Scottish History Department, Glasgow University, for various helpful suggestions regarding Morton's relations with the kirk; Mrs. Mary Manchester, librarian of Baillie's Library, and her indefatigable assistant, Mr. Angus McPhee, not only for all their help but also for making their library the most congenial in which I have ever worked; Mrs. Christine Saunders for producing such a splendid typescript; my wife, Agnes, to whom this book is affectionately and gratefully dedicated.

The jacket illustration, of James Douglas, 4th Earl of Morton, is reproduced by permission of the Scottish National Portrait Gallery.

Contents

1
Morton's Earlier Career

James Douglas, fourth earl of Morton, was the second son of George Douglas, known as the master of Angus, who was a brother of Archibald, sixth earl of Angus. His mother was Elizabeth Douglas, the only daughter of David Douglas of Pittendreich near Elgin.[1] Morton, in a royal letter written to him when he was deposed in March, 1578, had his age given as 'past threescoir ane zeiris' which would suggest he was born around the year 1516.[2]

In 1543, his father, once he had recovered his own estates forfeited, like most other Douglas possessions, to king James V fifteen years previously, began to make arrangements for the marriage of his son to Elizabeth, youngest daughter of James, third earl of Morton. This nobleman had also suffered at the hands of the crown but Sir George Douglas, acting on his behalf – the third earl of Morton enjoyed indifferent health – managed to obtain the restoration of the Morton estates shortly after the completion of the marriage negotiations between the two families. Thus, by April, 1543, Morton's father, in return for a payment of £2,000, had not only contracted this marriage but had also ensured as part of the settlement that the whole earldom of Morton became the inheritance of his son and daughter-in-law.[3] The new heir to the earldom was known as the master of Morton until the death of his father-in-law which probably occurred at the end of 1548.[4] Certainly, by the middle of 1550, on his return from captivity in England, as his signature on certain documents confirms, he had adopted the title of earl of Morton.[5]

Morton's inheritance was an impressive one including, apart from his principal residences at Dalkeith and Aberdour, baronies and estates with various ecclesiastical and other privileges attached to them in such diverse counties as Perthshire, Fife, Lanarkshire, Dumfriesshire and the Stewartry of Kirkcudbright as well as in several parts of east and south-east Scotland.[6] Besides, in 1557, on the death of his elder brother David, seventh earl of

Angus, he became the guardian, or 'tutor', of his two-year-old son Archibald and, after a protracted contest with Margaret, countess of Lennox, he won the right to administer his nephew's widespread territories during his minority.[7] These comprised the regality of Bothwell and the formidable fortress of Tantallon with, in addition, the 'landis, lordschippis and baroneys' of Abernethy, Jedburgh forest, Bonkle, Preston, Douglas and Selkirk.[8]

There can be little doubt that it was the monetary benefits accruing from his guardianship of Angus, combined with his lucrative marriage, which later enabled Morton to be in a position, on certain occasions, to render financial assistance to the crown.[9] It also made it possible for him to undertake elaborate alterations at Dalkeith as well as construct a new residence at Drochil in Teviotdale.[10] This latter edifice, which was probably built in or around the year 1578, was unusually large by Scottish standards with its main rooms grouped on either side of a central corridor, suggesting French influence on the design. In all probability, the royal masons, whom Morton undoubtedly employed at Aberdour, were similarly engaged at Drochil.[11]

Of Morton's early life and career, very little is known. In 1528, king James V, having quarrelled with his uncle, the over-mighty Archibald, earl of Angus, had driven him and Morton's father into exile in England, but whether Morton himself actually suffered banishment as well is uncertain. His kinsman and biographer Hume of Godscroft, for example, states that, for the remainder of James V's reign, 'he lived obscurely and lurked for fear of the king'.[12] According to this authority, he sought shelter for a time with his cousin Douglas of Glenbervie and, thereafter, in the north of Scotland where he learned those skills later to be applied so judiciously in managing the Morton and Douglas estates. On the other hand, there does exist a charter granted in 1536 naming Morton as heir to his mother.[13] On the basis of this testimony, there is just as much justification for concluding that, in these years, he led a comparatively untroubled existence on the family lands at Pittendreich.[14]

If Morton's formative years are somewhat obscure, one facet of his character, namely his attitude towards England, was, by the early 1540s, becoming fairly apparent. In this connection, the example of his father who, while exiled, had served Henry VIII both as a diplomat and as a border official, obviously had considerable influence on him.[15] One of the first occasions when Morton, and also his brother David, displayed their anglophile sympathies occurred in 1544 over their custody of Tantallon. In that year, the earl of Hertford, invading Scotland on Henry VIII's behalf, was clandestinely informed by both brothers that they were not only prepared to surrender their castle to him but that they were also willing to join his army at Coldingham and serve under him.[16]

Nonetheless, Morton, at this stage in his career, was not totally committed to the English cause since, four years after the Tantallon affair, he was closely involved in the defence of Dalkeith against English forces commanded by lord Grey. With both Angus and his own father the recipients of French pensions since the beginning of 1546, paternal influence again seems to have dictated his actions in 1548.[17]

The Dalkeith episode which took place in June, 1548 also resulted in Morton being 'sore hurt on his thigh' and captured by the English.[18] Consequently, the greater part of the next two years was spent in English captivity. Certainly, he was still imprisoned in May, 1549 when, in the instructions given to the commissioners negotiating with England about the return of Anglo-Scottish prisoners, he was described as 'George Douglasse soone'.[19] However, there is a reference in the treasurer's accounts to the delivery of a letter to him in June, 1550 so he had obviously returned to Scotland by that date.[20] In fact, his release probably took place as a result of an agreement between the two countries signed two months earlier.

With the onset of the reformation a few years after his return, Morton, who had become a privy councillor in 1552,[21] began to be involved in the religious turmoil of the period. However, although he was a signatory in December, 1557 of the 'First Band',[22] a resolution binding the signatories to strive for the recognition of a reformed church, he, initially, was a lukewarm participant. Indeed, by all accounts, Morton pursued at this juncture a policy of vacillation which caused John Knox to observe that 'he promised to be ours but never did plainly join.'[23] Thus, on 1st August, 1559, for example, he was reported as 'suspected of the regent and has left court'; yet, three months later, on 17th November, Sir Ralph Sadler the English ambassador was notifying his superiors that Morton's desertion of the regent, Mary of Guise, was only a passing phase and that, before his departure, he had secretly rejoined the queen mother in Edinburgh castle.[24] Moreover, throughout the early months of 1560, Morton continued to behave in this equivocal manner, at one moment apparently supporting the regent's opponents but, on other occasions, seemingly on her side.[25] In fact, it was not until May of that year when he signed the ratification of the treaty of Berwick, ensuring English military and naval assistance for the reformers, that Morton committed himself wholeheartedly to the cause of the reformation.[26]

The kindliest interpretation for Morton's conduct in these months would be that he required the support of Mary of Guise in the dispute, mentioned previously, between Margaret, countess of Lennox and himself. He had, for instance, contracted a bond of manrent with the regent in 1557[27] and obviously he had no desire to antagonise her permanently by rashly joining her adversaries. In fact, his predicament was perceived by at least one of the leading members of the reformers, William Maitland of Lethington who, in a letter to the English secretary William Cecil in December, 1559, observed that Morton could be won over to their side if he was made aware of the regent's real intentions 'anent the earldom of Angus'.[28] Clearly, Lethington held a different opinion from Morton of what the regent was contemplating!

Morton's irresolution in the period before the reformation had no visibly harmful effect on his career and, once the religious changes – limited as they were – were accomplished in the summer of 1560, he quickly emerged as one of the leading noblemen in the kingdom. Thus, in August, having participated in the parliament held that month in Edinburgh, he was appointed a member of the council formed to administer the country during queen Mary's absence.[29] In addition, he was delegated to be one of the commissioners entrusted with the delicate and ambitious task of negotiating a marriage between James, earl of Arran, eldest son of the duke of Chatelherault and queen Elizabeth.[30] This latter mission was undertaken towards the end of the year and, in December, Morton, Alexander, earl of Glencairn and Lethington, the three Scottish commissioners, presented, unsuccessfully as it transpired, 'a motion of the lordes of Scotland for a mariag of the Quenes Majesty to the Erle of Arren'.[31]

Morton returned from his abortive embassy to London in January, 1561 in time to sign the first Book of Discipline, the kirk's optimistic blueprint of ecclesiastical reform.[32] Meanwhile, queen Mary, widowed by the death of her husband Francis II in December, 1560, was considering returning to her native land. Morton, on learning of this and obviously eager to win her favour, contacted her before she departed from France. In a letter written to her before she sailed for Scotland, he conveniently ignored his devious conduct with her mother, Mary of Guise, and claimed that 'from the time the said Queen mother received the regency I was ever with her in service.'[33] Obviously, Morton was determined to ensure that Mary's personal rule would see the advancement of his own position in the government.

Whether or not Mary was impressed by Morton's efforts at ingratiating himself with her, he certainly featured prominently in her administration after she returned in August, 1561. Thus, in November, for example, he was assisting James, earl of Moray, her half-brother and leading supporter, restore law and order on the turbulent borders.[34] A year later, he was at

Corrichie in Aberdeenshire serving the queen in the campaign against the rebellious earl of Huntly.[35] Moreover, on this expedition, according to Thomas Randolph, the English ambassador, a plot by Huntly's followers to assassinate Morton, Moray, Lethington and Sir John Bellenden of Auchnoule, the justice clerk, was thwarted by 'only the hand of God'.[36] Morton's loyalty in these months was duly rewarded on 7th January, 1563 when he was appointed chancellor in succession to the recently executed earl of Huntly.[37] The office of chancellor was a key post in the governmental system, and Morton now not only presided over meetings of the privy council and parliament but was also in charge of the great seal. This latter responsibility brought, in addition, certain financial rewards in the form of an official salary and the traditional fee for every document issued under the great seal.

For over three years after this appointment, Morton remained on good terms with Mary – a fact underlined, to some extent, by her confirmation of his earldom in June, 1564.[38] Furthermore, although he was originally unenthusiastic about the proposed marriage of the queen to Henry Stewart, lord Darnley, in 1565, his attitude altered and he subsequently approved of the match.[39] This *volte face* was, doubtless, due partly to the bonds of kinship between the two families – Darnley was an Angus Douglas on his mother's side – and the settlement of Morton's dispute with Darnley's mother, Margaret Douglas countess of Lennox. This affair hinged on the fact that the countess of Lennox, as the only daughter of Archibald, sixth earl of Angus, had been persistently claiming her father's possessions since his death in 1557.[40] Patently, she posed a distinct threat to Morton's guardianship of the Angus estates. According to one account, the countess had, in fact, been persuaded by Morton to surrender her claims when he was on his mission to England in 1560 but her husband Matthew, earl of Lennox, had repudiated the agreement.[41] However, in May, 1565, undoubtedly eager for the chancellor's support for her son's forthcoming marriage, she came to terms with Morton and, by a mutual contract between both parties, she renounced any title to the Angus inheritance.[42]

Consequently, during the months of August to October, 1565, when Moray and certain other noblemen attempted to overthrow Mary and Darnley in what has been termed the Chaseabout Raid, Morton remained loyal to Mary. Indeed, in October, the chancellor was in command of some of the royal forces pursuing the insurgents over the border.[43] Nonetheless, it would seem that Mary had her suspicions of Morton's ultimate intentions. Shortly afterwards, for example, she insisted on the delivery into her custody of the great Douglas stronghold of Tantallon, an action only explicable if she distrusted her chancellor.[44] In fact, her estimate of Morton's loyalty in these months was shared by Randolph who observed that Morton and certain others were merely endeavouring 'to mak fayer wether untyll it come to the pinche'.[45]

Undoubtedly, 'the pinche', or turning point, in Morton's relations with Mary came about as a result of his complicity in March, 1566 in the murder of David Riccio, the queen's Italian secretary. As far as Morton was concerned, there were several reasons why he should become implicated in this affair. In the first instance, like most of his compatriots, he must have disliked Riccio's growing influence with Mary, not to mention his being a foreigner and a Catholic. Mary's negotiations with Rome, for example, begun shortly after her brother's insurrection in 1565, could be cited, at least from a jaundiced standpoint, as evidence of her secretary's pernicious advice.[46] Again, there was the rumour that the queen intended depriving Morton of his chancellorship and bestowing it on her Italian confidant. While this was probably mere idle conjecture, Randolph, nonetheless, seems to have given it some credence as, on 6th March, 1566, he informed his government that Morton had incurred Mary's displeasure and that 'the seale is taken from hym and as some saye shalbe geven to keape to David as Rubie (i.e. rumour) had yt'.[47] Furthermore, the elimination of Riccio seems to have been secondary to the real purpose of the plot which, so it has been argued, involved Morton and the other conspirators winning the support of the feeble Darnley by the removal of the secretary of whom he was uncontrollably jealous.[48] In return, the queen's husband would prorogue the parliament scheduled for the 12th of March at which Morton was allegedly convinced that an act of revocation would deprive him of certain of his possessions.[49] Moreover, Moray and his followers, who had been summoned to attend and would undoubtedly have received sentences of attainder, would avoid the consequences of their rebellious actions. Unquestionably, therefore, there was every incentive to win Darnley's favour. Besides, there is also the distinct possibility that Morton envisaged the exiled Moray returning to head a government in which Darnley was a mere figurehead, and essential control of the kingdom was invested in Moray and himself.

Morton, accordingly, committed himself wholeheartedly to the conspiracy against Riccio, and was present in person on the evening when he was murdered.[50] But the assassins underestimated both Mary's power of recovery and Darnley's duplicity so that, within a fortnight, she had detached him from his fellow-conspirators and had him divulging everything about the affair to her. In addition, she succeeded in dividing her opponents by astutely offering pardons to the Chaseabout raiders while depriving Morton of his chancellorship and summoning him, with certain others involved in the Riccio murder, before the privy council.[51] This was the signal for Morton, realising his schemes had gone badly awry, to depart in company with another conspirator, Patrick, lord Ruthven, for Berwick. There, on 27th March, the two noblemen wrote to Cecil justifying their actions on the grounds that they had forestalled a parliament 'quhairin determination wes takin to have ruinated the haill nobilitie that then wer banissit in this realme and lykewyis a great number that then wer resident within the realme'.[52]

For the next nine months, although there was some talk at the end of May of his leaving for Flanders, Morton remained in exile in the north of England.[53] His continued presence there was not entirely welcome to Mary's government since he posed an obvious security problem and, in June, for example, precautions were taken lest he attempted to return to Scotland during the queen's confinement.[54] However, his banishment ended on Christmas eve, 1566 when he, and most of his accomplices, were granted a remission for their parts in the killing of Riccio.[55]

This repieve, according to the earl of Bedford then on a mission to Scotland, was largely the work of Moray, John, earl of Atholl and James, earl of Bothwell.[56] Indubitably, it was done for a purpose, and it was to be Bothwell who first encountered Morton, as he returned, at Whittingham in Berwickshire to present him with the details of the conspiracy against Darnley. If Morton's own version of the meeting is to be believed, he refused to become actively involved in the affair although, as he was to admit later, he made no effort to inform the victim about the intended plot. Furthermore, he did nothing to prevent one of his kinsmen, the notorious Archibald Douglas at whose residence the conversations with Bothwell took place, from participating in it.[57] Undoubtedly, a guarded reaction by Morton at this juncture is understandable, especially when it is recollected that he had only just returned from being exiled over the Riccio affair. Consequently, while there could have been no love lost between Darnley and himself, he could have had his reservations about being too deeply implicated in the conspiracy and preferred to await the outcome of events. At the same time, even if Bothwell's allegation that it was Morton rather than himself who was the leading conspirator can be discounted,[58] there is no gainsaying the fact that he was more deeply involved than he was ever prepared to admit. Indeed, Darnley's dying words, 'Have mercy on me kinsmen for the sake of Him who had mercy on all the world', are generally understood to mean that some of his assassins were Douglases.[59]

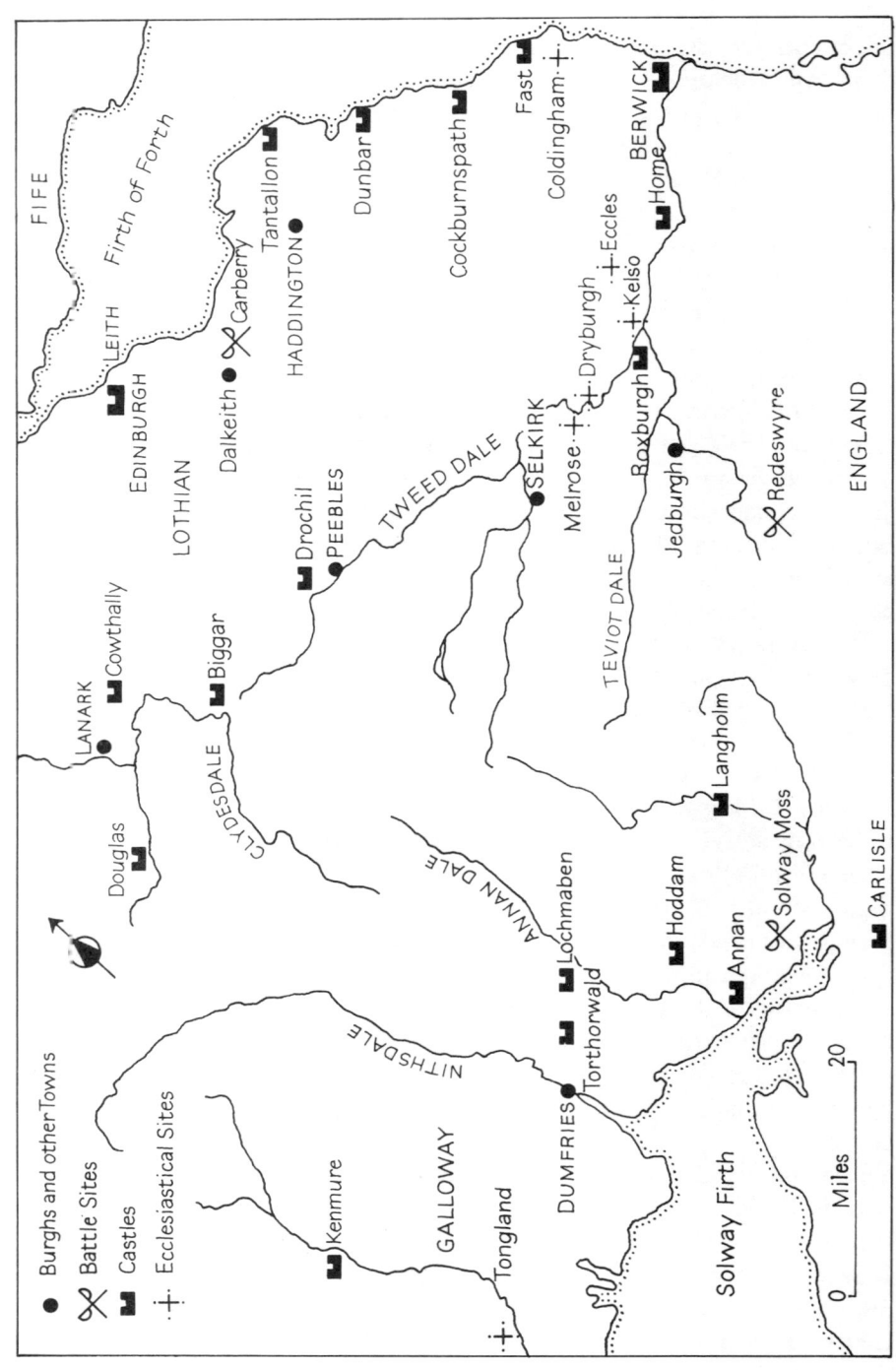

Burghs and other Towns •
Battle Sites ✗
Castles ◼
Ecclesiastical Sites +

FIFE

Firth of Forth

LEITH

EDINBURGH ◼

LOTHIAN

Dalkeith •

✗ Carberry

Tantallon ◼

HADDINGTON •

Dunbar ◼

Cockburnspath ◼

Fast ◼

Coldingham +

BERWICK ◼

Home ◼

Eccles +

Kelso +

Drochil ◼

PEEBLES •

TWEED DALE

SELKIRK •

Melrose +

Dryburgh +

Roxburgh ◼

Redeswyre ✗

ENGLAND

Jedburgh •

TEVIOT DALE

Cowthally ◼

Biggar ◼

LANARK •

CLYDESDALE

Douglas ◼

Langholm ◼

Solway Moss ✗

ANNAN DALE

Lochmaben ◼

Hoddam ◼

Annan ◼

CARLISLE ◼

Torthorwald ◼

NITHSDALE

GALLOWAY

DUMFRIES •

Solway Firth

Kenmure ◼

Tongland +

20

Miles

0

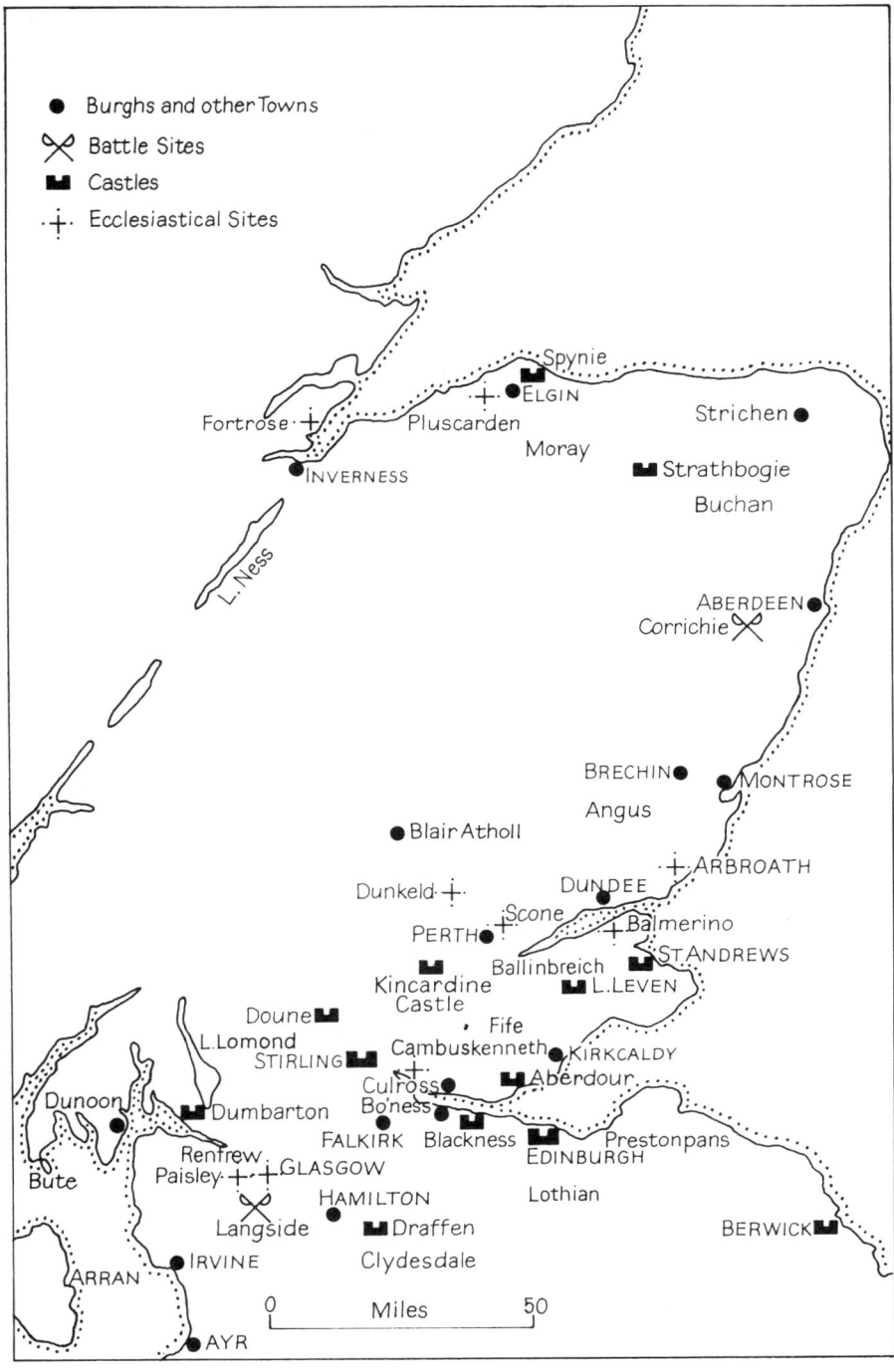

Burghs and other Towns
Battle Sites
Castles
Ecclesiastical Sites

Spynie
Elgin
Fortrose
Pluscarden
Moray
Strichen
Strathbogie
Buchan
Inverness
L. Ness
Aberdeen
Corrichie
Brechin
Montrose
Angus
Blair Atholl
Dunkeld
Dundee
Arbroath
Scone
Perth
Balmerino
St Andrews
Ballinbreich
Kincardine Castle
L. Leven
Fife
Doune
L. Lomond
Stirling
Cambuskenneth
Kirkcaldy
Culross
Aberdour
Dunoon
Dumbarton
Bo'ness
Falkirk
Blackness
Prestonpans
Renfrew
Paisley
Glasgow
Edinburgh
Lothian
Bute
Hamilton
Berwick
Langside
Draffen
Arran
Irvine
Clydesdale
Ayr
0 Miles 50

Whatever Morton's real part in the Darnley plot actually was, his overtly cautious behaviour did not prove disadvantageous as was underlined by the ratification of his earldom by parliament shortly after the Kirk o'Field explosion.[60] As for Morton's political allegiance after Darnley had been dispatched, he ostensibly lent his support to Bothwell, being one of the signatories, on 19th April, 1567, of what has been termed the 'Ainslie's Tavern Bond'.[61] This was a pact consenting to Bothwell's candidature for Mary's hand subscribed in an Edinburgh hostelry by Morton and several other distinguished noblemen. Yet subsequent developments would suggest that he and certain other magnates were only awaiting a suitable opportunity to wrest control of Mary from her paramour and, in all likelihood, compel her to abdicate. Bothwell's seizure of the queen, therefore, and his marriage to her shortly afterwards provided the pretext for a rebellion in which Morton undoubtedly played a conspicuous role.

The first instance of Morton revealing his true colours occurred at Stirling in May when he attended a convention of the disaffected nobility assembled to condemn Bothwell's actions.[62] Soon after this, he attempted, in company with Alexander, lord Home, to apprehend Mary and Bothwell at Borthwick castle near Edinburgh but the beleaguered pair successfully eluded them.[63] The next month, he was a member of the contingent of rebel lords who accepted the queen's surrender at Carberry, three miles southeast of Musselburgh.[64] Bothwell, on this occasion, perceiving, so it is said, the weak state of his forces, offered 'for triell of his innocencie' to settle the issue by single combat.[65] James Murray of Tullibardine and his brother William were the first to accept this challenge but they were rejected as unsuitable, Bothwell intimating that it was someone of Morton's eminence with whom he wished to do battle. Morton agreed to fight him, his only stipulation being that the contest should be fought on foot and with two-handed swords. However, at this point, Patrick, lord Lindsay intervened and convinced the other noblemen that he should represent their cause. Accordingly, Morton, doubtless secretly relieved that he was not having to fight someone much younger than himself, equipped Lindsay with the broadsword of his famous ancestor Archibald, fifth earl of Angus. But, at this juncture, Mary made the whole incident an anti-climax by refusing her permission for such an encounter and surrendering to her opponents.[66]

Mary's capitulation at Carberry was followed by her abdication on 24th July at Lochleven castle, the residence of Morton's cousin William Douglas of Lochleven. Undoubtedly, the queen's overthrow at Lochleven and the accession of the infant prince James was a significant milestone in Morton's career since it was from around this date that he began to consolidate his position as one of the most powerful men in the kingdom. Thus, on 29th July, he had a major role at the crowning of James at Stirling, taking the coronation oath on his behalf.[67] At the same time, his authority in the country was enhanced by his nomination as one of the council appointed to administer the state until Moray returned from France. Moreover, should the latter decline the offer of the regency made to him, Morton was designated one of the regents to govern in his stead.[68]

Further evidence of Morton's growing ascendancy during Moray's regency is provided by the various appointments which he received and the substantial acquisitions which he began to accumulate. In November, 1567, for instance, he was re-appointed chancellor and, less than a month later, he became sheriff of Dumbarton.[69] Shortly afterwards, in January, 1568, he took over the office of high admiral of Scotland – a position formerly held by Bothwell.[70] These were all appointments with lucrative possibilities but, in addition, he had also obtained, in August, 1567, the property of Sir Patrick Whitelaw of that ilk, denounced as a Darnley conspirator, and, the following month, the gift of the marriage of Sir Walter Scott of Branxholm, another perquisite of Bothwell's with obvious financial benefits.[71]

In May, 1568, when Mary's allies made their unsuccessful bid to restore her, Morton was a key figure on the king's side and, at the decisive battle of Langside, he commanded the vanguard of the royal army.[72] He was conspicuous too in the aftermath of this contest, accompanying Moray on his foray into south-west Scotland. This expedition, which assembled at Biggar on 10th June ostensibly 'for punyshinge of dysobedyent persons and theves', was more than just an ordinary judicial raid on the west march. Admittedly, some malefactors were arrested and punished but much of the effort expended was directed against Mary's adherents in this area. Gordon of Lochinvar, for example, had his fortress at Kenmure destroyed, while the garrison of Hoddam castle belonging to John, lord Herries, who was with the queen in England, was compelled to surrender. Morton's part in all this, besides occasionally commanding units sent 'to have drawen a chase on the theves and rebellis', was, as at Langside, to be in charge, along with lord Home, of the advance guard of the regent's forces.[73]

The army subjugating the west march dispersed at Peebles on 25th June but Morton's services were fairly soon to be required once again. This was at the enquiry instigated by queen Elizabeth into her exiled cousin's affairs. Accordingly, at the beginning of October, he and Moray were the two leading commissioners in the regent's party at the conference held at the dean of York's house in York to debate with representatives of Mary and Elizabeth the future of the former queen.[74] Morton, of course, possessed vital, if controversial, evidence in the shape of the celebrated casket letters which Mary's opponents alleged were incontrovertible evidence of her complicity in Darnley's murder. However, he was not able to reveal their contents officially until December when the commissioners were moved to Westminster for further discussions. Consequently, in a statement on 9th December, Morton described how, nearly eighteen months before, they had fallen into his hands. He had acquired them, so he declared, in Edinburgh on 19th June, 1567 when, having been informed that some of Bothwell's associates were present in the town, he had dispatched a number of his own henchmen to apprehend them. They had succeeded in capturing George Dalgleish, one of Bothwell's servants, who, on being interrogated, disclosed information which led, the next day, to the discovery under a bed in a house in the Potterrow of a silver box containing 'lettrez missives contractis sonettes and utheris writtes contenit therein'. Morton had retained this casket overnight but, the following day, in the presence of a number of noblemen and government officials, he had unveiled its contents.[75] Thus, the provenance of the letters having been outlined, their incriminating details were presented to the conference members.

Shortly before departing for England as a member of Moray's delegation, the regent had given Morton a receipt for this self-same casket which was described as 'overgilt with gold with all missive lettres, contractis or obligationis for mariage, sonets, or luif balletis . . . past betwix the Quene our said Soverane lordis moder and James sumtyme Erll Boithuile'.[76] Understandably, Morton and the others believed that these documents were their trump card against Mary and, consequently, they must have been bitterly disappointed at Queen Elizabeth's verdict when it was ultimately announced. The queen, so Cecil informed the Scottish commissioners on 10th January, 1569, had found nothing reprehensible in the conduct of Moray and his party but, at the same time, 'there had nothing beene sufficientlie produced nor showne by them against the Queen their soverane whereby the Queene of England should conceave or tak anie evill opinioun against the Queene her good sister, for anie thing yitt seene'.[77] It was with this inconclusive verdict that Morton and Moray returned at the end of January to Scotland and to a resumption of the civil war.

Moray's assassination at Linlithgow a year later resulted in an interregnum of approximately six months until, in July, 1570, the earl of Lennox, on queen Elizabeth's specific recommendation, became the new regent. In the interim, the two warring factions within the country had continued their internecine struggle, and Morton, as the head of the king's party, had given further evidence of his attachment to the English alliance by seeking

Elizabeth's assistance against his foes. Thus, in May, his own forces and an English one commanded by Sir William Drury, marshall of Berwick, had launched an attack on Hamilton territory in Clydesdale. The most spectacular incident in these operations was the destruction of the duke's palace and, in the neighbouring town of Hamilton, the razing of such buildings which, as Morton himself observed, 'we thought maist worthe to be brunte'.[78]

Lennox, in fact, was not an auspicious choice as regent, having little popular support and, within a year, had apparently alienated most of his councillors while Morton, on the other hand, was widely regarded as the person who ruled in the council.[79] The obvious question arises why, in the first place, he had backed Lennox's candidature instead of asserting his own obvious claims. The answer assuredly rests, to a large extent, on the fact that Morton still had doubts about his own strength. His failure, for example, shortly before Moray's death, to have Maitland of Lethington brought to trial in Edinburgh, largely because of the former secretary's powerful influence within the capital, must have given him grounds for acting cautiously.[80] Furthermore, it was to be another year yet before such outstanding figures as the earls of Argyll, Cassillis and Eglinton, along with lord Boyd, were to leave Mary and submit to the king's party.[81] For considerations such as these, Morton preferred waiting until he was absolutely certain the propitious moment had arrived. Similarly, in September, 1571, when Lennox was killed in a skirmish at Stirling and was succeeded by the ineffectual John, earl of Mar, Morton resisted the temptation of pressing his claims to the regency too forcibly.

Meanwhile, during these months, Morton was assiduously making further financial acquisitions to augment the not inconsiderable wealth which he already possessed. There was a wide variety of gifts from the crown in this period[82] but the most interesting is one supposedly given in April, 1571 as compensation for expenses incurred on another mission to England, *apropos* the fate of queen Mary, from which he had just returned. His reward on this occasion is said to have been the temporality of the archbishopric of St. Andrews.[83] This see had been vacant since 6th April, 1571 as a result of the execution at Dumbarton of the primate John Hamilton, a prominent Marian, who had been summarily hanged when the castle surrendered to the king's forces. Although there is no mention of such an award in the privy seal records, Morton, by his nomination in August of John Douglas for the vacancy, clearly exercised considerable influence in that diocese.[84] In September, 1571, for instance, he was assigned the lease for five years of the fruits of both the priories of St. Andrews and

Pittenweem,[85] and, unquestionably, his determined mind could have devised some means, albeit unofficially, of extracting its revenues for his own purposes.

At last, on 30th July, 1572, largely by virtue of Anglo-French mediation, a truce was signed between the two rival sides in the civil war, bringing a halt to the fighting which, in the last few months, had become increasingly ferocious. During this time, Morton was involved in two notable incidents. In the first of these, he was, so it was alleged, the intended victim of an assassination plot devised by none other than his kinsman Archibald Douglas in association with a servant called Thomas Binning. The latter, it was planned, should 'schote him with ane dag' but, fortunately for Morton, Binning's weapon proved unreliable and 'his piece faillit and misga'.[86] The complicity of Archibald Douglas in such a conspiracy must remain conjectural, although his involvement would not have been uncharacteristic. Certainly, he was imprisoned in Lochleven in May, although English enquiries about the reason for his incarceration produced the reply that it was a consequence of his being engaged in illicit correspondence overseas.[87]

The second episode concerning Morton in this period before the truce is the allegation in one contemporary account that he ill-treated and subsequently executed a minister who had the temerity to chastise him. Thus, according to the *Diurnal of Occurrents*, at the height of the bitter fighting of 1572 Morton had 'ane minister hangit in Leith and borne to jibbit because he was birsit with the battis'. This punishment was supposedly inflicted for having told Morton that 'he defendit ane unjust caus and that he wald repent quhen na tyme wes to repent'.[88] Admittedly, if Spottiswoode can be trusted, Morton, at this stage in the civil war, is said to have introduced the policy of not granting quarter to prisoners,[89] but that is a different matter from torturing someone so badly with the device called the boot that he had to be carried to the gallows. Indeed, there is no other reference to the deed, and its authenticity must remain very questionable.

One other matter resolved before the fighting temporarily ended was the fate of Thomas, earl of Northumberland. He had been a leading figure in the Northern rebellion of 1569 and had sought refuge in Scotland, only to be placed in the custody of William Douglas at Lochleven castle. Agreement about his return to stand trial for treason had been delayed by Morton's cousin driving a hard bargain about remuneration. Nonetheless, once the £2,000 he was seeking was guaranteed by the English government, the unfortunate earl was handed over, at the end of May, 1572, to Henry, lord Hunsdon, governor of Berwick.[90] Morton's part in all this, despite allegations by some authorities to the contrary,[91] would appear to have been minimal. It was Mar, for example, not Morton, who gave the instructions to Lochleven for Northumberland's release.[92] Furthermore, when Hunsdon's remarks that 'lord Morton was very much against the delivery of the earl'[93] are also taken into account, the charge that Morton betrayed Northumberland's trust in him has patently little substance to it.

Mar died suddenly on 28th October, 1572, and everything pointed to his successor being Morton. The latter, on the eve of becoming regent, was an extremely experienced royal councillor who, as chancellor, had enjoyed a privileged position at the council table. In addition, by his marriage, his tutelage of his nephew and his vigorous prosecution of his own interests, he had established himself as 'the wealthiest subject that had been in the kingdom for manie years'.[94] Although he could be provoked into violent action, as exemplified by his part in the murder of Riccio, his behaviour was more often characterised by a crafty caution rather than blundering impetuosity. His equivocal behaviour during the protestant revolution in 1559–60 or at the time of the Darnley conspiracy seems more typical of his nature. Besides acting circumspectly, Morton undoubtedly was becoming an increasingly prominent figure and had been the dominant person in Mar's administration – a fact well illustrated by an incident shortly before the latter's death. This occurred when Sir Henry Killigrew, the English ambassador, raised the subject with Mar of the possible return of queen Mary to Scotland, only to be informed by the regent that no decision could be given until he had heard Morton's opinion. This had prompted the acute comment from Killigrew to his superiors that 'Morton is the only man for her majesty to account of in this realm'.[95] That Elizabeth perceived this was unquestionably important, as a considerable amount of his confidence also stemmed from the knowledge of English support. This was the dividend for those anglophile sympathies which he had regularly displayed. In short, by November, 1572, Morton must have been convinced that the moment for which he had waited so patiently was now at hand and that he should accept the arduous and dangerous office of regent of Scotland.

Shortly before his election, Morton had a final deathbed conversation with John Knox. There had been one serious clash with the great reformer and his religious colleagues in 1571 over the nomination of John Douglas to St. Andrews but this controversy and certain other issues had been temporarily resolved at a conference held at Leith in January, 1572.[96] Now, at this last meeting, the dying Knox admonished the regent elect 'to use all thir benfites aricht and better in time to cum then ye have done in times bypast; first to Godis glorie to the furtherance of the evangle to the mainteanance of the kirke of God and his ministrie; nixt for the weill of the king, his realme and trew subjectis'.[97] Just to what extent Morton heeded, or was allowed to follow, this advice can only be judged in the light of his subsequent career, but clearly his first task was to consolidate his position and, if necessary, eliminate any factious opposition.

NOTES

1. Fraser, *Douglas*, ii, 298.
2. *Mort. Reg.*, i, 107.
3. Fraser, *Douglas*, ii, 166–67
4. There is a payment made 'afore his deces' in the treasury accounts for December, 1548, *T.A.* ix, 261.
5. *Laing Chrs.*, No. 580; *see* also *Scots Peerage*, vi, 361.
6. *Mort. Reg.*, ii, 276–80.
7. *R.S.S.*, v, No. 246; Calderwood, *History*, i, 327.
8. Fraser, *Douglas*, iii, 255–61.
9. *See* Chap. 8, 148-49.
10. Hume, *History*, ii, 239.
11. *R.C.A.H.M. (Peebleshire)*, ii, 223–29.
12. Hume, *History*, ii, 137–38.
13. *R.M.S.*, iii, No. 1541.
14. *See* Fraser, *Douglas*, ii, 298.
15. *Ibid*, 145–46.
16. *C.S.P. Henry VIII*, xix, pt. i, 213; *Maitland Misc.*, iv, 94–95, 98–99.
17. *C.S.P. Scot.*, i, 115; *Balcarres Papers*, i, 124–25.
18. *C.S.P. Scot.*, i, 118, 120.
19. *Ibid*, 175; Morton was imprisoned in the Tower along with his brother David, Robert, lord Maxwell and Robert Maule of Panmure, P.R.O. S.P. Dom. 10/5/10.
20. *T.A.*, ix, 422.
21. *R.P.C.*, i, 125.
22. Calderwood, *History*, i, 327.
23. Knox, *History*, i, 261–62.
24. *C.S.P. Scot.*, i, 236, 267.
25. E.g. *ibid*, 299, 349, 354 & 357.
26. *Ibid*, 403.
27. Donaldson, *James V – James VII*, 86.
28. *C.S.P. Scot.*, i, 279.
29. *Ibid*, 458.
30. *Ibid*, 465.
31. *Ibid*, 495–96.
32. Knox, *History*, i, 345.

33. *C.S.P. Scot.*, i, 528–31.
34. *Ibid*, 569.
35. *Ibid*, 662; *R.P.C.*, ii, 218–20.
36. *C.S.P. Scot.*, i, 668.
37. *R.S.S.*, v, No. 1186.
38. *R.M.S.*, iii, No. 1535.
39. *C.S.P. Scot.*, ii, 126.
40. Fraser, *Douglas*, ii, 323–25.
41. Hume, *History*, ii, 142.
42. *H.M.C.*, iii, App. 394; Fraser, *Douglas*, iii, 255–62.
43. *R.P.C.*, i, 379.
44. *Ibid*, 383.
45. *C.S.P. Scot.*, ii, 222.
46. Pollen, *Papal negotiations*, 232–34.
47. *C.S.P. Scot.*, ii, 264; Spottiswoode, *History*, ii, 35.
48. *See* Donaldson, *James V – James VII*, 121.
49. Melville, *Memoirs*, 148.
50. *C.S.P. Scot.*, ii, 270.
51. *R.S.S.*, v, No. 2696; *R.P.C.*, i, 436–37.
52. *C.S.P. Scot.*, ii, 271.
53. *Ibid*, 283–84.
54. *Ibid*, 289.
55. *R.S.S.*, v, No. 3149.
56. *C.S.P. Scot.*, ii, 308.
57. Bannatyne, *Memorials*, 317–20.
58. *Les Affaires du Conte de Boduel*, 12.
59. Pollen, *Papal Negotiations*, 369.
60. *A.P.S.*, ii, 562.
61. *C.S.P. Scot.*, ii, 322.
62. *Ibid*, 326.
63. Calderwood, *History*, ii, 361.
64. *C.S.P. Scot.*, ii, 332–33.
65. *Ibid*, 333.
66. Calderwood, *History*, 363–64.
67. *R.P.C.*, i, 542.
68. *Ibid*, 540–41.
69. *R.S.S.*, vi, Nos. 32 & 57.
70. *Ibid*, No. 92.
71. *Ibid*, Nos. 4 & 16.
72. *C.S.P. Scot.*, ii, 406, 408.
73. *Bannatyne Misc.*, i, 23, 25–27, 29; *Diurnal*, 132–33.
74. *C.S.P. Scot.*, ii, 576–77.
75. *Ibid*, 730–31.

76. *R.P.C.*, i, 641.
77. Calderwood, *History*, ii, 471–72.
78. *C.S.P. Scot.*, iii, 191–93.
79. *Ibid*, 633; *C.S.P. Foreign* (1569–71), 484–85.
80. *C.S.P. Scot.*, ii, 699–700; *Diurnal*, 148.
81. *C.S.P. Scot.*, iii, 642–43.
82. E.g. *R.S.S.*, vi, Nos. 1052 & 1112.
83. Calderwood, *History*, iii, 67; the text of Morton's speech to the English privy council is given in Trevor-Roper, 'George Buchanan and the Ancient Scottish Constitution', *E. H. R.* (Suppl. 3), 1966.
84. Calderwood, *History*, iii, 135.
85. *R.S.S.*, vi, No. 1285.
86. *Diurnal*, 292.
87. *C.S.P. Scot.*, iv, 235, 245, 252, 283.
88. *Diurnal*, 293.
89. Spottiswoode, *History*, ii, 174.
90. *C.S.P. Scot.*, iv, 198–99, 312.
91. *See* Spottiswoode, *History*, ii, 177; *Diurnal*, 298–99.
92. *Mort. Reg.*, ii, 74.
93. *C.S.P. Scot.*, iv, 313.
94. Calderwood, *History*, iii, 507.
95. *C.S.P. Scot.*, iv, 412–13.
96. *See* Chap. 6, 103-04.
97. Bannatyne, *Memorials*, 326.

2
The Conclusion of the Civil War

At Edinburgh, on Monday, 24th November, 1572 – the same day, in fact, as John Knox died – Morton was elected regent. The procedure adopted followed the precedent set at previous elections. Thus, when the nominations had been taken from among those present, the names of Morton and the earl of Glencairn went forward to a ballot in which the former was chosen 'be pluralitie of votes of the saidis estaittis'.[1] This 'pluralitie' comprised seven earls, three bishops, thirteen lords, nine commendators and over seventy lairds.[2] A closer examination of the composition of the convention would obviously be worthwhile if for no other reason than to determine how firmly those present were attached to the new regent.

Commencing with the earls who attended, Morton could really only definitely rely on his nephew Angus, his kinsman Robert Douglas, earl of Buchan, and William Cunningham, earl of Glencairn. Buchan, a son of Robert Douglas of Lochleven, owed his title to his marriage to Christina Stewart, countess of Buchan. He had been a loyal adherent of Moray and, on his assassination, had been appointed one of the four councillors entrusted with the administration of the kingdom. Glencairn, whose candidature had been a mere formality, was one of the earliest supporters of the reformation and, since Langside, he had been a prominent opponent of Mary.[3] However, if Morton could be sure of the allegiance of these three noblemen, he must have had his reservations about the affinities of the other earls who were present. David Lindsay, earl of Crawford, for example, belonged to a catholic family which had consistently supported Mary; Gilbert Kennedy, earl of Cassillis, was also a Marian who had been captured by the king's forces early in 1571 and had changed sides later that year in order to procure his release; John Graham, earl of Montrose, had, admittedly, always been on the side of king James VI throughout the civil war but rumour had it that he, in association with Cassillis and certain other magnates, would have preferred the earl of Argyll as regent instead of

Morton.[4] The latter, consequently, could not have placed a great deal of faith in the loyalty of any of this trio.

If support from some of the earls at the convention was, to say the least, questionable, there was, nonetheless, among the other peers, a group of half-a-dozen noblemen upon whom Morton could undoubtedly place much greater reliance. In this category were Alan, lord Cathcart, who had served on the royal council since the days of Moray's regency, John, lord Glamis who had a similar record of loyal service under king James VI, and Patrick, lord Lindsay who had been a leading advocate for Mary's deposition and who was shortly to become provost of Edinburgh – a sure indication of Morton's confidence in him. Andrew, lord Ochiltree, a noted supporter of the reformation who had been badly wounded at Langside fighting against Mary, William, lord Ruthven, royal treasurer since 1571, and Robert, lord Sempill, whose allegiance to Morton, at least in November, 1572, was underlined by his decision to name him as the tutor of his grandson during his minority, complete this coterie of Morton supporters.[5]

These, then, were the magnates whom Morton could consider as most trustworthy, but how committed to the king's and his own cause some of the others were must remain more conjectural. Although John, lord Herries did not attend, his son, William, master of Herries, did.[6] But, considering how his father had been one of Mary's most devoted followers and had, as a consequence, had his lands devastated on the instructions of Morton, it was unlikely that he was enthusiastic about the regent's election. Another nobleman present whose loyalty, at first glance, might seem suspect was Herries' nephew John, lord Maxwell. Yet, in his case, it should be remembered that he was related to the regent on his mother's side and, in addition, he had recently married Morton's niece. There was also Robert, lord Boyd, another ex-Marian. He had succeeded in becoming a privy councillor during the regency of the earl of Mar, and his subsequent acquisition of the regality of Glasgow, with the legal powers which such an award conferred, would indicate that Morton trusted him.[7] That still leaves lords Borthwick, Lovat, Sinclair, Somerville and Torphichen to be accounted for. While the motives of these more obscure individuals for being present could range from a dislike of the Hamilton or Huntly families to merely a desire to attach themselves to the side which seemed to be winning the civil war, their presence did imply a tacit acknowledgement of the new regime. They might have no great regard for Morton but at least they were prepared to accept him meanwhile.

At the same time, Morton had rather more support among the nobility than the number of noblemen present at the Edinburgh convention would tend to suggest. In other words, there were certain absentees whom he could reasonably assume were either on his side or were seriously considering joining it. In this category were William, lord Forbes and Alexander, lord Saltoun. Both families were enemies of the Gordons, especially lord Forbes, whose son had been a prisoner of Huntly's brother, Adam Gordon of Auchindoun, at Spynie castle since December, 1571.[8] In addition, there was William, master of Marischal, who had actually written to Morton confirming that he would 'obey and abyde to serve the Kinge and regent to be choisin' and that Andrew, master of Errol, would do likewise.[9]

Leaving aside the magnates, it must be conceded that Morton and the king's party had very limited support from the hierarchy of the church. In fact, only the archbishop of St. Andrews, in company with the bishops of Caithness and Orkney, were in attendance at Edinburgh and their presence was hardly unexpected. John Douglas, archbishop of St. Andrews, for example, was both a kinsman and a protégé of the regent whose candidature for the vacant primacy in 1571 had provoked controversy with the leaders of the kirk; Robert Stewart, bishop of Caithness, a brother of the regent Lennox, had always acted on the side of the reformers; Adam Bothwell, bishop of Orkney, was another ecclesiastic who had favoured the reformation and played a leading role in the government since 1567.[10]

If the bishops who attended were pretty predictable, the absence of the others can be readily attributed to two main causes. In some instances, it was loyalty to the Hamilton, Huntly or Argyll families, whereas, in others, their blatantly pro-Marian sympathies had compelled them to seek safety abroad. In the former category were William Gordon, bishop of Aberdeen, and his brother Alexander, bishop of Galloway, both of them uncles of the earl of Huntly; James Hamilton, bishop of Argyll, a natural brother of the duke of Chatelherault; James Paton, bishop of Dunkeld, and Alexander Campbell, bishop of Brechin, both of them clients of the earl of Argyll.[11] In the second group were James Beaton, archbishop of Glasgow and Mary's principal representative in France, William Chisholm, bishop of Dunblane, soon to be deprived of his see and, by 1572, the incumbent of a French bishopric, and John Leslie, bishop of Ross, imprisoned in the Tower for complicity in the Norfolk conspiracy.[12] However, the non-attendance of these prelates must have given Morton little cause for alarm. Unquestionably, much more important, as far as he was concerned, was the knowledge that he obviously had, at least for the time being, the backing of a much more significant and influential body, namely the ministers of the reformed kirk. In the latter's eyes, while not their ideal choice as regent, he did have the inestimable asset of being anti-Marian.

Although Morton, as in the case of the nobility and clergy, might have somewhat fewer members of the third estate present than might have been expected, some of the most important landowners, particularly from the Fife area, south-east and south-west Scotland, attended. The appearance, for instance, of such prominent borderers as James Hume of Colden-knowes, David Hume of Wedderburn, Sir Walter Ker of Cessford and his nephew Mark Ker, commendator of Newbattle, must have given the regent greater heart for the tasks which lay ahead of him. Likewise, he must have been heartened by the presence, from the south-west of Scotland, of such notable figures as Corry of Kelwood, Douglas of Drumlanrig, Jardine of Apelgirth and Kennedy of Bargeny. Unquestionably, these lairds and others like them had rallied to Morton for a variety of reasons. For some, like the Humes and the Kers, traditional enmity towards their rivals the Hepburns provided an additional incentive; for others, such as Bargeny and Drumlanrig, connected, respectively, to the Cassillis and Douglas families, it was clearly ties of kinship which prevailed. The motives of some of the others are less apparent, but the fact that Mary's cause was becoming an increasingly forlorn one could hardly have escaped the notice of most of them.

At the same time, if a comparison is made between those lairds who pledged their support for Mary in 1568 and those who appeared at the Edinburgh convention in 1572,[13] a feature of some significance which emerges is that only a handful of the earlier signatories are to be found at Morton's election. This, of course, is hardly surprising since some of them, like Gordon of Lochinvar and Ker of Ferniehirst, were still actively campaigning on Mary's behalf, whereas others such as Hepburn of Wauchton, Sinclair of Roslin, Blackadder of Tullialan and Brown of Colstoun were still under sentence of forfeiture for their allegiance to Mary.[14] Nonetheless, this comparison does serve to emphasise the divisions created within the country by the civil war as well as showing that the problems awaiting Morton in any attempt to unite the nation under him were formidable.

Finally, before ending discussion of the 1572 convention, it must be observed that there remains one group, namely the commissioners of the burghs, who have not yet been mentioned or considered. In fact, the burghs were strongly represented, and all the major towns in the kingdom, with the exception of Aberdeen (controlled by the Gordons), sent representatives. Patently, the burgesses wished to see an end to the economic dislocation produced by the civil war and regarded Morton as the person most likely to achieve this.

If Morton could be reasonably satisfied with the strength of his position in November, 1572, the same cannot be said of his opponents. By this date, their ranks were becoming decidedly thin – a consequence, undoubtedly, of Mary's imprisonment in England, and the assistance given by the English government to Morton and the king, not to mention the distinct hazards of remaining on the queen's side. Mary, indeed, was well aware of the difficulties attached to remaining one of her followers, as is evident from a letter written in May, 1571 to the earl of Cassillis before he deserted her. She realised, so she told him, that she was forfeiting his allegiance partly because he was afraid of his losing his possessions and partly 'be the crafty persuasonis of our enymeis'[15] Consequently, with John, lord Fleming the victim of a fatal leg wound accidentally sustained at Edinburgh castle in 1572, with James, lord Ogilvie overseas in France, and William, lord Livingston detained in England by Elizabeth,[16] Mary's principal followers were reduced to the representatives of the houses of Hamilton, Huntly and Atholl and the ever-faithful Seton family.

The head of the Hamiltons was James, second earl of Arran. Since 1549 – and this in itself epitomises a lifetime of devious political manoeuvring – he had also held the title of duke of Chatelherault, a French dukedom given to him by Henry II as a reward for his services. Chatelherault had a large family although only two of its members, John and Claud, his third and fifth sons, were politically active. Of the other male members of his house, his heir, James, third earl of Arran, the erstwhile suitor of queen Elizabeth, had been mentally unbalanced since 1562; Gavin, his second son, was dead, while David, the remaining offspring, suffered from a similar affliction to James. The Hamiltons, with a claim to the throne based on their ancestor James, lord Hamilton who had married Mary, a sister of James III, were next in line to the crown. Thus, they supported Mary both as heirs presumptive and because they also believed that, when she had been deposed in 1567, the duke should have become regent. Furthermore, there existed a bitter dispute between them and the Douglases over the custody of Arbroath abbey. The commendatorship of this benefice had originally been bestowed on Chatelherault's son John but, in 1568, much to the chagrin of the Hamiltons, it had been transferred to George Douglas, a natural son of Archibald, earl of Angus.[17]

Linked to the Hamiltons by his marriage to Anne, one of Chatelherault's daughters, was George Gordon, earl of Huntly. Although in the aftermath of Corrichie he and his brother, Adam Gordon of Auchindoun, had only just escaped the same fate as their father, his relations with Mary had subsequently improved considerably and latterly he had been chancellor in her government. In 1570, in recognition of his continuing loyalty to her, she had restored to him the hereditary appointment of lieutenant general of the north and, the following year, Huntly had played a leading part in the attack in Stirling which resulted in the death of regent Lennox.[18]

If the Hamiltons and the Gordons can be regarded as still actively engaged on Mary's behalf when Morton became regent, this can hardly be said of John Stewart, earl of Atholl. Although he adhered to the catholic faith and was also married to a sister of lord Fleming, he was remarkably inactive in the Marian cause. Indeed, by November, 1572, he gave the impression that he was waiting to see how Morton handled his opponents before committing himself any further.[19]

Lastly, among Mary's leading supporters, there is George, lord Seton and his family. He had been taken prisoner at Langside, fighting on the queen's side, and had subsequently gone to France where Mary had entrusted him with the formidable task of endeavouring to recruit military assistance from Scottish soldiers serving with Alva's forces in the Spanish Netherlands. By the latter part of 1572, he had returned to Edinburgh to become one of the main external sources of intelligence possessed by the Marians within the castle.[20]

So much for those noblemen whom Morton, at his accession to the regency, could clearly distinguish as adversaries of himself and the crown. Generally, the division between the rival sides was, in most instances, pretty clearly established. However, if the earls of Caithness and Sutherland are discounted, the former on the grounds that he was 'making always fair weather with those in authority', and the latter because he generally did as his domineering father-in-law told him,[21] there still remains one uncommitted figure of considerable importance, Archibald, earl of Argyll. A signatory of the Hamilton bond and officially in command of Mary's forces at Langside, Argyll, as it happens, had been prevented from participating in that contest by, at the last minute, becoming unwell. Thereafter, his loyalty to Mary had wavered and, ultimately, in 1571, he had submitted to Lennox's government.[22] Nonetheless, in November, 1572, at least according to Killigrew, the earl was the candidate of the queen's faction who, in the English ambassador's opinion, ensured 'there was great practice used to defer the election'.[23] In actual fact, once Morton was elected, any indecision on the part of Argyll was short-lived. Indubitably, he was influenced by several considerations, not least among these being the comparatively widespread support for the new regent, the prospect of being rewarded for his allegiance, and a desire to settle certain matrimonial problems which he had. Thus, in December, he attended the first meeting of the privy council and, a month later, was appointed chancellor with a grant of chamberlainry of the forfeited lands of the bishop of Dunkeld whose temporalities he had been collecting for the past year.[24] By April, 1573, Argyll was being described as the regent's right-hand man,[25] while, in June, in the first instance in Scottish legal history of a successful action on the grounds of desertion, he obtained a divorce in the Commissary court from his wife Jean, a half-sister of queen Mary.[26]

It has been seen that, in November, 1572, Mary's party consisted essentially of a number of disaffected noblemen to whom must be added the small garrison within Edinburgh castle commanded by Kirkcaldy of Grange. It was to be with Mary's noble followers that the regent's efforts at reconciliation were eventually to succeed.

On 10th December, Killigrew reported the possibility of talks between the new government and its leading opponents but the first meeting at Perth later that month proved unproductive. Apparently, only Atholl had met the English ambassador on the prescribed day, although Huntly did turn up afterwards. Nonetheless, by the end of January, by dint of further endeavours by Morton and Killigrew, a conference between the two sides was arranged to begin at Perth on 15th February, 1573.[27]

Morton, although he met Huntly shortly afterwards at Aberdour,[28] did not attend the negotiations which were presided over by the English ambassador. The regent was represented by Argyll, Boyd, Montrose, Ruthven, Robert Pitcairn, commendator of Dunfermline, the secretary, and Sir John Bellenden of Auchnoule, the justice clerk, while acting for the other side were Huntly and Chatelherault's son, lord John.[29] Obviously Morton hoped for a successful outcome to the Perth talks although, if they broke down, he had, as he announced beforehand, contingency plans ready. Thus, in such an eventuality, an expedition, scheduled to assemble at Brechin on 1st March and at Aberdeen two days later, would depart under his command with the avowed purpose of 'the establissing of justice and reduceing of the saidis dissobedient subjectis to thair dew obedience'.[30] This proclamation was undoubtedly a bluff – it was highly unlikely, for instance, that Morton would consider such a venture so long as Edinburgh castle remained intact – and what he had clearly done was to issue a stern warning in order to make Huntly and the others have second thoughts about rejecting his terms. In this aim he was successful, since an agreement was eventually reached at Perth.

By the main provisions of the settlement, the Hamilton and Huntly families, with their followers, must promise religious conformity, must recognise Morton as lawful regent, confess previous misdemeanours, agree

to eschew any support of the king's enemies, return all property seized by
them as well as prisoners still in their hands, and dismiss their respective
forces. In return, the leading members of the two houses, with most of their
adherents, would have all legal measures taken against them since 15th
June, 1567 declared null and void. In addition, they would have all their
lands restored and certain individuals, notably John Hamilton, the former
archbishop of St. Andrews, and Gavin Hamilton, erstwhile commendator
of Kilwinning, along with certain others previously denounced as rebels,
would be rehabilitated and all criminal offences forgiven except involvement in the murder of Moray or Lennox. This last matter and the question
of fruits and moveables taken since June, 1567, 'quhilkis are materis of sic
wecht and importance as the said Lord Regent of himself cannot con-
venientlie remit them', were to receive the arbitration of queen Elizabeth. If
remission was granted, it would be confirmed by act of Parliament. Regarding thirds of benefices and other matters affecting the kirk, the regent
would seek the advice of the general assembly. Disputes arising from the
settlement north of the Tay would receive the mediation of Glamis,
Montrose and Sir John Wishart of Pittarro while, in the southern half of the
kingdom, this task would be undertaken by Boyd, Mark Ker, commendator
of Newbattle, and Sir John Bellenden of Auchnoule.[31]

Although Atholl was not included in the Perth concordat, this was of
lesser importance now that his principal colleagues were detached from
him.[32] Moreover, he was to submit to the regent's authority in April when
he made a fleeting appearance in Edinburgh.[33] Even if this was merely a
token gesture since, in one contemporary estimate 'na man could judge
whais faction he inclynit maist unto',[34] Morton could not have been unduly
worried whether the earl was sincere or not. His main concern had been to
eliminate the threat from the Hamilton and Huntly nexus and, with the
completion of the negotiations at Perth, he was now in a position to concentrate on the sole remaining bastion of the Marians – the garrison of
Edinburgh castle.

Inside the fortress, Mary's cause was principally upheld by Sir William
Kirkcaldy of Grange and William Maitland of Lethington. Kirkcaldy was a
very able and experienced soldier who had initially fought on the king's side
and had been given the custody of Edinburgh castle by the royal government. However, after Lethington had sought refuge with him in September, 1569, he had subsequently changed sides and, in 1573, commanded, on
Mary's behalf, a garrison of about a hundred and sixty soldiers. His defec-
tion had infuriated, among many others, John Knox who had prophesised,
with considerable prescience as it so happened, that Grange's reward for his

treachery would be to 'hang from a gallows in the face of the sun'.[35]

Maitland of Lethington, who had been secretary during Mary's personal rule, had joined her opponents at the time of her marriage to Bothwell. But he had disapproved of her deposition which he believed would impair Anglo-Scottish relations and, by 1569, he was vigorously canvassing the proposition that the queen should divorce her third husband. His efforts at winning support for this proposal had antagonised Moray but, when the regent had attempted, in September, 1569, to have him arrested, he had been thwarted by Kirkcaldy's offer of protection. Since 1571 he had been lodged in Edinburgh castle, bedridden and in rapidly deteriorating health.[36]

The other individuals of any consequence within the castle were John Maitland, Alexander, lord Home, Robert Melville of Murdocairnie, Robert Crichton, and the governor of the castle, Henry Echling of Pittadro. Maitland was the former secretary's younger brother, destined in later life for high office under James VI, and, until his forfeiture in 1571, keeper of the privy seal and commendator of Coldingham.[37] Lord Home had fought on the side of the crown at Langside, sustaining facial and leg wounds in the process, but, in 1569, had transferred his allegiance to Mary. Following the capture in 1570 of Home castle by English forces pursuing fugitives of the Northern rebellion, he had joined the queen's faction in Edinburgh. The next year, accompanied by his wife and stepson, Robert Logan of Restalrig, he had entered the castle.[38] Melville of Murdocairnie, whose brother, Sir James Melville, the memoirist, had not joined the 'castilians', was, at this stage in his long career as a diplomatist, closely associated with both Mary and Lethington, having joined the latter in the castle about the same time as lord Home.[39] Robert Crichton was a former bishop of Dunkeld whose religious and political sympathies had resulted in his being deprived of his see in 1571 and left him with little alternative to enlisting with Grange and Lethington.[40]

Before the fighting restarted on 1st January, 1573, Morton offered Grange and the others the same terms as Mar had proposed when he was regent. Such a settlement would have restored all forfeited lands and possessions as well as producing an agreement similar to that subsequently formulated at Perth.[41] However, according to Sir James Melville, who acted as Morton's envoy in these negotiations, the regent insisted that it was to be a unilateral treaty excluding Grange's allies outside the castle. The reason for this stipulation, so Melville alleges, is that Morton felt the Hamilton and Huntly factions had committed 'great wrangis and extortions' and deserved to be punished. Furthermore, there were richer pickings to be had from these noble families than from Grange and his colleagues 'that have nother sa gret landis nor escheitis for us to wonne and for to be the reward of our laboures'.[42] But Grange, so Melville concludes in his account of the proceedings, was unhappy about deserting his confederates, and also sought to retain the castle for a further period of six months to prove that, despite 'wrang reportis and practises the ministers wer sterit up to cry out and preach against him', he was a man of honour.[43]

Obviously, it would be inadvisable to place too much reliance on Melville's version of the negotiations written, as it happens, many years afterwards. Indeed, the existing correspondence between Morton and Grange indicates that Melville has omitted at least one important detail, namely Grange's insistence on having 'the acts and deeds on either side . . . put into oblivion'. Not surprisingly, Morton baulked at the extent of this 'oblivioun desirit be the adversaris'.[44] In short, he was prepared to grant the leading 'castilians' a royal pardon for their actions but the question of satisfaction for all those parties who had claims against them as a result of the civil war was one which they would have to resolve themselves.

Thus, with attempts at a settlement between the two sides having broken down, Morton proceeded to take the necessary steps for the investment of the castle and, on 1st January, 1573, Grange signalled the resumption of hostilities by a bombardment of the town.[45] The fish market, according to one account, was the main target of the opening salvo with one person killed, several injured and 'the fishis blawin sa heich in the ayre that thay war sene to fall upoun the tops of heich houssis and sum of thayme to fall on the streits in great aboundance'.[46] The regent's official reason for ending the abstinence, as stated in a broadsheet published in January, was the garrison's rejection of 'all honest and equitable conditions'. Malpractices which were specifically condemned were the constant issue of 'counterfait and adulerat' coins and their provisioning of the castle far in excess of immediate needs.[47] At the same time, Morton was undoubtedly perturbed by the fear that there might be French intervention on Grange's behalf which could revive the Marian cause throughout Scotland. Consequently, if a satisfactory settlement was unobtainable, he wanted to see the castle taken as quickly as possible.

Nonetheless, on 27th March, Grange and company were offered similar terms to those recently accepted by Hamilton and Huntly at Perth.[48] This was at the request of Killigrew who was pointedly informed by Morton that he personally was reluctant to give the garrison another opportunity to surrender on favourable conditions since his own supporters disliked the generosity of the Perth agreement and were unwilling to make further sacrifices by which 'they should lose or render those livings of others which they possess'.[49] But the regent, of course, was only too conscious of the fact that he was dependent on English assistance and that there was really no alternative to acceding to Killigrew's request for one further effort at a peaceful solution.

Initially, on 27th March, Nicholas Errington, an agent employed by the English ambassador, was dispatched to the castle with full details of the Perth agreement but Grange insisted that there still remained 'some hard and dark points' which required further discussion.[50] Accordingly, on the 5th and 6th of April, Andrew, earl of Rothes, a nobleman generally regarded as sympathetic towards Grange and the Marians, entered the castle in the rôle of a mediator between the two sides.[51] However, Rothes' mission was no more successful than previous attempts, since Grange now insisted on a deal which included the payment of all his own debts, his retention of Blackness castle, an English guarantee of his life and an assurance, in the case of the queen's jewels that 'the said lord of Grange sall not be countable thairfore nor chargeit in ony sort to make reknying or deliverance of the same or any part thairof to ony persoun bot onelie to hir self'. Moreover, this was not all. Grange also sought the return of properties which had formerly belonged to his colleagues and himself. This latter demand would have entailed the English government restoring Home and Fast castles to lord Home, Morton surrendering control, in Fife, of Grange, Tyrie and Woodfield, Glamis renouncing possession of Kinghorn, north Pettudy and Bawbardie, Robert Pitcairn, commendator of Dunfermline, returning East Quarter to Murdocairnie and Sir James Balfour of Pittendreich dropping a lucrative action for damages against Grange's supporters in connection with St. Andrews castle. When these requests and the additional stipulation that the castle itself should be placed in the custody of Rothes are taken into account, it is not surprising that the negotiations ended in stalemate.[52]

The 'castilians' had been presented with the last opportunity of an honourable surrender, and Morton was now in a position to insist that the English forces and artillery, which Elizabeth had promised would be sent should it prove necessary, should be employed against the intransigent garrison. Consequently, the bombardment of the castle began on 17th May with the regent determined to consider nothing less than unconditional surrender.[53] This was forthcoming on 28th May and, by the terms of capitulation, the garrison was permitted to go free, most of them being recruited shortly afterwards for service with the Swedish crown.[54] On the other hand, Grange, the Lethington brothers, Home, Restalrig, Dunkeld, Drylaw,

Murdocairnie, Pittarro and two forgers of false coins were to be 'reserved and kept where the regent shall appoint' until queen Elizabeth's advice was forthcoming.[55] This meant, in effect, that, until this decision was given, Grange and the others were removed from the castle to be placed in custody within several residences in the town. Grange himself, along with Lethington, for example, was lodged for a few days with Drury, while Murdocairnie stayed with his brother, Sir James Melville.[56] However, most of the prisoners were ultimately confined in either Morton's own lodgings or at Holyrood.[57] One exception was lord Home, popularly believed to have too many friends in Edinburgh and consequently detained in the castle.[58] Although Elizabeth would have preferred that 'she should not have needed to intromit herself in advice for the punishment of offences done in another Prince's kingdom', she eventually did inform Morton, after a delay of nearly seven weeks, that she was referring 'the judgment and ordering of those matters to him and to the laws of that realm'.[59] This, of course, was precisely the sort of recommendation that the regent wanted. Not surprisingly, he was a strong advocate of the leading rebels receiving 'the due reward of their deserts'.[60]

Consequently, on Monday, 3rd August, 1573, Grange, with his brother Thomas Kirkcaldy, who had been captured in January at Blackness with a consignment of French money, and the two counterfeiters, James Mossman and James Cokky, were hanged in Edinburgh.[61] In Grange's case, there was one last-minute attempt at a reprieve by his nephew, William Mowbray of Barnbogle, who submitted bonds of manrent from numerous other lairds indicating their willingness to serve Morton both in peace and war. As well as this, he also had pledges for his uncle's future behaviour and information which would lead to the recovery of certain missing royal jewels.[62] The regent, however, remained unmoved, justifying Grange's sentence on two counts: firstly, it was 'quhat has bene and daly is spokin be the preacharis that Godis plague will not ceasse quhill the land be purgeit of blude', and, secondly, until Grange paid the supreme penalty 'such as are interested by the death of their friends' would not rest satisfied.[63] Thus, about four o'clock in the afternoon of 3rd August, Grange and Mossman were hanged together on the scaffold at the cross in Edinburgh's high street, the head of the former captain of the castle, as Knox had prophesised, finally swinging round to face westwards and into the sun.[64]

There were no further executions, although Lethington may only have escaped the gallows by dying shortly after the castle fell.[65] Indeed, it is possible that Morton, until he was restrained by queen Elizabeth, intended some grisly exhibition of his remains.[66] Of the others, Murdocairnie, again at Elizabeth's behest, was reprieved, remaining incarcerated for about another year.[67] Lord Home, on the other hand, had his life spared as the result of the intercessions of his kinsmen, the lairds of Manderston and Coldenknowes, but was not released from the castle until shortly before his death in 1575.[68] If his son is to be believed, he had been badly treated by the regent during his imprisonment.[69] As for John Maitland, the brother of Lethington, he was confined in Tantallon before being transferred, firstly to Callendar house in Falkirk, and then to Cowthally at the foot of the Pentland hills, the residence of his cousin, lord Somerville.[70] Finally, Robert Crichton, the former bishop of Dunkeld, was committed for a period to Blackness castle.[71] In the case of the lairds of Drylaw, Pittarro and Restalrig, the last-named at least was free by 1577 as, in August of that year, he was one of the signatories to a bond of surety for Robert, lord Stewart, feuar of Orkney and Shetland.[72]

NOTES

1. *A.P.S.*, iii, 78; Calderwood, *History*, iii, 242–43.
2. *A.P.S.*, iii, 77–78; William, master of Herries, also seems to have been at the convention, *C.S.P. Scot.*, iv, 433.
3. *Scots Peerage*, ii, 269–70; iv, 240.
4. *Ibid.*, ii, 471–74; iii, 29–31; vi, 232–33. For Montrose, see also *C.S.P. Scot.*, iv, 432.
5. *Scots Peerage*, ii, 514–16; iv, 263; v, 399–400; vi, 512–13; vii, 538–43; viii, 288–91.
6. *See* n. 2.
7. *Scots Peerage*, iv, 410–11; v, 155–61; vi, 482–83.
8. *Ibid*, iv, 55–57; vii, 411–412.
9. *C.S.P. Scot.*, iv, 433.
10. Keith, *Bishops*, 39–40, 215–16, 226–27.
11. *Ibid*, 97, 122–23, 166–67, 279, 289–90; John Campbell, bishop of the Isles, whose appointment was confirmed by the crown on 25th January, 1573, was also connected to Argyll, *Fasti*, 206.
12. Keith, *Bishops*, 180, 194–96, 259–60.
13. This can be done, to some extent, by an examination of the signatories of the Hamilton bond (Keith, *History*, ii, 807–10) and the subsequent escheats, remissions and respites under the privy seal.
14. *R.S.S.*, vi, Nos. 304, 363, 446, 282.
15. *H.M.C. Rep.*, *v*, App. 616.
16. *Scots Peerage*, i, 119; v, 441–42; viii, 544.
17. *Ibid*, iv, 352–53, 366–71.

18. *Ibid*, iv, 537–41.
19. *Ibid*, i, 444–45.
20. *Ibid*, viii, 585–87; *C.S.P. Scot.*, iv, 503.
21. *Ibid*, v, 253; *Scots Peerage*, ii, 338–40; viii, 343–45.
22. *Ibid*, i, 340–43.
23. *C.S.P. Scot.*, iv, 430, 432.
24. *R.P.C.*, ii, 172; *R.S.S.*, vi, Nos. 1421, 1820; *H.M.C. Rep.*, *iv*, App. 486.
25. *C.S.P. Scot.*, iv, 544–45.
26. *Scots Peerage*, i, 342–43; see also Riddell, *Peerage*, i, 546–52.
27. *C.S.P. Scot.*, iv, 443–44, 455–56, 478, 486.
28. *Ibid*, 503; *Diurnal*, 327–28.
29. *R.P.C.*, ii, 193.
30. *Ibid*, 177–78; *T.A.*, xii, 336.
31. *R.P.C.*, ii, 193–200; *C.S.P. Scot.*, iv, 494–98; *Warrender Papers*, i, 115–17.
32. Lord Seton also submitted to the crown in February, 1573, *Scots Peerage*, viii, 585–87.
33. *C.S.P. Scot.*, iv, 538; *R.P.C.*, ii, 211; *Diurnal*, 329.
34. *Historie and Life of King James the Sext*, 141.
35. *D.N.B.*, xxi, 209–12; Calderwood, *History*, iii, 283.
36. *Scots Peerage*, v, 293–95; see also Lee, *Maitland of Thirlstane*, Ch. ii, *passim*.
37. *Scots Peerage*, v, 298–99.
38. *Ibid*, iv, 461–62.
39. Fraser, *Melville*, i, 82–132, *passim*.
40. Keith, *Bishops*, 97; *R.S.S.*, vi, No. 2812; Alexander Crichton of Drylaw, who was also within the castle, was a kinsman.
41. Melville, *Memoirs*, 249.
42. *Ibid*, 250–51.
43. *Ibid*, 252.
44. *C.S.P. Scot.*, iv, 439.
45. *Ibid*, 459; *R.P.C.*, ii, 171–72; *T.A.*, xii, 331–32.
46. *Historie and Life of King James the Sext*, 125; on the other hand, according to Killigrew, the fighting was resumed by Grange 'by shot of harquebuses without any harm done', *C.S.P. Scot.*, iv, 459.
47. *Ibid*, 453–55.
48. *Ibid*, 526–28.
49. *Ibid*, 534.
50. *Ibid*, 533.
51. *Ibid*, 539, 543.
52. *Warrender Papers*, i, 120–25.
53. *C.S.P. Scot.*, iv, 570; Anglo-Scottish co-operation during the siege of Edinburgh castle is discussed in Chap. 7.
54. *C.S.P. Scot.*, iv, 571–72, 590. They formed part of a Scottish contingent,

reputedly of several thousand, many of whom were killed in 1574 in a battle with German mercenaries who were also employed by the king of Sweden, *ibid*, 674, 682; Berg and Lagercrantz, *Scots in Sweden*, 15–16.

55. *C.S.P. Scot.*, iv, 571.
56. Melville, *Memoirs*, 255.
57. *C.S.P. Scot.*, iv, 588, 590.
58. *Ibid*, 590.
59. *Ibid*, 582, 599.
60. *Ibid*, 575.
61. *Ibid*, 602.
62. Melvill, *Diary*, 35.
63. *C.S.P. Scot.*, iv, 602.
64. Calderwood, *History*, iii, 284–85.
65. *C.S.P. Scot.*, iv, 585.
66. *Ibid*, 600.
67. *Ibid*, 599, 622; Fraser, *Melville*, 101.
68. Melville, *Memoirs*, 256; *Scots Peerage*, iv, 462.
69. *H.M.C. Rep.*, xii, App. pt. viii, 102.
70. Calderwood, *History*, iii, 284; *History and Life of King James the Sext*, 145; Maitland was freed in September, 1578, *R.P.C.*, iii, 29.
71. *History and Life of King James the Sext*, 145.
72. *R.P.C.*, ii, 622.

3
Governance, Part I

For Morton, the fall of Edinburgh castle marked the real beginning of an ascendancy which was to last until March, 1578. During this period, the regent never summoned parliament although, as it so happened, he had held one earlier, in January, 1573. This had been called, as was normal practice, to confirm his appointment but, in addition, also passed some important religious legislation[1] as well as repealing certain measures previously enacted against the former Marians, Argyll, Boyd, Cassillis, Herries and Maxwell.[2] However, there was another parliament, summoned in the early part of 1573, conspicuous if only by its dearth of legislative measures.[3] Notice of this session was given at a meeting of the privy council on 1st March where it was announced that 'his Hienes Parliament now rynnand (was) to begin and of new to be fensit and holdin in the tolbuith of Edinburgh the xxiii day of Apryle nixt to cum'.[4] This, as stated, turned out to be a particularly unproductive meeting resulting in only a handful of social and economic statutes. Nonetheless, since the messengers intimating this parliament were also entrusted with announcing the terms of the pacification at Perth,[5] there seems every probability that Morton envisaged much more materialising from the April assembly than mere prohibitions on transporting salt 'furth of this realme' or the 'slauchter of Hering and quhyte fish'.[6] In other words, Morton had been confident that Grange and his colleagues would now perceive the futility of prolonging the siege any further and surrender on his terms. This capitulation and the recent agreement at Perth could then be conveniently ratified by the parliament which he had called. If these were not his intentions, then it is difficult to fathom why someone who never subsequently evinced a predilection for frequent meetings with the estates should order two such sessions within three months in 1573.

Although parliament did not meet thereafter until March, 1578, there was one very well-attended convention held at Holyrood in March, 1575.

Undoubtedly, as far as Morton was concerned, an important feature of this gathering was the presence of so many leading members of the nobility and higher clergy. Thirteen earls, including George, earl of Gordon, and that elusive individual, John, earl of Atholl, sixteen lords, seven bishops and fourteen commendators were there to indicate by their attendance the strength of the regent's position. The matters discussed embraced such topics as the controversy arising from Argyll's possession of certain royal jewels, church policy, 'the punisement of strang and idle beggaris', the currency, the exportation of salt, and legal reform.[7] But Morton called no further meetings of this nature during the remainder of his regency and, for the day-to-day administration of the country, he naturally depended on the governing body normally used for this purpose – the privy council.

On most occasions, the privy council comprised a handful of royal officials, and a scrutiny of its sederunts reveals that the commendator of Dunfermline, the bishop of Orkney, and lords Boyd, Glamis and Ruthven were easily the most frequent attenders. Robert Pitcairn, commendator of Dunfermline, royal secretary, was understandably rarely absent, but the presence so often of Adam Bothwell, bishop of Orkney, merits further comment. Since 1568, he had been commendator of Holyrood abbey, having surrendered the greater part of his bishopric to Robert Stewart, earl of Orkney, the former commendator of Holyrood.[8] Moreover, he was a bishop with legal training, being a judge of the court of session, whose expertise had been utilised by Moray in 1569 at Westminster during the enquiry into queen Mary's affairs.[9] Morton presumably appreciated his abilities, and this would account for the fact that, between June, 1573 and March, 1578, only Robert Pitcairn has a better record of attendance. As for Glamis, Ruthven and Boyd, they all held positions of responsibility in the government. Argyll, Morton's original chancellor, had died on 12th September, 1573[10] to be succeeded by Glamis on 8th October;[11] Ruthven had been treasurer before Morton's regency, having held that position since 24th June, 1571;[12] Boyd was installed as collector of thirds sometime in 1573.[13]

Unquestionably, it was Morton's policy to ensure that loyal service was adequately rewarded, especially in the case of Glamis and Boyd. Glamis, for example, received various escheats[14] and gifts of wardships[15] as well as, on 5th November, 1577, the shared lease for eleven years of lead mines in Ayrshire and Galloway with Morton's natural son, James, commendator of Pluscarden.[16] Boyd acquired the lands and barony of Grogar in Ayrshire forfeited by lord Home[17] as well as an assortment of escheats[18] and wardships.[19] In addition, on 25th March, 1575, he was appointed bailie and justiciar of Glasgow where his nephew, James Boyd, had been elected arch-bishop in November, 1573.[20] Then, on 3rd June, 1577, he was granted a pension of 1,000 merks per annum from the thirds of the archbishopric of Glasgow and Paisley abbey and, the same year, 'pro bono servitio', further lands in Ayrshire.[21] Ruthven's remuneration seems slender by comparison although he was able to procure a number of escheats for some of his 'servitors'.[22] Possibly his very position as treasurer was recognized, with its obvious opportunities for feathering his own nest, as sufficient reward. This was a viewpoint which, as it happens, was certainly held by some of his compatriots.[23] Obviously, there were other royal servants recompensed for their labours, notably Sir James Hume of Coldenknowes and John, lord Maxwell.[24] With both of them having the arduous task of administering the east and west marches respectively, this was only to be expected.

Not surprisingly, some of Morton's own relatives and kinsmen are to be found occupying positions in his administration and benefiting accordingly. Archibald, 8th earl of Angus, as has been seen, had become a ward of the regent on his father's death in June, 1557, and his uncle always appears to have done his best for him. The prolonged and ultimately successful struggle with Margaret, countess of Lennox, over her claims to his nephew's territories is a good example of his solicitude. Thus, Angus, who was another frequent attender at the privy council, was amply endowed with the forfeited property of the earl of Bothwell and Sir Thomas Ker of Fernihurst.[25] In addition, he received the escheated goods of several individuals put to the horn[26] as well as three gifts of marriage.[27] On 27th October, 1573, he was appointed sheriff of Berwick and bailie of Lauderdale[28] while, on 31st July, 1574, he became lieutenant of all the marches.[29] This appointment was renewed on 6th December, 1576,[30] and the following year, on 25th May, 1577, he also took over the wardenship of the west march.[31] Finally, on 16th December, 1577, he was created hereditary steward of Fife and captain of Falkland palace.[32] Indubitably, he was not only one of the principal recipients of the regent's favour but also a key figure in his government.

Angus, however, was not the only person related to Morton whose services were utilised and duly remunerated. Another was John Carmichael, younger of that ilk, whose father belonged to a cadet branch of the Douglases, while he had married a half-sister of Morton's.[33] He featured prominently in the regent's border administration, being referred to as keeper of Liddesdale in June, 1574, although he had probably been appointed the previous November.[34] He was also to play a leading part in the Redeswyre fracas the following year.[35] Sir James Melville relates that, shortly after the regent came to power, Carmichael was temporarily out of favour. However, as soon as he was suitably obsequious, a policy which Melville claims to have recommended, all was well.[36] Apocryphal as this · possibly is, it is undeniable that Carmichael did not really begin to accumulate his various escheats,[37] a wardship[38] and a pension from the superplus of the thirds of the priory of St. Andrews[39] until near the end of 1575.

Another relative who prospered during the regency was William Douglas of Whittingham. He was a cousin of Morton's who had married the sister of Maitland of Lethington and was a brother of that notorious individual, involved in so many dubious enterprises, Archibald Douglas.[40] He received an assortment of wardships for himself,[41] with grants of forfeited Bothwell property for one son,[42] and a prebend from the collegiate church of Corstorphine, as well as a pension for educational purposes from the treasurer of Moray, for the other.[43]

Two others who profited from their propinquity to the regent were George Douglas of Parkhead and Archibald Douglas of Milnton. The former was a half-brother of Morton's who was captain of Edinburgh castle and also, between 1576 and March, 1578, provost of the town.[44] He acquired several escheats,[45] wardships[46] and a fifty-year lease of leadmines at Glengonar and Wanlockhead in Lanarkshire for himself,[47] while, for his servant, Florence Douglas, he obtained the office of Rothesay herald.[48] Likewise, Douglas of Milnton, constable of Edinburgh castle, had his ties of kinship rewarded with several gifts under the privy seal.[49]

There remains one person within Morton's retinue who admittedly held no official post in his government yet whose name appears so frequently in matters concerning the regent that he merits closer scrutiny: this is George Auchinleck of Balmanno who, apparently, was related to Morton by marriage, being the husband of another half-sister of the regent.[50] Although one nineteenth-century account of his family states that 'there is little trace of them except for the occasional appearance as witnesses to local charters'[51] – a statement which seems to ignore a great deal of available evidence – Hume of Godscroft, on the other hand, believed Auchinleck occupied a position comparable to steward or chamberlain in Morton's household.[52] In fact, in the course of six years, he was a witness to at least a dozen charters involving Morton and his family,[53] as well as being entrusted with a considerable amount of the regent's business. Firm evidence of Auchinleck's stewardship, for example, is to be found in the treasurer's accounts where, for the month of April, 1576, is to be found the entry 'for furnishing and outredding of certain of his grace's affairs –

£500', while, in December of that year, he was assigned £2,000 by the treasury 'to be disbursed by him on his grace's affairs and business'.[54] Moreover, on 18th February, 1576, in the company of David Borthwick of Lochhill, King's advocate, lord Ruthven, Robert Pitcairn, Sir John Bellenden of Auchnoule, Sir Archibald Napier and James Reid, an Edinburgh burgess, he ratified a gold-mining contract between king James and Morton on the one part and Abraham Petersen, a Flemish mining entrepreneur, on the other.[55] That same year, he was also entrusted with receiving the 8,000 merks left as an educational bequest by Robert Reid, bishop of Orkney, which should have been handed over by one of the executors, Walter Reid, commendator of Kinloss. This sum had been bequeathed by bishop Reid in 1558 'to have bene employit upoun the bying of the tenement with the yaird and pertinentis of umquhile Schir Johnne Ramsay, knycht, liand on the south syde of the burgh of Edinburgh for to big ane college in the quhille was appointit to be thre scoillis . . . '[56] But the commendator of Kinloss, as it happened, was not particularly interested in the foundation of a university in Edinburgh and was eventually put to the horn for failing to deliver the money to Auchinleck.[57] Further evidence of the ubiquitious nature of Auchenleck's position is his presence as a commissioner on the justice ayre held at Roxburgh in November, 1576,[58] and again in March, 1578 at Edinburgh castle where he was one of Morton's witnesses when the latter surrendered the royal jewels, munitions and certain other items to the king's representatives.[59]

Auchinleck, in Hume's estimation, was an arrogant upstart, and he quotes two anecdotes involving him to substantiate this assertion. In one, he recounts the tale of the slaughter by Auchinleck during broad daylight in the streets of Edinburgh of a certain Captain Nisbet. In the other, he describes an encounter between Morton's servant and Oliver Sinclair, a favourite of king James V's. Sinclair, who had the misfortune of commanding part of James V's army at Solway Moss, reminded the regent's protégé, by pointing to his own circumstances, of the fickle nature of fortune.[60] Whether these accounts are authentic or otherwise, it is undeniable that Auchinleck received a lengthy catalogue of escheats,[61] wardships[62] and grants of land.[63] Furthermore, on 11th September, 1573, he was to be the recipient of £500 from 'the first and readiest compositions of the burghs',[64] with pensions, subsequently, from the spirituality and temporality of the archbishopric of St. Andrews and, when a new archbishop was installed, from the thirds of its priory.[65] Nor was that all, since his brother Archibald and even one of his servants also benefited from his influential position.[66]

This, then, was Morton's government, its principal members as well as the various relatives and kinsmen who assisted him. Outwith border raids, Morton left the capital infrequently but, on 3rd August, 1574, the regent departed from Edinburgh for Aberdeen on what Killigrew described as his 'northern voyage'.[67] The aims of this expedition, so it was proclaimed when it reached Aberdeen, were 'the establishment of justice and punishement of disordouris and enormittis attemptit aganis our Soverane lordis authoritie and commonweill of the realme'.[68] Within the capital, he left behind Angus, Lindsay and Ruthven in charge of affairs,[69] although he had also taken the precaution the previous month of confining George, earl of Huntly.[70] Thus, the most powerful nobleman in the north-east of the kingdom was placed under ward in the south-western province of Galloway, ostensibly on account of the behaviour of his brother, Adam Gordon of Auchindoun, now in France.[71] The latter, apart from being in danger of assassination from one of the sons of lord Forbes, had also been condemned by the privy council in 1574 for actions conducive to 'the raising of uprore and hostilitie aganis the trew religioun and the persoun of owre Soverane lord'.[72]

To assist him in his northern venture, Morton was accompanied initially by lord Glamis, Robert Pitcairn, Sir William Murray of Tullibardine, his comptroller, and David Borthwick of Lochhill.[73] The party was joined at some stage on the way by the earls of Rothes, Buchan and Errol whose principal houses were situated on the route northwards. This probably occurred at Brechin on 6th August when the regent's bodyguard of forty light horsemen, commanded by James Carmichael, younger of that ilk, was scheduled to be reinforced by the addition of levies from Fife, Kinross, Perthshire, Forfarshire and Kincardineshire.[74] Certainly, all three noblemen were present at the session of the privy council held at Aberdeen on 12th August when the master of Marischal and his brother, the commendator of Deer, were also in attendance.[75]

Morton's main business while in Aberdeen was to administer the law, which he did by convening a justice ayre. This court did inflict a few hefty fines. Andrew, earl of Errol, and George Hay, for example were fined £3,333 for imprisoning and committing grievous bodily harm on two individuals, including piercing the ears of one of them with a hot auger; the laird of Drum and his accomplices paid £1,000 as punishment for the abduction of Alexander Cumming of Culter.[76] However, the bulk of those found guilty of offences such as assisting Adam Gordon or supplying provisions to his forces or of such other malpractices as hoarding food and exporting barley without a licence paid much smaller amounts.[77] Many, indeed, sought, and obtained, remissions for felonies committed many years before which would underline the previous lack of good government in this area. One body which undoubtedly had incurred the regent's displeasure and suffered accordingly was the city council of Aberdeen. The councillors, Morton informed them on 21st August, 'haf nocht done thair dewetie and thankful service during the tyme of the lait truble and frequent tumult'.[78] Thus, their support of the Gordon family was to cost them an amercement of 4,000 merks, 3,000 merks payable before 20th October and the remainder to be spent on such social and religious projects as the regent determined.[79] As it transpired, 1,000 merks of the fine was remitted and another 1,000 merks was designated to the 'bigging and reparatioun of ane hospitall'.[80]

Morton departed on 4th September but not before he had extracted from the councillors a band of allegiance to king James VI and himself.[81] A similar compact was also procured from 'the Erlls, Lordis, Baronis, landit men and utheris' whereby they promised they would 'in all tyme cuming continew faithful and obedient subjectis to oure Soverane lord, his authoritie and Regent foirsaid'.[82] Morton's departure is unlikely to have been regretted since the members of the city council regarded their treatment as 'weray hourtfull',[83] and the author of one account observed that 'peipill thairabout gat na kyndnes'.[84] At the same time, it was important that some respect for law and order and royal authority should be implanted in this disaffected region. This seems precisely what the regent did achieve.

While Morton was at Aberdeen, another matter, namely the prolonged dispute with Colin, earl of Argyll, over certain royal jewels, seemed to be on the verge of a settlement. The origins of this affair went back to the parliament of January, 1573 which had authorised the regent to retrieve all of queen Mary's jewels and pursue 'the havaris, resettaris, sellaris and intromettors' of these items.[85] Once Edinburgh castle had fallen, this task was energetically undertaken by Morton. On 7th August, 1573, George, earl of Huntly, had restored 'ane garnysing of diamantes, sex rubies and twelf perlis all sett in knoppis of gold',[86] while, as a result of his interrogation of Grange and later Murdocairnie, the whereabouts of the bulk of the royal valuables was established. Some of them were dispersed among the hands of Ker of Fernihirst and the wives of lord Home and Maitland of Lethington but most of them had been given to Sir William Drury, marshall of Berwick.[87] Some of these were recovered on Morton's behalf in August by Drury's colleague, Sir Valentine Brown, while others appear to have been retrieved in October, 1573.[88] Certainly, the treasury accounts of that month contain a reference to £1,814.6s.8d. to Drury 'for redeming fra him of the Kingis jewellis . . . quhilkis wer laid in pledge to him be the layrde of

Grange'.[89] However, Morton's dealings with the marshall of Berwick were not yet concluded since, in a letter to Burghley on 3rd August, 1574, Killigrew noted that the regent had discovered the exact value of the jewels which Grange had given Drury and 'proposes to demand again'.[90]

Meanwhile, on 3rd February, 1574, Morton had raised the question in privy council of the royal jewellery in the possession of the Argylls.[91] Colin, sixth earl of Argyll, who had succeeded to the title on the death of his brother Archibald on 12th September, 1573, had married Agnes Keith, eldest daughter of William earl Marischal and widow of the earl of Moray.[92] This lady, the council declared, 'hes in hir handis thre greit rubyis and thre greit dyamontis of the saidis jewellis, with ane greit jewell in the forme of ane H set with dyamontis quhilk scho will not present befoir my said Lord Regent without scho be compellit'.[93] The countess, on the other hand, believed she was perfectly within her rights in keeping them since her late husband, as she later explained to queen Elizabeth, 'retained some part in his own hands for his relief on the debts contracted by him in the common cause whereof the burden comes on his bairns; in consideration thereof she has just cause to withold and retain the jewels after his decease until relief and payment of the said debts be made'.[94] Argyll and his wife attended this session of the council in February, 1574 but 'on na wayis did exhibit and present the saidis jewellis', and consequently they were put to the horn.[95] By August, however, following intervention on behalf of the Argylls by Killigrew, who had accompanied Morton to Aberdeen, and by queen Elizabeth herself, it looked as if a compromise had been reached. Thus, it was arranged that, on Morton's return to Edinburgh from the north, they would submit the jewels for inspection and, at the same time, state their case for retaining them.[96] But hopes of a settlement were soon dashed, apparently because Morton, despite the fact that the countess of Argyll had recently given birth to a stillborn child and was 'evil at point to travel', insisted the valuables should be produced in Edinburgh on 24th September.[97] Indeed, by 10th September, Argyll's wife was once again beseeching English assistance and forwarding a dossier of recent correspondence with the regent to strengthen her cause.[98] But all these endeavours made no impact on Morton who demanded a surety of £10,000 from Argyll that the jewels would be forthcoming on the date prescribed.[99]

Deadlock prevailed until the convention of March, 1575 when a satisfactory settlement was concluded. Argyll now relinquished the precious items but, in return, received a promise from Glamis, as lord chancellor, that he would 'tak consideratioun of the chargeis and expensis' of his wife and children.[100] In this manner, as Morton himself remarked, 'the occasion

D

of controversy (was) removed'.[101] Nevertheless, whether it was sound policy on the regent's part pursuing this vendetta with the Argylls so vigorously must be regarded as debatable. Certainly, Killigrew had been concerned about the schism between Morton and Argyll, regarding the latter as harshly treated.[102] This viewpoint – one, incidentally, also shared by his superior, Walsingham[103] – was, of course, largely determined by the English government's perennial preoccupation with developments in Ireland where Argyll, with his territory adjacent to the Irish coast, wielded some influence. On the other hand, Morton believed the countess had no claims whatsoever to the jewels once her husband had been assassinated. 'If any power over the King's jewels was granted to the regent Moray,' he had informed Argyll, 'they were not ordained to be witholden by his wife after his decease.' In any case, he added, 'concerning the late regent's debts contracted in the King's service, no such thing is yet found and declared by account'.[104] Clearly, the regent was convinced that Argyll must be taught respect for royal authority and not imagine he was above the law. In the light of the earl's subsequent behaviour, this does not seem an unreasonable attitude. If he was rather brusque with the countess at one stage, he does appear to have made some attempt to make amends. For example, in a letter to her on 15th May, 1575, in which he hoped she would give a friendly reception to the bishop of Moray, he also observed that he trusted she had found him 'a slaw uptaker of your escheat dewities out of the tenentis handes'.[105] Morton, in other words, was pointing out to the countess that, at least as far as certain escheated Campbell properties were concerned, he had deliberately neglected to take them into royal hands. In this way, and by virtue of his leniency, she could continue to enjoy the revenues of lands which should have reverted to the crown.

With the Argyll affair resolved in March, 1575, Morton's relations with the nobility for the rest of the year were generally felicitous. This mutual harmony is reflected in a letter written by him to Killigrew on 1st October in which he describes a leisurely and congenial excursion from his palace at Dalkeith to one of the other main residences at Aberdour. 'From Dalkeith,' he wrote, 'I was accompanied by the lord Claud Hamilton and Sir James Hamilton to Linlithgow and they departing from me there, the lord Livingston and his friends met and conveyed me to the Torwood where I found the earl of Mar, the earl of Buchan, Lochleven and other friends who returned together to Stirling; and there, besides the comfortable time spent with the King's majesty, to my great rejoicing I had good pastime hunting in the park and otherwise till my lord of Montrose and the laird of Tullibardine comptroller, coming hither accompanied me the first night to Kincardine, my lord of Montrose's house from which dining at Tullibardine in the morn I was at night with my lord of Rothes at Bambreich' (Ballinbreich). Lords Ruthven, Drummond and Oliphant were others visited or encountered before he finally reached his destination.[106] This mood of complacency was doubtless reinforced three weeks later when he learned of the sudden death at Strathbogie castle of George, earl of Huntly, a nobleman whose allegiance, as has been seen, was sometimes questionable.[107]

In February, 1576, however, there began the feud between the earls of Argyll and Atholl which was to dominate the latter part of Morton's regency and have important consequences for it. The first intimation of discord was at a privy council meeting on 28th February when Argyll, who was there in person, claimed in virtue of his heritable office of justice-general that a commission of justiciary formerly given by queen Mary to Atholl, over his own territory, should be dissolved. The council announced that it would reserve judgement until 20th April but, meanwhile, Atholl should not attempt to exercise any legal powers.[108] However, there is no record of any council session on 20th April, and the next occasion the two earls feature in the council minutes is 23rd June. On this date, the council, acting on reports of 'late slauchter and utheris enormities happynnit betwix the freinds, servandis and dependaris of the Erllis of Ergyle and Atholl', ins-tructed them to cease feuding to such time as they reached a decision regarding a settlement.[109] On 10th July, the two rivals were ordered to appear, each accompanied by not more than sixty followers, before the council on 16th November and also required to give guarantee that, in the intervening period, they would keep the peace.[110] This Argyll subscribed at Dunoon on 20th July, and Atholl two days later at Dunkeld.[111]

Notwithstanding the ruling of 10th July, the dispute between the two earls was not heard in the council until 2nd February, 1577. At this meeting, Atholl was ordered to produce two Camerons whom he had imprisoned at Blair Atholl as being the perpetrators of 'divers slauchters, heirschippis and oppressionis upoun certane the said Erllis men, tenentis and servandis'.[112] They were duly presented on 26th February when they were denounced for the murder of their late clan chieftain.[113] The relevance of the Cameron brothers to the Argyll-Atholl imbroglio is that they were apparently dependants of Argyll — a fact which became obvious when he and John Campbell of Caddell entered sureties for them and took them into protective custody.[114] This action, according to one authority,[115] was in retaliation for Atholl's refusal to hand over two of his servants whom Argyll had indicted on 30th July, 1576 and intended should stand trial on 18th October that year.[116]

It was not until 24th November, 1577 that Argyll was ordered to hand over the Camerons.[117] This delay may partly have been a result of attempts by Morton to mediate in the dispute. In January, 1577, for example, he had asked the lairds of Menzies and Fandowy to provide him with an assessment of the respective losses on either side. This involved them in the task of making 'cognitioun and jugement' about such details as 'how many ky and horss and quhat avale of insycht wer taken fra Johnne Campbell and his tenentis as alsua quhat quantitie of silver was takin fra the Erll of Athollis men . . .' Neither earl, as it happened, appreciated their efforts or was co-operative and the two commissioners, in fact, were 'evill handillit betwix the Campbellis and the Erll of Athole divers wyse'.[118]

As for Argyll's reply to the summons of 24th November, 1577, his answer was to ignore it altogether and have the messenger who delivered it to him, as he was hunting near Loch Eck, badly beaten up by his followers.[119] For this open defiance of royal authority, he was denounced on 17th January, 1578.[120] However, Argyll, seemingly impervious to condemnation, was by this date preparing to attack the laird of Glengarry, and the council on 18th February issued further orders declaring his actions treasonable and exhorted 'all and sindry oure Soverane lordis liegis dwelland within the boundis of the erldomes of Ross, Murray, the lordschippis of Badyeneuch and Balquhidder' to render assistance to Glengarry.[121] Next day, Thomas Fraser of Knocky, Colin Mackenzie of Kintail, John Grant of Freuchie, who had a perpetual bond of maintenance with Glengarry's father,[122] and several others were specifically instructed to help him.[123] More importantly, that same day, a mobilisation order was promulgated for the counties of Ayr, Dumbarton, Lanark, Renfrew and Stirling, the burghs of Ayr, Dumbarton, Glasgow, Hamilton, Irvine, Lanark, Paisley, Renfrew, Rutherglen 'and utheris townis and places on the coist syde quhair oistlary is used'.[124] From its detailed victualling and transport arrangements by land and sea, and its reference to the western seaboard, the regent was clearly planning to tackle the rebellious Argyll in uncompromising fashion. However, it was to be his misfortune that, just at this juncture, his attention was to be diverted by the conspiracy against him which was to bring his regency to an end.

The End of the Regency

The first signs of any significant opposition to Morton were observed on 28th June, 1577 by Robert Bowes, the treasurer of Berwick. Writing to the earl of Huntingdon that month, he noted the existence of a party headed by Atholl, Ruthven and Lindsay who had 'confederated themselves by oath for the maintenance of the King'.[125] They hoped, so he informed Burghley three weeks later, to end the dispute between Atholl and Argyll and thus add the latter earl to their faction.[126] Morton, apparently, was aware of the existence of this group,[127] and, in September, to measure the extent of its influence over the young king, he is reported as having set the dangerous precedent of offering to resign if James was dissatisfied with him.[128]

Meanwhile, as has been observed, the regent's quarrel with Argyll continued. In addition, Atholl was dissatisfied, partly on account of the affair with the Cameron brothers, but also, so Bowes noticed, because he was convinced that Morton was not seriously attempting to find a settlement between him and his rival.[129] Indeed, by July, 1577, he seems to have been of the opinion that the regent was deliberately prolonging the feud and, by this date, Atholl was seriously considering a reconciliation with Argyll.[130] Thus, on 22nd October, the two earls signed a bond promising jointly to assist the master of Mar in defence of the king.[131] Nevertheless, none of this came out until the end of February, 1578 when the situation was suddenly transformed. On 28th February, Thomas Randolph, who had just arrived as English ambassador, informed his superiors that 'the earls of Atholl and Argyll being lately reconciled have linked to them some personages of the house of Mar to favour their faction'.[132] In effect, Randolph was giving the first news of the conspiracy by the erstwhile adversaries and their confederates to overthrow Morton.

It is difficult to see how the regent could have prevented the formation of this alliance. Inevitably, as will shortly be shown, certain individuals, notably the earl of Montrose, the master of Mar, lords Maxwell, Herries and Ogilvie and the commendator of Newbattle had, during the course of his regency, either quarrelled with him or grown to dislike him. Understandably, they tended to gravitate to the Argyll-Atholl axis. If Morton did deliberately protract the dispute between the two earls for his own avaricious ends, then his overthrow could be regarded as a merited reckoning. But there is no concrete proof of this whatsoever – merely a reference of questionable veracity to such tactics in the *Historie and Life of King James the Sext*, a work definitely unsympathetic towards the regent.[133] If this allegation is dismissed as not proven, Morton was amply justified in taking such a determined stance towards the refractory earl of Argyll who was not only flexing his muscles against royal authority but other clan chiefs at the same time.[134] He certainly deserved to be put in his place, and it was unfortunate Morton was prevented from so doing.

On 2nd March, the regent received word from his cousin, Douglas of Lochleven, of developments at Stirling where Argyll had now arrived and been cordially welcomed by Alexander Erskine, master of Mar, the custodian of the king.[135] He also learned that Atholl was believed to be repairing there shortly. In reply, Morton told Lochleven that Randolph was departing for Stirling and would be accompanied by three of his council, namely Angus, Ruthven and Glamis. Initially, he recommended that he should contact Angus – 'Ye will understand be my Lord of Angus may awin meaning' – but, when his nephew decided to proceed to Stirling via Douglas in Lanarkshire, Alexander Hay, clerk-register, was substituted as the person whom he should consult.[136] This alteration was intimated to Lochleven on 4th March, by which date Morton would appear to have recognised his opponents' *fait accompli*, confessing to his cousin that he was quite prepared to resign 'how sone as evir his Majestie sall think himself reddy and able for his awin governament'.[137] This was to be four days thence, on 8th March, when the convention summoned by the Argyll-Atholl cabal assembled at Stirling.

The first session of the March convention was attended by six earls, four lords, two bishops, three commendators, the comptroller and the director of chancery,[138] all of them handpicked since 'the advertisement went only to those that were their own friends'.[139] Although Morton obviously could have gone personally to Stirling, he probably, as one authority suggests, had fears for his safety in such an undertaking.[140] At the head of the earls were Argyll and Atholl, both of them ambitious – Argyll was to succeed his old rival as chancellor on the latter's sudden death in 1579 – as well as inimical towards Morton. Of the others, the earl of Caithness had, doubtless, decided his best interests lay with Argyll and Atholl. This would seem to have been a judicious decision if charters subsequently confirming a yearly pension from the revenues of the bishopric of Caithness and to lands in Inverness are taken into account.[141] The earl of Montrose, by one account, deserted the regent over a disagreement about a feu charter which Andrew Graham, bishop of Dunblane, had granted him.[142] He was, in addition, one of those who, in August, 1576, had endeavoured to bring Argyll and Atholl together.[143] The earl of Mar, still a mere youth, very likely obeyed the wishes of his uncle, Alexander Erskine, master of Mar, a noted antagonist of Morton whom the latter regarded as one of the main instigators of the whole conspiracy.[144] The earl of Eglinton's presence is less easily deduced. Perhaps he still resented being imprisoned at Blackness for a time in 1574 for failing to answer charges brought by his first wife, Jane, one of Chatelherault's daughters, who alleged he had molested her tenants and uplifted their rents. Alternatively, he may have borne a grudge about being ordered in 1575, in his capacity as bailie of Cunninghame, to collect a tax which had been levied as far back as 1566 'for making and sustening of certane chargeis and expenssis maid at the baptisme of oure Soverane

Lord'.[145]

Of the lords, Maxwell is said to have objected to the regent's retention of the earldom of Morton, of which he apparently believed, as a nephew of the regent's wife, he was entitled to a one-third share.[146] Moreover, his dismissal from the wardenship of the west march on 25th May, 1577 and the restrictions subsequently placed on him must have strengthened his reolve to join the anti-Morton coalition and recover his position in the west march.[147] Lord Herries, Maxwell's uncle, it can be confidently assumed, was strongly influenced by family ties. Lord Ogilvie, however, was another nobleman motivated by resentment at imprisonment, being confined during 1576 in Linlithgow and later Glasgow.[148] Although he was later to plead that he had been detained 'for quat caus he knawis not',[149] his Marian sympathies, which extended to illicit correspondence with ex-archbishop Beaton in Paris,[150] not to mention a penchant for violent attacks on his neighbours,[151] would seem an adequate explanation. Lord Innermeath's presence can be attributed to his links as a Stewart with Atholl and by his dependance on Ruthven.[152] The latter, possibly purposely absent from the first session while he sat on the fence, was to attend the other meetings of the disaffected nobility and become a privy councillor in the new government.[153]

Regarding the bishops who attended the March convention, Alexander Campbell, bishop of Brechin, had alienated much of his bishopric to Argyll and, patently by his attendance, was giving further evidence of loyalty to the chief of his clan. However, the reasons for the presence of the other prelate, George Douglas, bishop of Moray, are impossible to ascertain. He may have quarrelled with Morton, yet there is no record of this, and he must serve as a caveat to too much emphasis on hypotheses based solely on kinship.

Finally, among the commendators, Adam Erskine of Cambuskenneth, clearly, on this occasion, sided with his half-brother, the master of Mar. Mark Ker, commendator of Newbattle, presumably was affected by a dispute which had arisen between his nephew, William Ker of Cessford, and the regent.[154] Furthermore, his appointment on 24th March to the new privy council and his son's promotion to master of requests four days earlier would suggest he was highly regarded by Morton's adversaries.[155] Robert Pitcairn, the secretary, would appear, like Sir William Murray of Tullibardine, the comptroller, to have sensed that a change of government was imminent and to have astutely taken the appropriate steps to ensure they were in the right place when this occurred. Lastly, there is the cantankerous George Buchanan, director of chancery and royal tutor, who, if Melville is to be believed, allowed an altercation over a favourite horse to affect his allegiance to the regent.[156]

The sole business of the first session of the March convention was Morton's dismissal. 'Having besyde his hienes,' it is stated in the minutes of the proceedings, 'a great nowmer of his nobilitie His maijestie hes thought convenient and necessary to advise with thame on the best wayes for the preservation of his hienes persoun and mainteinance of peace in this his realme.' This, it continued, was threatened 'be the apparent troubles quhilk arrysis throw the misliking that mony hes in the persoun of his right traist cousing, James, erll of Mortoun'. Thus, the king, 'perceaving all to remit the chois to his heines awin judgement', had decided to accept 'the burding of the administratioun' and replace Morton who 'be toung and last be writt produceit and red in the audience quhairupon his majestie cravit thair advices', had expressed his willingness to resign.[157]

Some further exposition of these minutes does seem necessary. For instance, there was hardly, as had been seen, 'a greit nowmer of the nobilitie' present. Again, *apropos* the phrase 'be toung', this could possibly refer to Morton's gesture of resignation the previous September but, more likely, was some statement about the future of his regency which he had made at the beginning of March. As for the written offer referred to in the parliamentary records, this undoubtedly was contained in a letter which the regent had given to Angus and which the latter read aloud to all those assembled at Stirling when he arrived there on 7th March. In its official version in the convention minutes, this declaration contains some brief advice about the royal revenues, the English alliance and the border situation as well as the important announcement that 'qhen it sould pleis your hienes to tak the regemen in your awin handis I wald maist willinglie according to your hines pleasure and commandment'.[158] Whether these were the exact contents of the Angus statement must remain conjectural. On the other hand, in certain 'notes appointit to be spokin before the upgeving of the regemen of the Erle of Morton', the regent, while repeating most of the above, does make some additional remarks. In particular, he reminds the king of the energy and resources he has expended in restoring Edinburgh castle and how he would be reluctant to surrender it to an unreliable person. In addition, he also points out that one reason why the royal revenues were not as substantial as they might be was a decline in the rental payments of both Argyll and Atholl.[159] Certainly, if Angus did make these comments on Morton's behalf, it is not surprising that they were subsequently omitted.

Morton, who was in Edinburgh on 8th March, received word of king

James' decision the same day as it was taken at Stirling and despatched Douglas of Whittingham with a message of acknowledgement.[160] On 10th March, the regent's resignation was confirmed by royal proclamation[161] and, two days later, another session of the convention was held.[162] This time, its personnel were augmented by the presence of Angus, lords Cathcart, Glamis, Lindsay, Menteith, Ruthven and Somerville, the bishops of Orkney, Caithness and Dunkeld, the commendator of Inchcolm and the masters of Gray and Rothes.[163] Undeniably, this was a more impressive gathering than the previous one, even more so when the number of noblemen, ecclesiastics and lairds actually present in Stirling on this date but not actually in attendance is taken into account. Their presence is corroborated by an examination of the signatures on the document entitled 'The nobilitei's obligatioune for ratifeing my lord of Mortoun's discharge maid by the King in Parliament'. This reveals a total of ten earls, eight lords, four bishops and eight commendators, with the names of the earls of Crawford, Errol and Mar, lord Borthwick, the masters of Mar and Seton and the commendators of Deer, Coldingham and Dryburgh appended in addition to those already noted as in attendance at the convention. Moreover, influential lairds such as Ker of Fawdonside, Hume of Coldenknowes, Hume of Manderston, Kennedy of Bargeny and Douglas of Lochleven also subscribed.[164] Incontrovertibly, the centre of government had now been temporarily transferred from Edinburgh to Stirling and the position of the palace revolutionaries greatly strengthened by Morton voluntarily accepting his deposition without any struggle.

At the meeting on 12th March, a lengthy document entitled 'The Discharge by the Privy Council of Scotland to James Earl of Morton of his regiment' was drawn up. This made generous reference to Morton's governance and the 'faithful and trew service done be the said lord regent to his hienes in his tender aige' but studiously excluded mentioning 'the jowellis and plenissingis of his hienes' housses, claithing, artailzerie and munitioune pertening to his Majestie or his darrest moder intromettit with and recoverit be the said lord Regent'.[165] Since these items were located in Edinburgh rather than Stirling, what was really being insisted upon was the submission of Edinburgh castle, obviously a cardinal objective for the coalition party. However, Morton, in reply to a communiqué informing him of the proposed commission, was once again co-operative. Nonetheless, he did remind the king of the loyal service performed by the captain of the castle, his half-brother, George Douglas of Parkhead, as well as his own not inconsiderable outlay on behalf of the crown on assuming the regency. Moreover, he continued, in reply to a suggestion that he had allowed the royal palaces to decay, 'his majesty's houses are now in better case than they were at the beginning of the regiment and his rent is now in good order'. Finally, ending on a conciliatory note, he consented to the dismissal of his border administrators, Angus, Carmichael and William Douglas of Bonjedburgh, whom his opponents clearly regarded as too influential.[166]

Meanwhile, at Stirling on 17th March, Glamis was killed in a scuffle between his followers and those of the earl of Crawford.[167] Although Calderwood and Hume of Godscroft both suggest that the chancellor had joined the opposition immediately the crisis of 1578 erupted,[168] nevertheless, considering Morton had demitted office voluntarily, he would seem to have had little alternative and, in any case, there is distinct evidence which would confirm that the ex-regent still regarded him as a trusted friend. This comes in a letter written by Morton to him on the day before his death when he asked him to use his influence with the king in order to deny various malicious rumours circulating about his fortifying Edinburgh castle, retaining control of the mint and preparing to resist royal authority.[169] Besides, on learning of Glamis' melancholy fate, he observed to Angus that his demise was 'an unhappy chance quhilk na doubt is to my greit greif'.[170] These hardly seem the sentiments of someone who felt aggrieved.

Previously, on 15th March, Glamis, Ruthven and Herries had arrived in Edinburgh requesting that Morton should hand over the castle to the new government so that new custodians of it might be installed. In addition, 'The irenis of the counyie hous wes desirit with tene thousand pundis money'. In return, the commissioners delivered the exoneration 'dischairging him of all thingis and intromissionis that micht be layd to his chairge sen entrie in the regiment . . . '[171] Their business with the ex-regent concluded, the representatives of the new regime left Edinburgh the following day, obviously with some reservations about Morton's reaction since they took the precaution of asking the town council to keep a careful watch on his supporters within the castle.[172]

These instructions, as it happened, led a day later to an ugly clash between the garrison and some of the townspeople. The latter, obediently observing the commissioners' orders, had tried to prevent a couple of small cannons being taken into the castle. In retaliation, a small detachment had sallied out of the fortress and 'be schotis of hagbutis and pistoletis slew thrie tounsmen and hurt fyve or sex'.[173] Again, Morton would appear to have been anxious to play down the whole episode which he described to Lochleven as a trivial business 'come foolishelie on'. His only ambition, he confided in the same letter to his cousin, was 'to leif quietlie, to serve my

God and the King, my maister'.[174] This objective he would seem to have been on the point of realising when, shortly afterwards, he handed over the castle and its contents to the reconstituted commission in which Rothes took the place of Glamis.[175]

NOTES

1. *For details,* Chap. 6.
2. *A.P.S.,* iii, 71–77.
3. *Ibid,* 81–83.
4. *R.P.C.,* ii, 204.
5. *T.A.,* xii, 341.
6. *A.P.S.,* iii, 82–83.
7. *Ibid,* 84–94.
8. Keith, *Bishops,* 226–27.
9. Donaldson, *Trial of Mary,* 128; Brunton and Haig, *Senators of the College of Justice,* 119.
10. *Scots Peerage,* i, 343.
11. *R.S.S.,* vi, No. 2148.
12. *Ibid,* No. 1191.
13. The first reference to this appointment is in the minutes of the privy council, 15th December, 1573, *R.P.C.,* ii, 313.
14. *R.S.S.,* vi, No. 2681; vii, No. 897.
15. *Ibid,* vi, No. 2682; vii, Nos. 494, 775, 786–87.
16. *Ibid,* vii, No. 1271.
17. *Ibid,* vi, No. 1961.
18. *Ibid,* Nos. 2434, 2548; vii, Nos. 183, 1007.
19. *Ibid,* No. 8; vi, No. 2771.
20. *R.M.S.,* iv, No. 2407; *R.S.S.,* vi, No. 2175.
21. *Ibid,* vii, No. 1059; *R.M.S.,* iv, No. 2717.
22. *R.S.S.,* vii, Nos. 272, 279, 334, 1199, 1318.
23. *C.S.P. Scot.,* v, 396.
24. *See* Chap. 7, Maxwell, however, was not particularly well rewarded.
25. *R.M.S.,* iv, Nos. 2111, 2248, 2344–47; *R.S.S.,* vii, No. 811.
26. *R.S.S.,* vi, No. 2283; vii, Nos. 1072, 1353.
27. *Ibid,* Nos. 111, 1311; vi, No. 2542.
28. *R.M.S.,* iv, No. 2152.
29. Fraser, *Douglas,* ii, 327.
30. *R.P.C.,* ii, 572.
31. *R.S.S.,* vii, No. 1048; *R.P.C.,* ii, 613.
32. *R.M.S.,* iv, No. 2753.

33. *Scots Peerage,* iv, 578–79; Fraser, *Douglas,* ii, 342.
34. Rae, *Scottish Frontier,* 244.
35. *See* Chap. 9, 177–78.
36. Melville recommended that Carmichael should 'grace him at every word, find na fault with his procedingis bot serve all his affections with gret deligence and continowell onwating', *Memoirs,* 260–61.
37. *R.S.S.,* vii, Nos. 374, 607, 696, 955, 1080.
38. *Ibid,* No. 926.
39. *Ibid,* No. 378.
40. *Scots Peerage,* ii, 161; v, 298.
41. *R.S.S.,* vi, Nos. 2594, 2790; vii, Nos. 249, 714, 1242.
42. *R.M.S.,* iv, Nos. 2400, 2628.
43. *R.S.S.,* vi, No. 2255; vii, No. 540.
44. *Scots Peerage,* i, 188; *Edin. Rec. (1573–89),* 576.
45. *R.S.S.,* vi, Nos. 2696, 2058; vii, Nos. 368, 939.
46. *Ibid,* Nos. 263, 1312.
47. *Ibid,* No. 793.
48. *Ibid,* No. 43.
49. *Ibid,* vi, No. 2265; vii, Nos. 71, 76, 835, 1325, 1333, 1448.
50. Fraser, *Douglas,* ii, 170. However, cf. *R.P.C.,* iii, 294, where Morton is referred to as Auchinleck's 'moder broder'.
51. Jervise, *Memorials,* ii, 111–12.
52. Hume, *History,* ii, 238.
53. *R.M.S.,* iv, (1546–80).
54. *T.A.,* xiii, 101, 149.
55. *R.P.C.,* ii, 506.
56. *R.S.S.,* vii, No. 1209.
57. *Ibid,* No. 1209; *see also, R.P.C.,* ii, 528–29.
58. *T.A.,* xiii, 348.
59. *C.S.P. Scot.,* v, 283.
60. Hume, *History,* ii, 244–45; for Auchinleck's menacing behaviour towards the provost of Edinburgh in August, 1578, *see* Chap. 8, 157.
61. *R.S.S.,* vi, Nos. 2346, 2431, 2581, 2743; vii, No. 1409.
62. *Ibid,* vi, Nos. 2500, 2526; vii, Nos. 1324, 1339, 1346, 1400, 1454.
63. *R.M.S.,* iv, Nos. 2181, 2288, 2309.
64. *T.A.,* xii, 360; in addition he was awarded expenses of £666.13.4. in August, 1574, *T.A.,* xiii, 28.
65. *R.S.S.,* vi, Nos. 2700–01; vii, No. 788.
66. *Ibid,* vi, Nos. 2518, 2598, 2782.
67. *C.S.P. Scot.,* v, 36.
68. *R.P.C.,* ii, 388.
69. *C.S.P. Scot.,* v, 35.
70. *R.P.C.,* ii, 381.

71. *Ibid*, 420, 423.
72. *Ibid*, 356; *Scots peerage*, iv, 538.
73. They are all to be found in attendance at Aberdeen; *R.P.C.*, ii, 388.
74. *T.A.*, xiii, 24, 27.
75. *R.P.C.*, ii, 388.
76. *T.A.*, xiii, App. ii, 323 & 328.
77. *Ibid*, 318–29.
78. *Abdn. Counc.*, 11–12.
79. *Ibid*, 12–13.
80. *Ibid*, 15; *R.P.C.*, ii, 402–03.
81. *Abdn. Counc.*, 13–15; *R.P.C.*, ii, 394–96.
82. Those who subscribed included the earls of Errol and Buchan, lords Glamis, Innermeath and Sinclair, the masters of Marischal and Forbes, the commendator of Deer and over sixty lairds; *R.P.C.*, ii, 398–40.
83. *Abdn. Counc.*, 13.
84. *Diurnal*, 342.
85. *A.P.S.*, iii, 74.
86. *H.M.C. Rep. ix*, App. 192.
87. *C.S.P. Scot.*, iv, 585, 621–23; *H.M.C. (Salisbury MSS)*, ii, 56.
88. *C.S.P. Scot.*, iv, 608.
89. *T.A.*, xii, 364.
90. *C.S.P. Scot.*, v, 36.
91. *R.P.C.*, ii, 330–31.
92. *Scots Peerage*, i, 344–45.
93. *R.P.C.*, ii, 330.
94. *C.S.P. Scot.*, v, 53.
95. *R.P.C.*, ii, 331.
96. *C.S.P. Scot.*, v, 37, 42–44.
97. *Ibid*, 50–51.
98. *Ibid*, 49–55; there is a draft copy of the countess of Argyll's letter to queen Elizabeth in S.R.O., Moray Muniments, i, Box 15, 632.
99. *C.S.P. Scot.*, v, 52.
100. *A.P.S.*, iii, 84 and 86; *R.P.C.*, ii, 435.
101. *C.S.P. Scot.*, v, 114.
102. *Ibid*, 26, 64.
103. *Ibid*, 119.
104. *Ibid*, 50.
105. *H.M.C. Rep. vi*, App. 655.
106. *C.S.P. Scot.*, v, 197.
107. Huntly's death was apparently the result of a rashly undertaken game of sixteenth-century football, *Scots Peerage*, iv, 540.
108. *R.P.C.*, ii, 500.
109. *Ibid*, 533.

110. *Ibid*, 538–39; *T.A.*, xiii, 133–34.
111. *Ibid*, 546.
112. *Ibid*, 587–88.
113. *Ibid*, 597.
114. The exact date is not given but they forfeited their sureties on 1st January, 1578, *Ibid*, 661.
115. Gregory, *History of the Western Highlands*, 215.
116. *R.P.C.*, ii, 547.
117. *Ibid*, 660–61; *T.A.*, xiii, 186.
118. *H.M.C. Rep. vi*, App. 696–97.
119. *R.P.C.*, ii, 661, 663–64.
120. *Ibid*, 663.
121. *Ibid*, 673–74; *T.A.*, xiii, 193.
122. Fraser, *Grant*, iii, 143–49.
123. *R.P.C.*, ii, 674.
124. *Ibid*, 674–75.
125. *H.M.C. Rep. (Hastings)*, ii, 10.
126. *C.S.P. Scot.*, v, 229–30; it would appear there had been attempts at such a settlement for nearly a year, *Argyll Letters*, 13–14.
127. *H.M.C. Rep. (Hastings)*, ii, 10.
128. *Ibid.*, 10; *Historie and Life of King James the Sext*, 162; Teulet, *Papiers*, ii, 363.
129. *C.S.P. Scot.*, v, 230.
130. *Historie and Life of King James the Sext*, 159–60.
131. *H.M.C. (Salisbury MSS)*, ii, 162.
132. *C.S.P. Scot.*, v, 274.
133. *Historie and Life of King James the Sext*, 159–60.
134. Gregory, *History of the Western Highlands*, 216–17.
135. N.L.S., Morton papers, 77, f.28; printed in *Mort. Reg.*, i, 87–89.
136. N.L.S., Morton papers, 77, f.29; printed in *Mort. Reg.*, i, 90.
137. N.L.S., Morton papers, 77, f.29 and 30; printed in *Mort. Reg.*, i, 90–91.
138. *A.P.S.*, iii, 115.
139. Spottiswoode, *History*, ii, 206.
140. Moysie, *Memoirs*, 1.
141. Confirmed on 1st & 4th June, 1578; *R.M.S.*, iv, Nos. 278 and 283.
142. *Scots Peerage*, vi, 233.
143. *Argyll Letters*, 13–14.
144. 'Our freindlie dealing and confidence in the house of Mar is not thankfully acquite', N.L.S. Morton papers, 77, f.33; printed in *Mort. Reg.*, i, 91.
145. *R.P.C.*, ii, 303, 326–27, 436.
146. Fraser, *Carlaverock*, i, 232.
147. *R.P.C.*, ii, 613, 631, 729; he was, in fact, re-appointed warden of west march in March, 1578, *ibid.*, 678–79.

148. *Ibid,* 527–28.
149. *A.P.S.,* iii, 117.
150. S.R.O., Airlie Muniments, ii, GD16, 569.
151. *R.P.C.,* ii, 479.
152. He was said to 'depend wholly on Ruthven', *C.S.P. Scot.,* v, 254.
153. *A.P.S.,* iii, 119.
154. *See* Chap. 7, 128–29.
155. *A.P.S.,* iii, 118; *R.S.S.,* vii, No. 1527.
156. Melville, *Memoirs,* 260.
157. *A.P.S.,* iii, 115.
158. *Ibid,* 117; *C.S.P. Scot.,* v, 276–77.
159. *Warrender Papers,* i, 135–36.
160. *C.S.P. Scot.,* v, 275.
161. *Ibid,* 275–76.
162. *A.P.S.,* iii, 115.
163. Absent on this occasion were the earls of Eglinton and Mar, lord Innermeath and the bishop of Brechin.
164. *Mort. Reg.,* i, 100.
165. N.L.S., Morton papers, 77, f.34; printed in *Mort. Reg.,* i, 92–95.
166. *C.S.P. Scot.,* v, 276–77.
167. *Ibid,* 283.
168. Calderwood, *History,* iii, 395; Hume of Godscroft, *History,* 255.
169. N.L.S., Morton papers, 77, f.36; printed in *Mort. Reg.,* i, 101–02.
170. N.L.S., Morton papers, 77, f.38; printed in *Mort. Reg.,* i, 105.
171. Moysie, *Memoirs,* 3.
172. *Ibid,* 3.
173. *Ibid,* 4; Calderwood, *History,* iii, 396.
174. N.L.S., Morton papers, 77, f.40; printed in *Mort. Reg.,* i, 103.
175. N.L.S., Morton papers, 77, f.42; printed in *Mort. Reg.,* i, 106; his surrender of the castle and his voluntary demission were confirmed by act of parliament on 31st March, 1578, *A.P.S.,* iii, 120.

4

Governance, Part II

On Tuesday, 1st April, 1578, Edinburgh castle was handed over to John Cunningham of Drumquassel and James Seton of Touche, its temporary custodians, and Morton retired to Lochleven castle, the residence of his cousin, William Douglas.[1] Here he had time to reflect on recent events, and it may possibly have occurred to him that he should have endeavoured to reach an agreement with Atholl and thus detached him from his powerful ally, Argyll, which is certainly what the English government would have preferred him to attempt.[2] Yet his demission 'was indeid sa quicklie performit', as one source observes, 'that before the regent could get intelligence thay war all conspyrit in myndis and body aganis him and voitit all that the king sould accept the regement'.[3] Again, on second thoughts, he may have concluded, as did some of his followers, notably lord Boyd, that he had resigned too hastily.[4] However, this would have meant ignoring the formidable strength of his adversaries who were not only firmly entrenched around the king at Stirling but also had the support of the citizens of Edinburgh. As far as the members of the town council were concerned, there were two main reasons for their antagonism towards Morton. There was his unpopular financial policy,[5] and there was his treatment of some of them in the aftermath of the siege of 1573. In the latter instance, compositions had been taken from Marian supporters, ostensibly to assist the crown and compensate loyal citizens for damages sustained during the civil war. The regent, however, so one account alleges, 'causit bring the haill to the castell of Edinburgh, and wald not pairt with ane penny'.[6] Thus, in the interval between his abdication and the capitulation of the castle, the town council were thanked on two separate occasions 'for thair gryt travellis and guid service'.[7] Finally, he doubtless noted — and his subsequent behaviour suggests that he did — that his opponents' success had depended to a large extent on the influence which they exercised over the king. There was nothing exceptional about this during a royal minority, yet the hostility of the master of Mar and the conspiratorial activities within the royal household had done great harm to Morton's cause despite, apparently, a last-minute attempt by the regent 'to bestow part of his gold unto sa many of them as he beleved wer wonnable'.[8] Therefore, should he wish to retrieve his position, an essential prerequisite was control of the king and his guardians.

'First Rowme and Place'

The incident which signalled that Morton's return was a distinct possibility took place at Stirling castle on Saturday, 27th April. It would appear, according to the most reliable account, that the master of Mar, residing in the gatehouse of the castle, was suddenly awakened at 6 a.m. that morning by his nephew, John, earl of Mar, and his two brothers, the commendators of Cambuskenneth and Dryburgh, accompanied by a number of servants. Their business was not hunting, as they had originally seemed to indicate, but to accuse the master of treating his nephew in an unsatisfactory manner and, as guardian of the king and his castle, far exceeding the powers which he had been granted. A mêlée now ensued, in the course of which the master's son was mortally injured, and meanwhile, Argyll, who was also staying in the castle, arrived on the scene with some of his followers. But, by this time, 'the fray was pacified' and the protagonists had adjourned to seek a compromise. There followed a joint statement informing the council in Edinburgh that the two parties were reconciled and recommending they 'proceed forwards in the course determined for the government as though no such matter had happened'.[9]

Not surprisingly, there was an emergency meeting of the council at which Montrose was dispatched to ascertain the true state of affairs at Stirling. Despite his reassuring message that everything was 'well pacified, and that this government shall not by this accident be impeached', there was a general exodus of the council from Edinburgh to Stirling.[10] In addition, captain David Preston of Craigmillar was ordered to move the troops under his command to the scene of the action.[11]

That the upshot was a peaceful solution must be due in no small measure to the wise precaution taken by the earl of Mar's faction in issuing a proclamation limiting the number of followers each member of the council could bring to Stirling 'to the effect that the godlie and gude werk intendit may the better proceed'.[12] Under these arrangements, each earl was restricted to twenty-four followers while 'every lord or uther persoun being of the same counsale' to a maximum of sixteen.[13] Thus, on 3rd May, the council was able to announce that the earl of Mar had displaced his uncle and that he took upon himself 'the charge of the attendance upoun his

Majesteis persoun preservation thairof and keping of his said Castell of Striveling during his Hienes being thair'.[14]

Although Sir Henry Killigrew could write in April that Morton 'meddles with nothing',[15] it has been generally assumed that the ex-regent did not spend all of his time at Lochleven in mere contemplation or gardening. 'He seemed to do nothing but to make alleys and gardens,' wrote Calderwood, 'yet was he contriving deeper matters.'[16] 'Making the allees of the garden even, his mynd was occupied in the mean tym upon cruked paithes, with a complot how to be brocht in again to be maister of the court', was Sir James Melville's more sardonic estimate of his activities at Lochleven.[17] At the same time, Morton never subsequently admitted being involved in the events at Stirling on 27th April, specifically denying any complicity when questioned before his execution,[18] and perhaps, therefore, the earl of Mar and his two uncles had acted spontaneously though confident of support from the Douglas family for their enterprise. Morton certainly was not present at Stirling on 27th April, as Melville would have us believe,[19] although he was soon aware of developments at the castle. This information was provided by Douglas of Lochleven who, having been contacted by the commendators of Cambuskenneth and Dryburgh on the Saturday, had joined them later that day. Morton, in turn, had wasted no time in notifying the earl of Angus and urging him, unnecessarily as it so happened, to raise as many supporters as he could.[20]

Whether, as the Argyll-Atholl party was later to proclaim, the earl of Mar and his associates were 'his apostat and subornit instruments'[21] or not, there is no controversy about the significance for Morton of these events. Undoubtedly, he was in a much stronger position to effect his reinstatement, a fact, as his subsequent policy proves, which he clearly appreciated.

Morton's first move was to make overtures to his former opponents, Atholl and Argyll, about the possibility of a reconciliation. On 2nd May, for example, Sir James Balfour of Pittendreich, whose services as an intermediary had been utilised earlier at Perth in 1573, submitted details of recent negotiations he had been conducting on the ex-regent's behalf with Atholl. He also enclosed a bond of friendship from the latter for Morton's consideration, but Morton was not completely satisfied with some of the articles in this bond nor, for that matter, with the omission of 'some particular heads commonit betwix the laird of Carmychaell and George Drummond'. Moreover, his request to be permitted to rejoin the court at Stirling had been rejected meantime and this obviously upset him. 'It appears,' he replied, 'gif my lord had been willing to have endit matters with me he would not have refusit my coming to Striveling at this tyme'.[22]

This, however, was only a temporary setback to Morton's plans for a settlement. Queen Elizabeth was supporting his efforts and, in her correspondence with James VI, was exhorting him to reinstate his former regent on his council.[23] At the same time, she exerted diplomatic pressure on Argyll, pressing him 'to be a mean to the king and the rest of the nobility for the calling of the earl of Morton about him as a councillor'.[24] Consequently, as a result of these endeavours, Morton now participated in discussions with Argyll and Atholl which took place at Craigmillar castle on 23rd May.

What decisions were actually reached and Morton's behaviour therafter have been the subject of contrasting interpretations. In Calderwood's account, the leaders of the two factions, having met at Craigmillar, retired to Morton's residence at Dalkeith where they 'embraced (each) other, dynned and supped' before returning that evening to Edinburgh. The three noblemen, so Calderwood states, had agreed to ride together the next day to Stirling for a joint meeting with the king, but Morton ignored this arrangement by rising early and setting off before the others. Once at Stirling, he had persuaded Sir William Murray of Tullibardine to admit him and his followers to the castle where he quickly assumed control over both Tullibardine and the earl of Mar, king James' youthful custodian.[25] However, this version of the sequel to the Craigmillar conference differs both from that of Robert Bowes, who was actually present, and from that given by the Edinburgh notary, David Moysie, in his *Memoirs* which are a contemporary narrative of these events. As far as the English ambassador in concerned, he is quite definite that the three principal noblemen had 'agreed very friendly together', although he does concede that Argyll and Atholl would have preferred if Morton had waited until Monday before proceeding to Stirling.[26] Again, in Moysie's account, there is no hint of serious disagreement between the two sides. Indeed, he affirms that six days elapsed before 'the erle of Mortoun and ather of thame red be thair owin companeis all to Sterling'. Moysie, nonetheless, does stress the point that Morton's influence with the king was now considerable and that he enjoyed 'more familiaretie with the Kingis Majestie then the erles of Ergyle, Atholl, Montroise or ony utheris of thair factioun'.[27]

Whether or not Morton upstaged his rivals by riding ahead of them to Stirling, the most feasible explanation of the subsequent conduct of Argyll and Atholl is that, having recognised that the *coup* of the earl of Mar and his accomplices had made it virtually impossible to prevent Morton's appearance at court, they decided to resolve the situation by calling for a full meeting of the royal council. Accordingly, on 2nd June, 'His Majesteis haill Counsale' was summoned, ostensibly to examine 'wechtie caussis concerning his Hienes and the publict weill', but assuredly also to obtain a vote of confidence for the two earls and their faction.[28] A defeat for Morton in these circumstances would convince the king that he did not have the backing of most councillors.

Unfortunately, they had underestimated Morton's prestige and, at the convention on 12th June, twenty-five of the forty-eight members voted for him 'to be of his Majesteis ordinar privy counsale' with 'first rowme and place' on that body.[29] Of those present at the assembly which had deposed him on 8th March, the earl of Mar, the commendators of Dunfermline and Cambuskenneth, the bishop of Moray and Sir William Murray of Tullibardine now endorsed his return to power. In only three months, Morton had been restored, if only by a narrow majority, to a position apparently comparable in all but title to his former office.

Two days later, Morton, in a move obviously designed to ensure that he remained close to the king, announced that the parliament due to be held in Edinburgh on 10th July was to be transferred to Stirling where it would re-assemble on 15th July.[30] The first indications of any reaction to this came shortly afterwards at a privy council session on 17th June when Argyll, with several others, strongly criticised a mission to England due to be undertaken by the commendator of Dunfermline. Although the secretary was being sent to assess the possibilities of a league whose aims included the 'suppraising of domestic sedition'[31] – clearly an item likely to arouse the suspicions of Morton's opponents – the real motive for Argyll's disapproval was more probably resentment at parliament being switched to Stirling.

When parliament did convene at Stirling on 15th July, it was more a gathering of Morton's supporters than a representative assembly. Thus, of the twenty-five members present with Morton and the king in the great hall of Stirling castle that day, the earls of Angus, Buchan and Mar, lords Boyd, Cathcart, Oliphant, Ruthven and Somerville, the archbishop of Glasgow, the bishops of Aberdeen, Caithness and Moray, and the commendators of Cambuskenneth and Dryburgh were incontrovertibly on Morton's side.[32] The others in attendance were also his adherents, at least for the time being. To indicate its disapproval, the Argyll-Atholl faction boycotted these proceedings, sending as its commissioners the earl of Montrose, lord Lindsay and the bishop of Orkney. Its spokesman was Lindsay who, immediately after the opening preliminaries, protested about the legality and freedom of a parliament held within a castle and, the following day, when the Lords of the Articles were being chosen, launched another attack on the nature of the parliament.[33] Lindsay's complaints provoked king

James, supposedly at Morton's prompting, to reply that, 'least anie man sould judge this not to be a free parliament I declare it to be free and those that love me will thinke as I think'.[34] By the same token, Morton, whose council had already publicly declared that the king was in no way 'detenit aganis his will', now held an emergency council meeting where it was agreed that the recent declaration by the king should be given widespread publicity.[35] Moreover, in an effort to guarantee solidarity, it was also affirmed that everyone presently in attendance at this parliament would remain in Stirling until it was dissolved.[36] The three dissident commissioners were now summoned before the Lords of the Articles where they were accused of attempting to disrupt parliament and requested to withdraw their allegations.[37] The bishop of Orkney acquiesced but Lindsay and Montrose, remaining adamant, were ordered 'for certaine ressonabill caussis and considerations moving his Hienes . . . to remaine within thair ludgeingis within the burgh of Striveling'.[38]

On Friday, 25th July, at its final session, parliament ratified, among other items, the earl of Mar's custody of the king and Morton's restoration, and appointed various commissions for legal, university and church reform. Finally, a new council was approved consisting of the earls of Morton, Argyll, Buchan, Eglinton, Glencairn, Lennox[39] and Rothes, lords Boyd, Cathcart and Ochiltree, the commendators of Cambuskenneth and Dryburgh, and those who occupied official positions in the government. Of the latter, the most important were the chancellor, Atholl, the treasurer, Ruthven, the secretary, the commendator of Dunfermline, and the comptroller, Sir William Murray of Tullibardine. There was also an arrangement whereby there would be a rota of four councillors who would be in permanent residence with the king at Stirling for two months at a time. By this device, Morton, Cathcart, Lennox and Cambuskenneth would be the first group in regular attendance followed by Argyll, Boyd, Buchan and Ochiltree.[40]

The overall impression arising from these proceedings is that Morton was prepared to tolerate the presence of Argyll and Atholl on the council but was determined that none of their colleagues would sit on it. Indeed, he seems to have made some kind of attempt to separate Argyll from his allies, not only by having the king specially request his presence at the new council but also by writing to him in a similar fashion himself.[41] Although Argyll did not reply favourably, his colleagues do seem to have been somewhat disorganised at this juncture, with Atholl on the point of returning home, the earl of Caithness already in Fife and heading northwards, and lord Herries apparently unwell or unenthusiastic.[42] In fact, it would appear to have been Montrose's escape from house arrest at Stirling and his arrival at Edinburgh on 23rd July which spurred the disaffected nobility to a more determined course of action.[43]

Argyll and Atholl, with their cohorts, now congregated in Edinburgh where they not only ignored privy council orders to disperse[44] but assaulted those who were attempting to enlist loyal forces within the town. Thus, to quote Calderwood, 'When the drum was beattin, and the trumpet blowin, for leveing of soldiours to Captan Hume, the lords caused breake the drum, and take the trumpet from the trumpeter'.[45] Claiming to be 'the chosin counsellors of the King's majestie and remnant of the nobilitie heere assembled', they published their own proclamation in defence of their actions. Morton, they declared, had seized control of the king, transferred parliament from Edinburgh to Stirling, had ill-treated Montrose and Lindsay, and now was making military preparations against those who sought nothing but 'the King's majestie's deliverance and libertie'. His purpose in all this had solely been 'to mainteane this his usurped authoritie, to worke the utter wracke and exterminion of the King's Majesties faithfull and obedient subjects'.[46] Not surprisingly, Morton and his council issued a strenuous denial of this proclamation, asserting it was the work of men whose 'querrel (was) groundit upoun untreuth' and who had 'poysoun lang lurking in thair hartis'.[47]

Meanwhile, Morton and his allies faced up to the prospect of a civil war. The first order for an armed levy came on 26th July and, despite the statement that it was a consequence of 'the monyfauld reiffis, slauchtaris, heirschippis, oppin robbereis and oppressionis quhilkis hes bene and dalie is committit and usit in diverse partis of this realme bot speciale be the inhabitantis of his Hienes bordouris', it gave the impression from the wide recruitment area of being distinctly more than a mere border muster.[48] This was confirmed the following day partly by the terms of the earl of Angus's commission, as its commander, whereby he was instructed 'to pas and persw the saidis dissobeydient personis . . . be fyre, swird and all uther kynd of hostilitie, quhairevir thay may be apprehendit',[49] and, on 29th July, by orders summoning all able-bodied men to assemble at Stirling on 10th August.[50] At the same time, numerous letters were urgently despatched all over central Scotland to those regarded as faithful supporters[51] while, on 31st July, no doubt to strengthen the king's forces, Sir David Hume of Fishwick, Thomas Crawford of Jordanhill, James Preston and Andrew Lambie were commissioned to recruit 'certane bandis of men of weare for furthsetting of his Majesteis authoritie and service'.[52]

On 12th August, the rival armies faced each other at Falkirk. Angus was in command of the government forces, while the insurgents' troops comprised the various units attached to the earls of Argyll, Atholl and Montrose, lords Innermeath, Livingston, Maxwell and Seton and the masters of Cassillis and Lindsay.[53] In addition, there were the borderers who came with Cessford, Coldenknowes and Hume of Manderston, although these lairds, since lord Hunsdon, governor of Berwick, had instructed Bowes to warn Cessford of his intentions, must have been aware of the possibility of English intervention on Morton's behalf.[54] Contemporary opinion is unanimous in its verdict that, although the two sides were numerically roughly equal, Morton's opponents were better-equipped and more reliable.[55] Moreover, the latter, as Bowes observed, 'either for their own causes or their friends' bore Morton a deadly hatred and so were desirous of revenge, 'which was but in a few of the king's side against any of the other lords'.[56] In fact, Morton, in all likelihood, doubted the reliability of his men as, on two separate occasions, on 12th and 13th August, he ordered Angus to withdraw rather than engage the enemy.[57]

However, an actual showdown was averted since, on 14th August, as a result of the mediatory efforts of Robert Bowes and two Edinburgh ministers, James Lawson and David Lindsay, both parties accepted a truce and signed a joint agreement. The main provisions were that both sides agreed to disband their forces; Argyll and Atholl, since the king was convinced their actions arose 'from the love and tender affection they bear to him', were assured there would be no reprisals; Argyll was to have free access to the king; Montrose and Lindsay were to be added to the privy council, and a commission of eight noblemen nominated on queen Elizabeth's recommendation was to be appointed to examine the outstanding differences between the two parties.[58]

Morton, by this settlement, had clearly survived a perilous threat to the position which he had lately retrieved and, it might be imagined, had turned a dangerous corner. Bowes, however, still had serious reservations about the permanence of this recent peace formula. 'I traist,' he wrote to lord Scrope, governor of Carlisle, 'ye sall heire tell the lords sall cum shortelie to this towne of Edinbrough again for thair gayes so manye evill reaportes betwix the lords and the erle of Morton that I thinck yt sall be als evill as evir it was before and wars for thay will nevir be peacifyed in quyet maner till thay meit (each) other in the feldes.'[59] Although, on this occasion, Bowes' estimate was somewhat too pessimistic, Morton did have problems with the date and rendezvous for the proposed meeting between the contending commissioners. His opponents insisted that it should be held on 30th November at Edinburgh, whereas Morton adhered to the 20th of

September at Stirling[60] and, 'Because the haill aucht nobill men writtin for be his Majestie convenit not at Striviling the said XX day of September throw the schortnes of the warning or utheris impedimentis', the meeting was re-arranged for Stirling one month hence.[61] That this conference did occur is confirmed by Bowes[62] and by David Moysie, who is the only authority to give full details of the proceedings. Apparently, Montrose, Sir James Balfour of Pittendreich, the laird of Bargeny and Peter Hay, bailie of Errol, attended representing the Argyll-Atholl party, while the earl of Buchan, lord Boyd, the commendator of Dunfermline and Sir John Gordon of Lochinvar were there on Morton's behalf. As a result of these discussions, according to Moysie, Argyll and Montrose were reconciled to Morton, and it was also agreed that there should be a convention at Stirling in January, 1579, to be followed by the summoning of parliament in March.[63]

That some such agreement was concluded in October, 1578 is confirmed partly by the presence of Montrose and Argyll for the first time at the council in November[64] and by certain bonds of friendship contracted about this date between Argyll and the earl of Mar and Morton himself.[65] Further confirmation of the improved relations between the two sides is provided by a report by the French ambassador in London who, on 15th November, 1578, informed his government that 'Les countes D'Arguil, d'Athol, de Cadenesse, de Montrosse et de Linnesay se sont si bien accordez avec le counte de Morton qu'ilz sont aujourd'hay ensemble comme freres'.[66] Corroboration that a convention was also intended can be found in both the treasurer's accounts[67] as well as in the Edinburgh burgh records where the orders both to attend such an assembly and the reasons for its postponement due to short notice, the inconvenience and bad weather are given.[68]

The Hamilton Vendetta

No parliament or convention was actually held in March, 1579 but, significantly, from 12th March and for over a week, the privy council was augmented by so many unfamiliar faces as to have the appearance of a convention. The explanation for the presence of, in the first instance, Atholl and such uncommon figures as lords Drummond, Herries, Innermeath, Oliphant, Sinclair and Stewart,[69] the archbishops of St. Andrews and Glasgow, the bishops of Brechin and Dunkeld, the commendators of Balmerino, Cupar, Culross, Deer and Inchcolm, in addition to the regular council members, did not become apparent until the discussion of business on 17th March.[70] On that day, David Borthwick of Lochhill and Robert Crichton of Eliok, the royal advocates, delivered a report concerning an 'Actioun aganis Lord Claude Hammiltoun, commendator of Paislay for the superplus and omittit thriddis, fruittis and rentis quhatsumevir not gevin up in the rentall of the said Abbay of Paislay off all yeiris and termes bigane sen the said Claudies awin interes and possessioun to the fruittis of the same Abbay'.[71] In other words, the pretext of discrepancies in Claud Hamilton's administration of Paisley abbey was to be the signal for a combined assault on the house of Hamilton, and it was this prospect which had brought together the Douglases, Stewarts, Campbells, Grahams, Leslies and the others. This was to be the first manifestation of what was intended.

During the earliest part of Morton's regency, there had been some ill-feeling between the Hamiltons and the Douglases, mainly on account of the slaughter, by the former, of James Johnstone of Westerhall, a dependant of Angus. Nevertheless, relations were greatly improved when, at Holyrood, on 7th March, 1575, lords Claud and John Hamilton publicly atoned for their actions before Angus. This atonement took the form of a rather dramatic ceremony at which the two Hamilton brothers, walking barefooted and bareheaded across the inner court of the palace, suddenly knelt down and, in a gesture implying they placed themselves at his mercy, each presented Angus with a naked sword.[72] A bond of friendship was then signed between the two brothers and Morton and his nephew.[73] The latter, in return, with Westerhall's widow, who was to receive 2,000 merks as compensation,[74] subscribed a remission to the members of the Hamilton family involved in the affair.[75]

However, one member on the Douglas side, namely William Douglas of Lochleven, Morton's cousin, proved irreconcilable. Claiming to seek revenge for the assassination of his half-brother, the earl of Moray, he continued a single-handed vendetta against the Hamiltons.[76] Consequently, he was involved in a serious incident in Fife in the summer of 1575 in which, although accounts are widely divergent, he undoubtedly behaved in a violent manner towards lord John Hamilton as he sought to pass through his land.[77] Morton, on this occasion, was preoccupied with the Redeswyre crisis but, when there was a similar disturbance in February, 1577, he acted decisively. On 2nd March, he summoned the lieges to assemble at Kinghorn and Cupar on 5th March 'to pass furthwart and accumpany his Grace as thay sal be commandit for quieting of the saidis troublis'.[78] Whether the services of the inhabitants of Lothian and Fife were actually called upon seems improbable since Morton certainly was not in Fife on 5th March when, in fact, he attended a meeting of his council in Edinburgh.[79] It is more likely, therefore, that the proclamation was intended as a salutory warning. On 22nd March, Lochleven and lord John were instructed to appear before the council on 20th May and meanwhile give assurances for their good behaviour.[80] Lochleven 'marvellit' at being asked for such a guarantee, only to be sternly rebuked by his cousin who reminded him that it was requested so that 'gude order and rule be kepit in the countrie quhilk during the tyme of oure office and charge we are bound of dewty to see the same observed and kepit and trustis that all our friendis will respect the same and not gif occasion to the contrary'.[81] But Lochleven remained intransigent and, on 17th May, an order was issued for his imprisonment in Edinburgh castle.[82]

Morton, therefore, in his years as regent, had never displayed personal animosity towards the Hamiltons and, as has been seen, was prepared, for the sake of law and order, to incur the displeasure of his cousin rather than allow him to take justice into his own hands. This being his past record, why did he sanction the persecution of the Hamiltons in 1579? There are at least two convincing arguments for his tactics.

In the first instance, the Hamilton purge could serve as a useful diversion so that the other nobility would not have what Hume of Godscroft has described as 'leisure to think of him and his late greatness'.[83] Furthermore, because of hereditary claims of the Hamiltons to the succession as well as the involvement of certain prominent members of their family in such events as the assassination of Moray and the death of Lennox and their generally chequered political record, it was an operation for which he could expect widespread support. Killigrew, writing in 1575, at the time of the first episode with Lochleven, was then of the opinion that Morton's cousin was merely one representative of an anti-Hamilton party whose membership included Argyll, Atholl, Buchan, Ruthven, Lindsay and the house of Mar.[84] A scrutiny of those present during the crucial dates in March, 1579 when the enlarged council planned the attack on the Hamiltons, reveals the English ambassador's earliest estimate as a fairly accurate one and that, in the space of four years, the attitudes of certain noblemen to the Hamiltons remained unchanged.

Secondly, obvious targets for a penurious monarchy, such as James VI's, were the vast family estates of the Hamiltons. These stretched from the isle of Arran on the west coast through Lanarkshire, where lord Claud was both commendator of Paisley and hereditary sheriff of Clydesdale and where their chief residences, Hamilton and Draffen, were located, to their territories in the north-east which lord John held as commendator of Arbroath. The forfeitures and fines which could be realised from these and all the other possessions in the hands of the house of Hamilton unquestionably provide a second motive for the campaign against them. Indeed, this need to enrich the crown was later specifically mentioned in the proclamation of 15th May, 1579, in which it was announced that there would be no disposition of Hamilton lands until parliament convened.[85]

The exact date when Morton first conceived the stratagem of utilising the general antagonism towards the Hamiltons to his own and the crown's advantage cannot be established with absolute certainty. In July, 1578, for example, lords Claud and John had evinced alarm about 'the whisperings of certain particulars present about the King'.[86] This, however, could simply indicate their misgivings about the effect of the influence of the house of Mar on the king's impressionable nature. A more probable occasion was in October at the discussions which resulted in Argyll and Montrose being reconciled to Morton. The promise of an officially backed campaign against the Hamiltons could well have been the inducement which enabled the two parties to eschew their differences. Indeed, one contemporary account does make just such a suggestion. Thus, the anonymous author of *A Chronicle of the Kings of Scotland*, referring to the meeting between the rivals in October, asserts that 'thay being agreitt, entirrit in ane gritt friendschip and all thair dewyiss wes aganis the name of Hamiltoun and for the revendge of the slachtter of the twa Regentis'.[87]

Whenever the seeds of the plot were sown – and it should be remembered that Morton was later to deny it was his idea at all[88] – it was the council's announcement on 17th March, as has already been stated, that it intended prosecuting lord Claud for his maladministration of Paisley abbey which was the earliest overt signal. Why there should be a hiatus of six weeks before further measures were taken is problematical, but the delay was probably caused by a divergence of opinion among the councillors as to the appropriate course of action to be pursued. Some members, at least according to Spottiswoode, advocated that the Hamiltons should be summoned to stand trial, whereas others believed that, since they had already been condemned by a previous statute, they should simply be arrested forthwith.[89] In the end, as the order for their apprehension confirms, it was the second viewpoint which prevailed. Lords Claud and John, now that the king was of age, so it was declared, were no longer protected by the pacification of Perth, and his majesty believed it was his bounden duty to see that 'the saidis decreittis and sensamentis of Parliament gevin and pronuncit aganis the said Johnne and Claude Hammiltonis sal be execute without delay; and to that effect thair personis to be serchit for an apprehendit that they may ressave puneisment according to thair treasonabill deservingis'.[90]

This order was swiftly followed on 1st May by the appointment of Morton, Angus, Mar, Eglinton, Ruthven, Boyd and Cathcart as the commissioners empowered to put it into effect.[91] The next day, lords Claud and

John were proclaimed traitors, and mobilisation instructions were issued ordering those affected to muster at Hamilton or, if necessary, at any other point where their presence was deemed essential.[92] By this date, Morton and his assistants had departed from Stirling, leaving behind them a caretaker government to publish further advice over the next few days. From the tenor of these edicts with their prohibitions on conveying the Hamiltons overseas, it is obvious that the two brothers had eluded the grasp of the commissioners and were trying to escape from the country.[93] Then, on 11th May, because prolonged investments were obviously expected at Hamilton and Draffen castles, both of which had now been under siege for about a week,[94] rather ambitious military arrangements were announced by the council. Under these proposals, each part of the kingdom would provide forces to perform siege duty on a rota basis.[95] That this was an unrealistic proposal was corroborated the following day by an amendment confining those required for service to 'All and sindrie erllis, lordis, frehaldaris landitmen, gentilmen and substantious yemen men dwelland within the boundis of the sherefdomen of Edinburgh principale and within the constabularie of Hadingtoun, Linlythguow, Lanerk, Air and Renfrew and baillieis of Kyle, Carrik and Cunninghame'. This body was ordered to assemble on 20th May at Hamilton, fully armed and with fifteen days' provisions.[96] However, this host was found to be unnecessary since the infantry and artillery were more effective than had been envisaged and, on 19th May, the occupants of Hamilton castle were compelled to surrender unconditionally, while at Draffen the defenders evacuated the fortress under cover of darkness.[97] Meanwhile, at Paisley, the master of Glencairn took possession for the crown of another Hamilton stronghold.[98]

Although lords Claud and John evaded capture, the former, eventually, to England and the latter to France,[99] their deranged brother, James, earl of Arran, with their other brother, David, and their mother, the duchess of Chatelherault, were taken at Draffen and conveyed to Linlithgow.[100] Here, Arran was persuaded to subscribe a document condemning his brothers for disobeying a command requesting them to present him before the privy council,[101] a procedure, in Spottiswoode's estimation, designed to facilitate royal acquisition of the Hamilton estates. The earl, because of his mental condition, so the same author affirms, could not be accused of complicity in his brother's offences but, by this declaration, he was placing both himself and his possessions in the protective custody of the crown.[102]

The fates of the lesser figures attached to the house of Hamilton are clearly indicated by the spate of denunciations and cautions for attendance before the privy council which now ensued. Eventually, a dozen individuals, including James Hamilton of Bothwellhaugh, John Hamilton, provost of Bothwell, Gavin Hamilton of Raploch and Robert Hamilton of Dalserf, had sentences of treason against them ratified by parliament in November, 1579.[103] The remainder, with one notable exception, namely Arthur Hamilton of Mirretoun, captain of Hamilton castle, who was hanged at Stirling on 30th May,[104] 'war compellit', according to one source, 'to answer as law wald'. This entailed a journey to Edinburgh and the exaction of 'great soumes of money for pardoun of sik crymes as ather actuallie thay had done or that could be allegeit aganis thayme'.[105] With a general order of 28th October banishing virtually all Hamiltons from Edinburgh and the court, the process against them was completed.[106]

Finally, before leaving the affair altogether, there is the question of the political wisdom of Morton's anti-Hamilton vendetta. King James, admittedly, seems to have been impressed and supposedly stated, in the presence of the English amabassador, that 'no nobleman's service in Scotland was to be compared to Morton's'.[107] Again, despite the expensive nature of the campaign,[108] the financial position of the crown by means of fines and confiscations must, to some extent, have been improved. Moreover, the various gifts disposed by the crown under the privy seal all had compositions attached to them. Here, a gift of escheat received by Alexander Hamilton, commendator of Kilwinning, a member of a branch of that family unaffected by events, might serve as a typical example. He was given 'the coirnes, cattell, maillis, fermes, proffeittis and dewties of the Manis of Monkcastell within the regality of Kylwynning and schirefdom of Air quhilkis pertenit to Claude Hamilton sumtyme commendator of Paislaw' but was still, however, required to pay a composition of £40.[109] On a different note, another justification for Morton's actions would be that it provided an opportunity to settle old scores against the Hamiltons, and consequently rallied many of the more important members of the nobility to his side at a time when he still needed such support to consolidate his position.

On the other hand, Morton did not retain his king's affection for any length of time. Esmé Stewart, for instance, was shortly to establish himself at court and his own influence was soon to be rapidly eroded. Furthermore, despite the financial plight of the crown, two of the most lucrative Hamilton possessions were relinquished, both of them, ironically, to enemies of Morton. Thus, Esmé Stewart received Arbroath abbey, while his partner, captain James Stewart, was ultimately to acquire the earldom of Arran.[110] Lastly, even if the assault on the Hamiltons did provide Morton with the backing of a substantial number of magnates, it was still a somewhat primitive and barbaric way to govern a country, and queen Elizabeth, for example, criticised his treatment of the Hamiltons on several occasions.[111] Morton, admittedly, was no worse in this respect than his contemporaries but, if he had possessed qualities of superior statemanship, he should either have accepted the advice of those councillors who recommended prosecuting the Hamiltons via the existing legal machinery or he should have desisted from the enterprise altogether.

On 24th April, shortly before the proscription of the Hamiltons got properly under way, there occurred the death at Kincardine castle, near Auchterarder, of the earl of Atholl,[112] an event, in its own way, of some importance. The circumstances surrounding the demise of the earl who had recently attended a banquet at Stirling with Morton soon gave rise to controversy. His son, John, fifth earl of Atholl, for example, writing only a few days later, is to be found referring to 'venemus and extreme poysoun'.[113] Then, at the formal inquest on 15th June before the privy council, his widow, Margaret, countess of Atholl, voiced her suspicions about the manner of her husband's death.[114] Unquestionably, her doubts had been reinforced by the depositions of the physicians present, all but one of whom had declared that her husband had been poisoned. Moreover, the medical expert who had disagreed with his colleagues, a certain Dr. Preston, on being requested to sample some of the evidence, 'having tasted a little of it with his tongue, almost had died, and was after, so long as he lived, sickelie'.[115] Morton, at least according to one source, was one of the prime suspects. 'Whether be advyce of Mortoun,' says this version, 'or be the auld countess of Mar it is uncertayne sik mightie poyson was gevin to the lord Chancellor that upon the fourt day after that bancat he departit this lyff.' However, when it is recollected that the decision to attack the Hamiltons was taken over a month before Atholl's death, some doubts about the reliability of this source are raised. This is especially so when it proceeds to allege that it was only afterwards that Morton, afraid lest the chancellor's friends would bring the Hamiltons to the court and 'that the young king ... sould delyte in new faces and new counsall', instigated the programme against them.[116] Nevertheless, there were, clearly, persistent rumours, much to the alarm of certain members of the Mar family and to the annoyance of Morton.[117] Adam Erskine, commendator of Cambuskenneth, for example, concerned at the outcome of the post mortem, wrote to Robert Erskine of Dun, son of the superintendent of Angus and Mearns, seeking his father's presence at the relevant privy council meeting.[118] Morton, on the other hand, dealt severely with William Turnbull and William Scott, two pamphleteers who, although they had made no reference, specifically, to Atholl, had published scurrilous attacks on him.

Both men were arrested and executed at Stirling in August.[119] This sentence, according to a gift of escheat of Turnbull's goods on 1st September, was condign punishment 'for the inventing and making of leyis of sum of the nobilitie to oure said soverane lord incontrair the tennour of the actis of Parliament maid thairupon'.[120] As might be expected, both families ensured that the parliament of November, 1579 cleared their names officially from any complicity in Atholl's death.[121] However, it seems unlikely that Atholl was poisoned, especially when the statement of his wife that she was also unwell after dining at Stirling is considered,[122] and the fragile constitution of the earl, who had applied in June, 1578 for a licence to go abroad on account of his ill-health, is taken into consideration.[123] Admittedly, this may only have been a safeguard taken by Atholl during a period of considerable political uncertainty, but Andrew Lang's conclusion that it was more likely a surfeit of 'haggis, friar's partens, sheephead and cockie-leekie' does appear a more satisfactory diagnosis of Atholl's fatal illness.[124]

The significance of Atholl's departure is that one of the most powerful figures in the kingdom was removed from the political scene. Thus, Morton, while his opponents had lost an invaluable ally, could regard the situation, at least momentarily, with some satisfaction. In the summer of 1579, understandably, 'he estimit himself to leve in securitie from the dangers of any great enemies in Scotland'.[125] His complacency, however, was to be short-lived since, with the arrival at Leith on 8th September of Esmé Stewart, lord d'Aubigny,[126] there emerged a new challenge to his pre-eminence.

Morton's Downfall

Esmé Stewart was the son of John Stewart who was a brother of Matthew, earl of Lennox, former regent and royal grandfather, and also of Robert Stewart, the present earl of Lennox. John Stewart, while in France, had acquired the title, lord d'Aubigny, which, on his death, had been inherited by Esmé.[127] Whatever Esmé's motives were for arriving at this moment, king James was immediately impressed by his French relative and, in November, as a measure of his favour, rewarded him with the vacant commendatorship of Arbroath abbey,[128] ensuring, also, that it was excluded from any parliamentary statute prohibiting the disposition of forfeited Hamilton lands.[129] Then, in March, 1580, having persuaded Robert, earl of Lennox, to relinquish his title,[130] James presented Esmé with that earldom.[131] In addition, the new earl of Lennox, although his attendance is not recorded at any meetings until June, 1580, was now admitted to the privy council and was also reported as being offered the governorship of the strategic stronghold of Dumbarton castle.[132]

Up until this juncture, there would appear to have been little that Morton could have done to prevent the king, who was clearly infatuated with Lennox, betowing favours on him. At the beginning of 1580, Morton, as it happened, was engaged in another round of that intermittent friction which sporadically erupted between the earl of Argyll and himself. The pretext, on this occasion, was a rumour, first current in February and supposedly at Argyll's instigation, that Morton recently 'had devised something for the alteration of the state'.[133] What, exactly, he was supposed to have planned remains obscure, although the 'fellowship of Falkirk' were reported as believing 'some practice was intended for their overthrow'.[134] That he had conspired anything whatsoever was strenuously denied by Morton and, eventually, on 28th April, at his insistence, the council issued a statement completely exonerating him from any such intrigue.[135]

Morton's conduct, however, during these weeks was distinctly unstatesmanlike. His reaction, for example, to the Argyll allegation was to leave Edinburgh in a pique for Dalkeith where, apparently, he sulked, 'minding to forbear the court until he be called'.[136] Moreover, he had also contrived to quarrel with his nephew, Angus, one of his most reliable supporters, and this at a time when, as English observers had already noted,[137] there was a serious rival imminent. The origins of this dispute with Angus are uncertain although Bowes, on one occasion, refers, among other things, to 'the great quarrel betwixt the Laird of Cleish and George Afflecke, servant to the Earl of Morton'.[138] Now, since the English ambassador observed about a month later that 'the variance is only for matters of money',[139] and bearing in mind that Auchinleck's protagonist was, in fact, Robert Colville, clerk to the treasury,[140] it is pretty likely that some financial squabble, in which Colville supported Angus, was the root cause of the disagreement.

Whatever the reasons for the friction between Morton and his nephew, his maladroit tactics probably encouraged Lennox's followers, if not that nobleman himself, to consider the seizure of the king. Granted this in itself was a shadowy business rumoured to have been planned to take place on 9th April as the king returned from Doune castle in Perthshire to Stirling,[141] yet it is unquestionably an indictment of Morton's tactics in these months.

However, Morton's position at this stage, at least in the opinion of Robert Bowes, analysing the situation in mid-May, was not necessarily a hopeless one. Morton, he conceded, 'had fallen from his former state and leading in the government which chiefly grows from his absence from court, divisions betwixt him and Angus and temporizing with Lennox'. 'Yet,' he affirmed, 'the experienced here think that he may again be enabled to repossess his wonted grace and to reduce matters to a better course'. This, Bowes believed, could be best achieved by Morton utilising the unique influence with king and council which he still retained, settling his differences with Angus and displaying much greater resolution. If he was to 'lay away the vizor' and act with greater determination, his old colleagues would rally to him, and those place-seekers who had drifted to Lennox would, 'according to the common disposition of this changeable nation', return to him.[142]

Apart from his observations on the need for a reconciliation between Morton and Angus which seems to have been realised by the end of May,[143] the keynote of Bowes' assessment was clearly that Morton must seize the initiative against Lennox. Unfortunately, Morton's subsequent actions provide little evidence for concluding that he perceived the direction in which his best interests lay.

On 23rd May, the court left Stirling and the king commenced his tour of the north-eastern part of his kingdom.[144] Morton, however, was an absentee from the earlier stages of this expedition, ostensibly suffering from a leg injury sustained from a horse but actually because, so Bowes reported, he feared a *coup* was imminent.[145] Melville may also be correct in suggesting that another reason for his absence was his disapproval of Lennox's presence.[146] The latter certainly accompanied the king, making his first appearance in the privy council at Dundee on 9th June,[147] and, a fortnight later, winning the plaudits of the Aberdeen magistrates by helping to revoke an infeftment of certain salmon-fishing rights on the Dee and Don, originally granted by Morton to George Auchinleck and now restored to the town council.[148] Morton joined the other councillors at St. Andrews on 29th July[149] where, while attending the performance of a play, he was given a prophetic warning by a 'phrenetick man' called skipper Lindsay that 'his judgment was neir and his dome was dichten'. This incident occurred in one of the buildings forming part of the priory of St. Andrews and was also witnessed by king James and Lennox. Apparently what happened was that, as Morton, who was impatiently 'gnapping on his staffe', was awaiting the commencement of the play, the stage was taken over by Lindsay, a character popularly believed to be 'bereft of his witt'. Indeed, his initial appearance was greeted with laughter which quickly subsided, nonetheless, once he began to address his audience. James Melvill, for example, an eye witness of the events, compared him favourably with many preachers he had heard and, in his opinion, Morton was 'mikle movit with this first interlude . . . sa that during all the sportes that followed he altered never

F

the gravitie of his countenance'.[150]

Whether Morton was affected by this experience or not, he seems to have, at least temporarily, changed his strategy, and there were now reports of the possibility of a settlement being reached between him and Lennox.[151] But, by the end of August, the chances of such an *entente* were becoming less likely and, instead, the political situation grew even more confused with various rumours of governmental changes in the offing.[152] In addition, there were, as Bowes assiduously reported to his superiors in London, the untoward episodes in Edinburgh when, on two separate occasions, the town gates were dramatically shut on Lennox's orders. The explanation given for the first closure was that it was carried out in order to arrest Cunningham of Drumquhassel who, despite his captaincy of Dumbarton castle having been revoked by the privy council in July,[153] had failed to deliver possession of it to Lennox. As for the second incident, when the gates were shut until eight o'clock the next day, this was justified by Lennox as a precautionary measure against 'some hurt (which) was devised against him, that Angus or other friends and servants of the Earl of Morton should have executed the same immediately in the night'.[154] The whole business certainly suggests a confused state of affairs within the town although, if Morton and his followers had been planning some *coup* or other, it had clearly been thwarted.

By mid-September, Morton had obviously been out-manoeuvred and eclipsed by Lennox. Bowes, writing on 13th September to a worried English government, observed that Lennox's authority was now so formidable that 'few or none will openly withstand anything that he would have forwards and such as be willing to give the attempt distrust both their own power and company at home and also their backing abroad'. In the same enclosure, he also submitted a list of those who could be regarded as members of the Lennox faction. In this category, he included lords Ruthven, Lindsay, Herries, the commendators of Dunfermline, Newbattle and Inchcolm and the lairds of Cessford and Coldenknowes.[155] Of these, Dunfermline was aptly described by Bowes as 'running the course of Lennox in some parts which he perceives he does more in desire thereby to retain his office and credit than any love to join with or set forward Lennox's devices'.[156] Ruthven, on the other hand, was both ambitious and probably disgruntled over the dispute which had arisen between him and Morton's cousin, Douglas of Lochleven. This concerned a gift of ward and nonentry of the heritage of the earl of Buchan, who had died in August, 1580, granted to Lochleven by king James, and contested by Ruthven on grounds of legal irregularity and the crown's financial plight.[157] Of the others named by

Bowes, all of them could be regarded as members of the Argyll-Atholl confederacy of 1578. Argyll, although not prominent in affairs at this particular moment, was undoubtedly an inveterate opponent of Morton and, when it is recalled that both Montrose, who was reported as an adherent of Lennox in August, 1580,[158] and the master of Mar can be regarded as his followers, there does seem considerable validity in Calderwood's assertion that one motive for Lennox's presence in the country was to replace Atholl in the partnership against Morton.[159] Whether John Maitland and Robert Melville, two notable survivors of the siege of Edinburgh castle in 1573, were as deeply implicated, as Calderwood and Hume of Godscroft both insist,[160] must remain a matter for conjecture but, certainly, neither could have regarded Morton very amicably.

On 24th September, as further confirmation of the ascendancy of Lennox and his followers, the council, with Morton supposedly absent on legal business, recommended the appointment of a lord high chamberlain with a deputy and twenty-four gentlemen of the chamber.[161] The real significance of this proposal became apparent on 15th October when, with Morton actually present, Lennox was nominated to the principal position and the master of Mar was named as his assistant.[162] Moreover, when, on closer examination of the composition of the gentlemen of the chamber, Ruthven's brother, the sons of lords Herries and Lindsay, several Kers and Humes, not to mention Stewarts are seen to be members, it can safely be assumed that it was a handpicked body with virtually all of it supporting the new lord high chamberlain.

The last significant episode before Morton's overthrow was the dispute between lords Ruthven and Oliphant which was sparked off on 1st November.[163] On that date, Ruthven, in the company of certain members of the Stewart family, had been returning from the wedding of the earl of Mar when their proximity to the lands of Oliphant and the existence of some ill-feeling already between the two families provoked the master of Oliphant to attack them. In the resultant fracas, Alexander Stewart of Schutingleyis, brother of Stewart of Traquair, was shot and killed.[164] Oliphant, consequently, at Ruthven's petition, was summoned before the privy council, placed in ward at Doune and ordered to stand trial for murder.[165] Although Oliphant was ultimately acquitted of this charge which, interestingly enough, included the use of a poisoned bullet,[166] the affair had ramifications which affected Morton. His cousin, Douglas of Lochleven, one of whose daughters was married to the master of Oliphant, had been a prominent figure in his son-in-law's defence while Morton himself had eventually taken Oliphant's part.[167] This could not have improved his relations with Ruthven who, according to one account, subsequently withheld information about the conspiracy against him,[168] nor, for that matter, with the house of Stewart. In short, the whole affair, if anything, weakened his own position even further and, correspondingly, strengthened that of his adversaries.

Lennox, by the end of December, must have been convinced that he now had sufficient support to dispose of Morton without fear of serious repercussions. Among his adherents, in addition to those already indicated, he could also depend on lords Maxwell, Robert Stewart and Seton. Lord Maxwell, who had originally opposed Morton in 1578, was ultimately on such good terms with Lennox as to be promised Morton's earldom once he was eliminated.[169] Lord Robert Stewart had spent most of his time since 1576 in prison for serious offences committed in Orkney, where he had oppressed the islanders in a nefarious fashion,[170] but had recently been released and admitted to the council[171] to become an embittered opponent of Morton.[172] Lastly, lord Seton was, in Calderwood's estimation, one of those who had 'particular quarrels against him'.[173] This was undoubtedly the case since there was evidence, as recently as May, 1579, of blatantly Marian sympathies which had led to the arrest of Seton and three of his sons on a charge of sheltering a servant of Archbishop Beaton, Mary's agent in Paris.[174] In addition, they had also been accused of assisting the Hamiltons.[175] As well as these noblemen, there was also the notorious Sir James Balfour who had been in France at least since April, 1580 supposedly searching for incriminating evidence against Morton,[176] and, more importantly, captain James Stewart. The latter was the second son of Andrew, lord Ochiltree, who had returned from military service abroad and was first recorded at court on 3rd June, 1579.[177] In October, he had been among those appointed gentlemen of the king's chamber[178] and, slightly earlier, he had acquired two substantial gifts under the privy and great seal respectively. In September, by the former, he had received a gift of 'teind schaves, fruitis, rentis, proventis and emolumentis of the kirkis of Sanctandrois and Leucheris' forfeited by the earl of March as the result of an action for debt by an Edinburgh burgess.[179] By the latter, a month earlier, he had obtained certain lands in Lanarkshire formerly in the possession of Claud Hamilton.[180] An unprincipled adventurer who would most likely have been supporting Morton had his star been in the ascendant, he now grasped the opportunity to play a vital role in his overthrow.

On Saturday, 31st December, either during a regular meeting of the privy council or, possibly, at an extraordinary one specially summoned for the purpose, Morton was accused by captain James Stewart, in the presence of king James, the earls of Angus, Argyll, Eglinton and Lennox, lords Cathcart and Lindsay and David Borthwick of Lochhill, of being an accessory to Darnley's murder.[181] Morton, who supposedly had some inkling that such a plot was imminent,[182] reacted violently and bitterly attacked his accuser. Physical conflict seeming a distinct possibility, they were both removed from the council chamber and Borthwick of Lochhill, the royal advocate, was consulted regarding the correct legal procedure. On his recommendation, it was decided that Morton, until he stood trial for the accusations against him, should be placed in custody. In the words of the official indictment, signed by king James, Argyll and Lennox, 'Forasmekle as James erll of Mortoun lord of Dalkeith is suspectit and delaitit in presens of the Kingis Majestie and lordis of secreit counsall to have committit treasoune Quhairfoir his majestie with awise of the saidis lordis Ordanis ane maser or uther officiar of Armis To pas and in his hienes name and auctoritie command and charge the said James erll of Mortoune To remain and keip waird in the abbay of Halierudhous in the hous quhairin he presentlie remainis . . . '[183] Morton, apparently, accepted the decision calmly and, eschewing any thoughts of escape, confined himself within Holyrood house until Monday when, by a further privy council order, he was taken to Edinburgh castle[184] by an escort consisting, appropriately enough, of captain James Stewart, the master of Mar and the lairds of Coldenknowes and Manderston.[185]

NOTES

1. Calderwood, *History*, iii, 398; Moysie, *Memoirs*, 5.
2. *C.S.P. Scot.*, v, 252.
3. *Historie and Life of King James the Sext*, 164.
4. Calderwood, *History*, iii, 396; Spottiswoode, *History*, ii, 208.
5. *See* Chap. 8, 156–57.
6. *Diurnal*, 336.
7. *Edin. Recs. (1573–89)*, 66–67.
8. Melville, *Memoirs*, 266.
9. This is the version of Robert Bowes, English ambassador, writing to Walsingham the following day, *C.S.P. Scot.*, v, 287.
10. *Ibid*, 287–88.
11. N.L.S. Advocates MSS, 29.2.6, No. 140.
12. *R.P.C.*, ii, 696–97.
13. *Ibid*, 696.
14. *Ibid*, 688–90.
15. *C.S.P. Dom.Add.*, 540.
16. Calderwood, *History*, iii, 408.

17. Melville, *Memoirs*, 264; for a similar viewpoint, see *Historie and Life of King James the Sext*, 165.
18. Bannatyne, *Memoriales*, 322.
19. Melville, *Memoirs*, 265.
20. *C.S.P. Scot.*, v, 288.
21. *Historie and Life of King James the Sext*, 168.
22. *Warrender papers*, i, 136–40.
23. *C.S.P. Scot.*, v, 293.
24. Elizabeth to Argyll, 20th May, 1578, *Ibid*, 293–94.
25. Calderwood, *History*, iii, 408–09.
26. *H.M.C. (Hastings)*, ii, 11–12.
27. Moysie, *Memoirs*, 8–9.
28. *R.P.C.*, ii, 703.
29. *A.P.S.*, iii, 121; *C.S.P. Scot.*, v, 296.
30. *R.P.C.*, ii, 705.
31. *Ibid*, 707–08.
32. *R.P.C.*, iii, 6–7.
33. Calderwood, *History*, iii, 413.
34. *Ibid*, 414.
35. *R.P.C.*, iii, 3.
36. *Ibid*, 7–8; Morton astutely saw to it that the King's declaration was also recorded in the official account of the proceedings, *A.P.S.*, iii, 94.
37. Calderwood, *History*, iii, 416.
38. *R.P.C.*, iii, 8; *see also* Calderwood, *History*, iii, 417.
39. I.e. Robert Stewart, bishop of Caithness, and a great-uncle of the King who had become earl of Lennox in June, 1578, *R.M.S.*, iv, No. 2785.
40. *A.P.S.*, iii, 94–116.
41. *H.M.C. (Hastings)*, ii, 13; *C.S.P. Scot.*, v, 305.
42. *H.M.C. (Hastings)*, ii, 13; *C.S.P. Scot.*, v, 306.
43. *H.M.C. (Hastings)*, ii, 13; *C.S.P. Scot.*, v, 305; Calderwood, *History*, iii, 417.
44. *R.P.C.*, iii, 10, 15–16; *T.A.*, xiii, 213–14.
45. Calderwood, *History*, iii, 419; *see also* Moysie, *Memoirs*, 13; *Historie and Life of King James the Sext*, 167.
46. Calderwood, *History*, iii, 419–22; also in *Historie and Life of King James the Sext*, 167–72.
47. *R.P.C.*, iii, 15–16.
48. *Ibid* 9; *T.A.*, xiii, 213.
49. *R.P.C.*, iii, 12–14; *T.A.*, xiii, 213.
50. *R.P.C.*, iii, 16–17; *T.A.*, xiii, 214.
51. *Ibid*, 214.
52. *R.P.C.*, iii, 18.

53. The fullest details are in Calderwood, *History*, iii, 423–24 and Moysie, *Memoirs*, 14–15.
54. *C.S.P. Scot.*, v, 317.
55. Calderwood, *History*, iii, 424; *C.S.P. Scot.*, v, 318; *Historie and Life of King James the Sext*, 172.
56. *C.S.P. Scot.*, v, 318.
57. Calderwood, *History*, iii, 423–24.
58. *C.S.P. Scot.*, v, 316; *R.P.C.*, iii, 22; Calderwood, *History*, iii, 424–26.
59. *H.M.C. (Hastings)*, ii, 14.
60. *C.S.P. Scot.*, v, 318–19; *R.P.C.*, iii, 25–26.
61. *Ibid*, 33–34.
62. *C.S.P. Scot.*, v, 327.
63. Moysie, *Memoirs*, 19–20.
64. The first time they attended was 15th November, 1578; *R.P.C.*, iii, 45.
65. The bond between Argyll and Mar is specifically dated 27th November, 1578, N.R.A. 6 (Argyll Muniments).
66. Teulet, *Papiers*, ii, 391.
67. *T.A.*, xiii, 228.
68. *Edin. Recs. (1573–89)*, 98.
69. I.e. Lord Robert Stewart, feuar of Orkney.
70. *R.P.C.*, iii, 108–116.
71. *Ibid*, 115.
72. Calderwood, *History*, iii, 346; *Diurnal*, 346; *Historie and Life of King James the Sext*, 152.
73. S.R.O., Johnstone of Westerhall papers, GD1/510, No. 6.
74. N.R.A. 859 Douglas-Home Box 56/4.
75. Fraser, *Douglas*, iii, 269–70.
76. Moray was the illegitimate offspring of James V and Margaret daughter of John, 5th Lord Erskine and Lochleven's mother. Her legal husband was Lochleven's father, Sir Robert Douglas of Lochleven, *Scots Peerage*, vi, 369.
77. E.g. *C.S.P. Scot.*, v, 178–79; Calderwood; *History*, iii, 346; *Historie and Life of King James the Sext*, 155–57.
78. *R.P.C.*, ii, 598; *T.A.*, xiii, 161.
79. *R.P.C.*, iii, 598.
80. *Ibid*, 605–06; *T.A.*, xiii, 164.
81. N.L.S., Morton Papers, 77, f.24; printed in *Mort. Reg.* i, 85–86.
82. *R.P.C.*, ii, 612.
83. Hume of Godscroft, *History*, ii, 262.
84. *C.S.P. Scot.*, v, 179.
85. *R.P.C.*, iii, 159–60.
86. *C.S.P. Scot.*, v, 302.
87. *A Chronicle of the Kings of Scotland*, 133.

88. In a statement to Nicholas Errington, the English agent in Edinburgh in December, 1579, *C.S.P. Scot.*, v, 369.
89. Spottiswoode, *History*, ii, 264.
90. *R.P.C.*, iii, 146–47.
91. Details of this military commission are to be found in *A.P.S.*, iii, 159–62.
92. *R.P.C.*, iii, 148; *T.A.*, xiii, 262.
93. *R.P.C.*, iii, 148–65; *T.A.*, xiii, 264.
94. Morton and company are reported as having begun the siege of Hamilton on 4th May, *C.S.P. Scot.*, v, 336.
95. *R.P.C.*, iii, 153–54.
96. *Ibid*, 156.
97. *C.S.P. Scot.*, v, 337.
98. Moysie, *Memoirs*, 22.
99. *C.S.P. Scot.*, v, 351–52; *Historie and Life of King James the Sext*, 175; Spottiswoode, *History*, ii, 264.
100. *C.S.P. Scot.*, v, 337.
101. *R.P.C.*, iii, 160–62.
102. Spottiswoode, *History*, 264–65.
103. *A.P.S.*, iii, 125.
104. *C.S.P. Scot.*, v, 338.
105. *Historie and Life of King James the Sext*, 176.
106. *R.P.C.*, iii, 232.
107. *C.S.P. Scot.*, v, 337.
108. See *T.A.*, xiii, 267–72 and Chap. 8, 148.
109. *R.S.S.*, vii, No. 2000.
110. *R.M.S.*, iv, No. 2920 and v, No. 167.
111. See Chap. 9, 181.
112. Calderwood, *History*, iii, 442–43; Spottiswoode, *History*, ii, 263; Moysie, *Memoirs*, 20.
113. *H.M.C. (App) xii*, pt. viii, 24.
114. *R.P.C.*, iii, 184–85.
115. Calderwood, *History*, iii, 443; see also N.L.S. (Atholl), 3157.
116. *Historie and Life of King James the Sext*, 174.
117. Queen Mary for example, the following year in a letter to the countess of Atholl, referred to the possibility of the Mar family being involved, *H.M.C. (App) xii*, pt. viii, 9.
118. *H.M.C. (App.) v*, 635; *Spalding Misc.*, iv, 61–62.
119. Calderwood, *History*, iii, 770–72; Moysie, *Memoirs*, 24; Spottiswoode, *History*, ii, 263–64; *Historie and Life of King James the Sext*, 177.
120. *R.S.S.*, vii, No. 2031.
121. *A.P.S.*, iii, 175–76.
122. *Ibid*, 176.
123. *R.S.S.*, vii, No. 1561.

124. Lang, *History*, ii, 263.
125. *Historie and Life of King James the Sext,* 177.
126. Calderwood, *History*, iii, 457.
127. *Scots Peerage*, v, 355–56.
128. *R.M.S.*, iv, No. 2920.
129. *A.P.S.*, iii, 151.
130. He now became earl of March, *R.S.S.*, vii, No. 2244.
131. *Ibid*, No. 2252.
132. *C.S.P. Scot.*, v, 384.
133. *Ibid*, 378, 385.
134. *Ibid*, 378.
135. *Ibid*, 404, 411; *R.P.C.*, iii, 281–83; Calderwood, *History*, iii, 461–62.
136. *C.S.P. Scot.*, v, 378.
137. Walsingham was the first to make this observation in January, 1580, *C.S.P. Foreign* (1578–80), 146.
138. *C.S.P. Scot.*, v, 397.
139. *Ibid*, 436.
140. *See T.A.*, xii, Intro. xvii.
141. *C.S.P. Scot.*, v, 392–93, 409.
142. *Ibid*, 422–24.
143. *Ibid*, 436.
144. *Ibid*, 431.
145. *Ibid*, 441–42.
146. Melville, *Memoirs*, 265.
147. *R.P.C.*, iii, 289.
148. *Ibid*, 294–95.
149. *Ibid*, 295.
150. Melvill, *Diary*, 81–82; Calderwood, *History*, iii, 462–63.
151. *C.S.P. Scot.*, v, 465–66, 479–80.
152. *Ibid*, 487–88, 498, 503.
153. Drumquhassel had been relieved of this position on 27th July (*R.P.C.*, iii, 295).
154. *C.S.P. Scot.*, v, 490.
155. *Ibid*, v, 500.
156. *Ibid*, 526; queen Mary, who described the secretary as 'crafty, wily, made by Morton and to serve all changes and turns', obviously had a similar opinion of him, *Ibid*, vi, 86.
157. *R.P.C.*, iii, 312–13; *R.S.S.*, vii, No. 2521.
158. *C.S.P. Scot.*, v, 474.
159. Calderwood, *History*, iii, 457.
160. *Ibid*, 457; Hume of Godscroft, *History*, ii, 264.
161. *R.P.C.*, iii, 316; *C.S.P. Scot.*, v, 510.
162. *R.P.C.*, iii, 322–23.

163. Calderwood (*History*, iii, 479) dates the incident in October, but 1st November is the date given at Oliphant's trial, Pitcairn, *Trials*, i, 90.
164. Calderwood, *History*, iii, 479; Moysie, *Memoirs*, 28.
165. *R.P.C.*, iii, 329, 333–34.
166. Pitcairn, *Trials*, i, 90–92.
167. Calderwood, *History*, iii, 479–80.
168. Hume, *History*, ii, 268.
169. Fraser, *Carlaverock*, i, 250–52.
170. *See*, for a detailed account of his activities, *Oppressions in the islands of Orkney and Shetland*, Maitland Club, 1859.
171. *R.P.C.*, iii, 327.
172. Melville, *Memoirs*, 263–64.
173. Calderwood, *History*, iii, 483.
174. *Hist. MSS (Salisbury)*, ii, 257.
175. *C.S.P. Scot.*, v, 336; *R.P.C.*, iii, 182–83.
176. *C.S.P. Scot.*, v, 387.
177. *Ibid*, 339.
178. *R.P.C.*, iii, 322–23.
179. *R.S.S.*, vii, No. 2544.
180. *R.M.S.*, v, No. 5.
181. According to Calderwood (Calderwood, *History*, iii, 481), it was an ordinary council session, whereas Bowes (*C.S.P. Scot.*, v, 569 and 576–77) states that it was specially convened. Between them, they give the best account of events on 31st December.
182. Oddly enough, lord Robert Stewart, according to Bowes, was one of the informants, *ibid.*, 569.
183. N.L.S., Morton Papers, 77, f.54; printed in *Mort. Reg.*, i, 124–25.
184. N.L.S., Morton Papers, 77, f.56; printed in *Mort. Reg.*, i, 125.
185. Calderwood, *History*, iii, 482; *C.S.P. Scot.*, v, 576–77.

5
The Financial Affairs of the Kirk

While Morton's downfall was a direct consequence of factional intrigue among the magnates, his relations with the kirk, both with regard to its patrimony and polity, unquestionably form another important part of his administration. At the same time, it is helpful, for a clearer understanding of these two aspects, to separate his handling of the financial affairs of the kirk from matters affecting its organisation and government.

The question of the kirk's patrimony was a major problem from the onset of the reformation and, in February, 1562, the privy council, on behalf of the reformed church and the state itself, had introduced a system whereby, between them, they hoped to obtain one third of most of the available revenues of the old church. Accordingly, on 1st March, 1562, Sir John Wishart of Pittaro had been appointed the first collector-general in charge of twelve provincial sub-collectors of thirds. This system had not worked well for the kirk and, subsequently, in the wake of the revolution against queen Mary, it had been decided, in December, 1567, that the thirds should be assigned firstly to the ministers as part of their stipends, and only the remainder or 'superplus' should be allocated to the government. Shortly afterwards, the kirk had been permitted to name its own collectors who were answerable to the exchequer, and the office of collector-general became redundant. However, a breakdown of the whole organisation had followed these alterations. This had occurred partly as a result of the civil dislocation of the period but also because the kirk's collectors lacked authority and were ineffective. Consequently, in January, 1572, the crown had come to an agreement with the kirk that the government should receive £7,000 annually from the thirds and had, in addition, appointed its own officials for the collection of this sum.[1]

Morton, therefore, on his accession, found the collectory in a chaotic condition. Out of eleven sub-collectors' accounts for 1569, for example, only those for Lothian had been audited by the date of his appointment.[2] This deficiency was clearly a matter requiring his immediate attention since, not only would the crown benefit, but so too would his own standing with the kirk – a consideration which, in the closing stages of the civil war, he could not afford to ignore. Thus, in March, 1573, the general assembly, at the regent's request, nominated a commission of ten members headed by John Douglas, archbishop of St. Andrews, 'to hear the saidis collectoris compts with the rest of the Lords of our Sovereign Lords Chekker, allow and approve or disallow according to their wisdom and conscience and after the said compts shall be made to subscrive the same according to the order taken'.[3] By March, 1574, as a result of their endeavours, the bulk of the sub-collectors' accounts between 1568 and 1572, although there were still some omissions, had been audited.[4]

Morton's next undertaking, which his council announced on 5th May, 1573, was to set on foot the arrangement by which ministers or readers were given the right to collect thirds or other dues from the members of their local parishes. 'General assemblies,' the council declared, 'have earnestly cravit that they mycht have speciall assignations of payment of their stipends' and now, in answer to their demands, 'Thair stipends sal be assignit and appointit to thame als neir and commodiouslie as may be to the place of thair residence'. The council also informed the members of the kirk that, in order to facilitate this task, it had 'appointit the names of the kirkis to be collectit and the ministeris to be distributit amangis thame as also assignations to be maid for payment of thair stipendis'. By 10th August, when Morton outlined the final details of his financial reorganisation, this information had been obtained and 'the names and nowmer of the parroche kirkis hes bene collectit and the present nowmer of ministeris and pre-acheouris distributit throuchout the realme'.[5]

The most significant alteration which the regent now proposed was the revival of the office of a collector-general who would be responsible for administering the collection of the thirds of benefices and whose revenues, it was intended, should support both the kirk and 'the commoun and neidfull effairis of the realme'. Additionally, in an effort to obtain a more realistic overall contribution, the collector-general was empowered to take appropriate action for the uncovering of omissions, evasions and other malpractices perpetrated in the previous assumption.[6]

Morton, who, in the space of about eight months, had effected a number of important changes affecting the finances of the kirk, found his actions received a mixed reception from its members.

One measure about which there could be little complaint was the powers given to the collector-general to assist him in his re-assessment of the thirds.

The first enquiries in this connection appear to have been made in August, 1573 and continued thereafter although, in the case of Melrose abbey, for example, instructions were still being issued in January, 1578 to the collector-general and his deputies to procure 'ane rentale of the said Abacie of Melrose as the samin presentlie extendis to and assume ane thrid thereof'.[7] In another instance, in October, 1573, in what appears to have been an attempt to bring Argyll and the Isles, which hitherto had escaped assessment, into line with the rest of the country, John Campbell, bishop of the Isles, gave a guarantee 'to bring and present ane sufficient and perfite particular rentall of the haill rentis and fruittis of the bishoprik of Ilis and Abbay of Ycolmkill as alsua of the priorie of Ardchatten'. He promised, in addition, a list of the names of all churches, their possessors and rentals in his diocese.[8] While, since Argyll and the Isles remained outwith the collectory, this was a notably unsuccessful attempt, the endeavours of the collector-general undoubtedly did produce substantial rewards. Thus, in 1573, over a hundred 'new enterit benefices' were added to the accounts yielding a total of £1,106 with further, if less spectacular, augmentations during the rest of Morton's administration.[9]

The payment of ministers' stipends from the locally available thirds, a provision actually advocated by several past assemblies,[10] did not, in itself, provoke unfavourable comment. However, it had been necessary to replace the old register of ministers and their assistants which had been in use since 1567 by a new one which, at least in prototype, was ready by August, 1573 and which appeared in its final version a year later as the 'Buik of Assignations of the Ministeris and Reidaris Stipendis'. Under this new disposition, with its redistribution of ministers, readers and parishes, the displacement of the clergy varied markedly. There were, on the one hand, badly served border areas such as Teviotdale, Ettrick and Tweeddale, within the diocese of Glasgow, where there were only eleven ministers and forty readers for fifty-nine churches. Conversely, there were other better-provided areas like the diocese of St. Andrews where, for sixty churches, there were twenty-four ministers and fifty readers. However, on average, one minister was responsible for three or four parishes, and it was this ratio which became a source of contention between the regent and the kirk.[11]

Initially, on the understanding that it was an interim expedient 'to remaine quhill God of his mercie sall thrust out more labourers into his harvest', the members of the general assembly appear to have raised few objections to Morton's reorganisation.[12] But there was one outspoken critic, namely John Davidson, regent of St. Leonard's college, St. Andrews, who was the author of 'The Dialogue betwixt the Clerk and the Courtier', a turgid attack in verse on the new arrangements. 'Foure parish kirks,' he was later to state in his defence, 'are over great a charge for one minister and therefore the order that would appoint so manie or more to one man . . . [he believed] to be evil and consequentlie devilish.'[13] For his temerity in having the verses published, although he denied this was his intention, he was summoned before Morton at the justice ayre held at Haddington in January, 1574. There followed the first of several interrogations and periods of detention until, in June, due to stand trial and convinced he would not receive a fair hearing, he sought refuge in exile, firstly in Argyll and then England.[14]

Although Davidson had his well-wishers, both among the clergy and the laity, some of whom succeeded in persuading lord Boyd to intervene, not very successfully, on his behalf with Morton,[15] he appears to have lacked the unanimous support of the general assembly. Certainly, one member, John Rutherford, provost of St. Salvator's college, St. Andrews, criticised 'The Dialogue' apparently because he believed it contained unfavourable references to himself.[16] It is possible, as Calderwood claims, that the assembly feared Morton's displeasure. 'The brethrein,' so he states, 'deputed to trie would nather damne nor allow [his book] but passed over with silence, least the regent should be offended, pretending their number was not full.'[17] Perhaps this was the case, yet, the same churchmen could be pretty outspoken when they felt so inclined.

As it happened, in the religious atmosphere of the sixteenth century, Morton's treatment of the disputatious regent of St. Leonard's was unremarkable. In fact, Davidson's main criticism of the re-organisation of the parishes was the effect it would have on the religious teachings of the ministry rather than its financial aspects, and it is Calderwood, by remarks such as 'the regent and counsell had made an act before, to cast so manie kirks in the hands of one preacher that the kings revenues by the superplus of the thrids might be the greater', who implies that Morton's motive was merely a pecuniary one.[18] Nevertheless, he had written critically of government policy, causing the justice-clerk, Sir John Bellenden of Auchnoule, to observe that, 'To a privat man to write against the conclusions of princes is damnable and the writer worthie of punishment'.[19] Davidson, in short, presented no serious threat to the authorities, and his condemnation of Morton's re-arrangement of the parishes was essentially a spurious form of agitation. It had little to do, in reality, with the kirk's finances as there were insufficient ministers available in Scotland to fill the existing vacancies, and it seems very unlikely that there was some reservoir of exiled divines who would have returned to their native soil if only stipends were made available. Davidson's significance, therefore, was as a forerunner of that more radical section of the kirk which was to feature more prominently as Morton's tenure of office progressed and pose problems both to him and, subsequently, to king James VI.

The fact that the collection of the thirds was once more in governmental hands would appear to have brought little immediate response from the kirk. In March, 1574, for example, the general assembly was asked by Morton 'the substantial cause if any be of mislyking the order agreed upon for payment of minister's stipends and assignation of the same and what better order can be proposed and devised for the same'.[20] A committee duly deliberated the matter but the upshot was a somewhat oblique statement by its chairman, Sir John Erskine of Dun, superintendant of Angus and Mearns, that 'nothing should be imputed to them or laid to their charge as done and concluded by them with my Lord Regent's Grace, that might prejudge the brethren or the Assembly'.[21]

Morton, therefore, as with the redistribution of ministers, did not feel the real weight of opposition from the kirk regarding lay collection of the thirds until after his return to power in 1578 when the assembly, in October that year, repeated the demand made during his demission that it should intromit with its own thirds.[22] This request that 'the Kirk of God within this realme may be restored to the benefit of the Act of Parliament concerning the thirds' was made more forcibly in July, 1580 when the king was reassured that the kirk's uplifting of the thirds would not have a deleterious effect on the royal revenue.[23]

The kirk's eventual hostility to the crown's collection of the thirds should not obscure the fact that, under Morton, they were far more efficiently collected and administered than hitherto. That this was the case is confirmed by a comparison between the insubstantial register of ministers kept between 1567 and 1573 and the much more impressive registers kept thereafter.[24] Stipends in many instances might be inadequate but, at least while Morton was in control, far more ministers were in receipt of some form of remuneration than formerly had been the case.

The accounts of the regent's successive collectors-general of thirds, Robert, lord Boyd and Adam Erskine, commendator of Cambuskenneth, are completely extant for all but the years 1574 and 1575. With regard to expenditure, there is firstly the 'discharge' or payment of stipends to the commissioners, ministers and readers by diocese 'according to the modification and assignation of the said buik'. This is followed by grants to students and bursars, the disbursement to the royal household and various remissions, pensions and extraordinary expenses. Finally, there are the lists of 'rests depending' indicating individuals against whom proceedings for non-payment are pending, 'rests by horning' where the defaulters are officially denounced, and, completing the accounts, a short list of salaries to royal officials.[25] Since it is of some relevance to discover whether Morton extended further the iniquitous practice of granting remissions from the thirds and just how effective he was in reducing the numbers of those who evaded payment of their thirds, the items of greatest significance are the remissions and the details of those who were in arrears.

There had always been a large number of thirds remitted. In 1562, the first year they were collected, the total was forty-two and, among those benefiting on that occasion were Archibald, earl of Argyll, James Beaton, archbishop of Glasgow, John, master of Maxwell, James, earl or Moray, George, lord Seton and Robert Stewart, commendator of Holyrood abbey.[26] In addition, John, lord Erskine, (subsequently earl of Mar and regent) refused to pay thirds for Cambuskenneth and Dryburgh abbeys as well as Inchmahome priory.[27]

Under Morton, there was a similar, if slightly larger, catalogue of exonerations – on average, fifty between 1573 and 1580.[28] Among the forty-eight exemptions granted in 1576,[29] which can conveniently be regarded as a typical year, are certain individuals whose presence in the accounts can be readily explained. David Cunningham, for example, subsequently bishop of Aberdeen, was a chaplain attached to Morton's household at that time;[30] James Hume of Coldenknowes was warden of the east march;[31] William McDowell, who also enjoyed with the 'puir beidmen of the hospitall of St. Paulis Werk' the third of that preceptory, was the royal master of work;[32] Robert Pitcairn, commendator of Dunfermline, to whom several benefices were 'gevin fre', was, of course, royal secretary; Robert Pont was both a senator of the college of justice and, like John Winram, another recipient, a superintendent of the kirk.[33] All these remissions, therefore, can be regarded as the predictable perquisites of office. So, too, can the exemption given to Morton's kinsman, the ubiquitous Archibald Douglas, for both the money and the victual of the parsonage of Glasgow. What might appear in this instance to have been evidence of the regent's patronage can, in fact, be explained by his membership of the court of session, normally a guarantee of excusal.[34]

Less deserving, no doubt, were the remissions to Thomas Lyon, master of Glamis, and brother of the royal chancellor and 'the bairnis of Robert Stewart fueare of Orkenay' who were allowed part of the revenues of Holyrood abbey.[35] However, the least justifiable concession was almost certainly 'the rest of the third of the priorie of Pittenweme . . . gevin fre by our soverane lord at the advyss of my lord regent's grace to James Balfour, prior thairof'.[36] Balfour, whose conduct since his participation in the Darnley murder had given him a deservedly notorious reputation which was undoubtedly well known to Morton,[37] had, nevertheless, proved himself valuable as an intermediary at Perth in February, 1573, and this was doubtless one way in which he profited. In any case, as it happened, he had not paid his thirds for Pittenweem in either 1570 or 1572.[38]

If Morton was not granting remissions too gratuitously, the question then arises, who did benefit? The answer, in many cases, undoubtedly must be those who probably most deserved to. Thus, for example, the towns of Ayr, Dundee, Dumfries, Montrose, Perth and Stirling and the 'puir hospitall of Inverness' all received exonerations for 'the sustenation of the puir' or for 'the puir and hospitalitie thairof'.[39] Another beneficiary was the grammar school of Dunkeld which was excused its contributions for the prebends of Inchmagranoch, Craigie and Caputh as well as the chaplaincy of Inver.[40] In this instance, however, Morton's administration was merely repeating previous concessions,[41] and some other allowances, which have been described as 'compassionate remissions',[42] had likewise been awarded before his accession. 'The puir sisters of the Scenis' in Edinburgh, for example, were still being treated favourably in 1576, as were the occupants of the hospital of St. Nicholas beside St. Andrews who continued to enjoy the £20 annual rent once paid by the lairds of Balcomy to the Blackfriars of St. Andrews.[43]

The collectors' accounts after 1576 reveal no spectacular changes from the pattern already observed. Admittedly, in 1579, David Erskine, commendator of Dryburgh, George Douglas, bishop of Moray, and William, lord Ruthven were all added to the list of recipients while Robert Stewart, bishop of Caithness, successfully retained his privileges.[44] This might give rise to the consideration that Morton was looking after the interests of a particular faction. But, when it is recollected that Erskine's brother was the new collector-general and that he had appealed successfully in 1573 against an indictment for non-payment on the grounds that he had 'his saidis thridis alwayes dischargit be the Quene',[45] that the bishop of Caithness was the king's uncle, had previously had the thirds of his bishopric remitted to sustain the ministry in his diocese,[46] and had merely done so again in 1579,[47] and that Ruthven as treasurer had frequent recourse to his own resources on the crown's behalf,[48] these concessions seem less remarkable and no part of any deliberate design.

Thus, it would be inadvisable to draw any definite conclusions from Morton's handling of the remissions of thirds. Certainly, to some extent, he took care of his relatives and kinsmen, as indicated by the concession already noted to the bishop of Moray, and another, in 1576, to his natural son James, who had the superplus of the thirds of the bishopric of Galloway remitted.[49] However, even when the similar treatment in 1577 of William Douglas, commendator of Melrose and second son of the regent's cousin, William Douglas of Lochleven, is taken into account, it hardly amounts to blatantly excessive patronage.[50] Accordingly, apart from this and some increase in the amount of allowances for charitable purposes to the poor of certain towns, it would seem impossible to detect the presence of any conscious policy on the part of Morton where the thirds were concerned.

Excluding those who obtained official exemptions, there was always a larger group attempting illegal evasion and against whom legal action was either pending or had been taken. In this latter category of 'restis by horning' are to be found, between 1573 and 1577, such notable personages as William, lord Yester, John, lord Herries, George, lord Seton, Hugh, lord Somerville, James Paton, bishop of Dunkeld, Alexander Colville, commendator of Culross, Adam Erskine, commendator of Cambuskenneth, David Erskine, commendator of Dryburgh, Walter Reid, commendator of Kinloss, Claud Hamilton, commendator of Paisley, Sir James Douglas of Drumlanrig, Thomas Turnbull of Bedrule, John Carmichael of Meadowflat, John Johnstone of that ilk, Sir Alexander Jardine of Apelgirth and Robert Boyd of Baddineath.[51] Two typical examples, from Dumfriesshire, of somewhat less eminent individuals who could also apparently act with impunity are Thomas Campbell, commendator of Holywood and Douglas of Drumlanrig's son, Robert, provost of Lincluden college. In 1567, Campbell, for example, had been proclaimed an outlaw for non-payment of part of the third of Holywood abbey and, a decade later, he was still not contributing; Robert Douglas, likewise, was first delated in 1567 over the third of the common kirk of Glencarne and, ten years later, he was still in arrears.[52]

Overall, in this period, the average number of hornings annually amounted to seventy-seven with, in many instances, the offenders' names being constantly repeated.[53] Inevitably, this would confirm the view that, even under Morton, the process of putting individuals to the horn was still 'little more than a formality'.[54] On the other hand, Morton's administration, especially during the earlier years of his regency, did make some attempt at rectifying this situation. On 14th December, 1573, for example, the council, while permitting the collectors of thirds an extension until 20th January, 1574 for the presentation of their accounts, warned them 'upon thair perrel and under the pane of rebellion and putting of thame to the horne . . . to mak compt reknying and payment of thair said intromission during the space foirsaid'.[55] Furthermore, the next day, in connection with deficiencies in the bishopric of Aberdeen, 'the fewaris, firmoraris, tenentis, takksmen, parochynaris and all utheris intromettouris with the fruitis of the said Bischoprik' were ordered to render to the collector-general, or risk denunciation, 'the haill fruitis, rentis, kind, teindschavis and emolumentis of all landis and kirkis pertening to the said Bischoprik'.[56] Again on 29th May, 1574, 'divers personis' in Stirling, Dumbarton, Lennox and Renfrew, at the horn for non-payment, were sent warning letters either reminding or informing them of their offence.[57]

As well as this activity, there was, between 1575 and 1580, about a score of grants made under the privy seal associated with failure to pay thirds, fruits or teindsheaves which resulted in forfeiture for someone or other.[58] One victim of this policy was Thomas Hay, commendator of Glenluce and parson of Spynie. On 9th February, 1575, being 'ordourlie denuncit rebell and put to the horne for nonpayment to Harry Smyth collector of the thrid of his said benefice of Glenluce of the cropis and yeiris 1567-71', his parsonage of Spynie was presented to Alexander Winchester. On 20th February, escheat of the fruits of his parsonage was given to Alexander Innes of Crommy. Finally, on 10th March, the proceedings against Hay were completed by the appointment of Robert Charteris of Kelwood as chamberlain of Glenluce abbey.[59]

Although certain pressure was exerted on defaulters and some were punished for their temerity – Alexander Hume, commendator of Cold-ingham priory, for example[60] – when the large numbers known to remain immune are taken into account, not to mention the complaints of the kirk on this subject, it becomes obvious that Morton was either unable or unwill-ing to do very much to alter the situation. In August, 1575, for instance, the general assembly had vainly requested some kind of an arrangement whereby 'Quher ministers produces letters of horning to the general Collectour upon sick persons as are assignit to them for payment, the said collectour may be causit to make payment to the saids ministers'.[61] In short, despite the efforts of officials like Patrick Davidson, Ross herald, and James Purdy, Islay herald, who, in November, 1579 claimed, when pleading exemption from a tax being imposed by the Edinburgh magistrates, they were 'all the dayis of the yeir occupit in his Hienes continewall service about the inbringing of the superplus of the thriddis',[62] there was clearly widespread retention of wealth which was rightfully the kirk's or the crown's.

Although the collectors' accounts also provide evidence of the number of pensions from ecclesiastical sources granted by the government, they are, as has already been noted, incomplete, and a more comprehensive impression of the various awards and the principal beneficiaries can be obtained from the gifts made under the privy seal.

Crown officials, especially members of the legal profession, emerge as the main group whose salaries were provided by this source. Thus, in 1573, Robert Pont, senator of the college of justice, received 300 merks from the thirds of the bishopric of Moray,[63] while, the following year, Alexander Hay, clerk register, was awarded an annual pension of 500 merks from the superplus of the thirds.[64] In 1576, James Meldrum, fiar of Segy and another senator of the college of justice, 'having onlie the appearance of ane leving qußen it sall pleis God to call his father frome this lyff', was granted a pension consisting of five chalders of victual from the superplus of Haddington priory.[65] Two other awards made that year were to James Millar, writer to the signet, and to the advocate, Nicholas Elphinstone of Schank.[66] Further donations were made in 1577 to William Baillie of Provand, president of the college of justice,[67] to John Skene, an advocate whom the crown had 'chargit . . . to serve and travell with certane utheris in the reviewing of the auld municipall lawis of this realme',[68] to Thomas Bannatyne, justice-depute and lord of session,[69] and two writers, John Forsyth and Henry Sinclair.[70] Others, outwith the judiciary, who profited were Gilbert Primrose, royal surgeon,[71] Peter Young, the king's tutor,[72] and the two border administrators, James Hume of Coldenknowes and John Carmichael of that ilk.[73]

Although certain members of the nobility also acquired such gifts, most of these can be regarded as rewards for faithful service. Thus, in 1579, the countess of Mar, in consideration for her 'long, gude and cairfull service done to his majestie', was given £1,100 annually, of which £600 was to be forthcoming from the thirds of the archbishopric of St. Andrews and the remainder from the revenues of Strathearn.[74] Likewise, her son John, earl of Mar, received his award of £400 per month in 1578 out of the thirds in order that he could meet the extra expenses he had incurred as custodian of the king.[75] Similarly, it can be presumed that lord Boyd received his subvention of 1,000 merks per annum as recompense for his efforts at the collectory.[76]

For that matter, neither Morton's own family and relatives nor his servants were enriched directly to an abnormal degree by the crown, either by the thirds or such branches of the kirk's patrimony as gifts of prebends and forfeited church property. Certainly he made adequate provision for Patrick Adamson, before he became Archbishop of St. Andrews, as well as another chaplain, Patrick Auchinleck, while they served him in the capacity of 'minister of Goddis word in my lord Regentis grace house'. Thus, both received pensions of £300 which, although above the scales recommended by Knox for the ministry, were, in the circumstances, hardly extraordinary.[77] Consequently, apart from George Auchinleck, whose peculiar links with Morton have been examined elsewhere, only the acquisitions of his eldest natural son, James, could be regarded as, in any way, exceptional. The latter, in one year, for example, obtained the escheat of the fruits of the deanery of Brechin, the chantory of Moray, the subdeanery of Ross and a number of other benefices forfeited by James Thornton, chantor of Moray.[78] When two other less substantial awards that year are also taken into consideration,[79] it is clear the commendator of Pluscarden could have no grounds for complaint about parental neglect!

Morton, it has been seen, certainly utilised some of the resources from the thirds as well as such other sources as gifts of prebends and escheats of forfeited property to provide pensions or other forms of remuneration for various candidates. Moreover, despite privy council announcements about the revocation of pensions out of the superplus which were ultimately ratified in parliament in November, 1579,[80] the practice undoubtedly continued.[81] However, there is no evidence of blatant patronage by the regent, and Morton, in making such awards, far from being an innovator, was merely following a precedent established for over a decade. Indeed, while the practice of using church revenues in the public interest may be ethically debatable, it should be remembered that Morton was not innovating and that, even in the second Book of Discipline, it was conceded that a residue of ecclesiastical finances might be used 'for the commoun welth, gif neid require'.[82]

On the other hand, there still remain for consideration those gifts made by certain prelates from their own fruits. Unquestionably, there was a number of such donations during Morton's regime although only five of the bishops seem to have been involved. These were James Paton, bishop of Dunkeld, Robert Stewart, bishop of Caithness, William Gordon, bishop of Aberdeen and his successor, David Cunningham, and Patrick Adamson, archbishop of St. Andrews.

Paton had been nominated by the crown on 8th September, 1571 to succeed Robert Crichton,[83] and he was the subject of constant strictures for his behaviour from the kirk in the 1570s.[84] The only significant award he made, however, was an annuity of £220 from the thirds of bishopric to a 'servitor' of the regent, David Crawford of Blackcraig.[85] Robert Stewart, who was an uncle of the king, had originally been appointed to his Caithness diocese as a young man in 1541 and had subsequently permitted considerable dilapidation of both this see and the priory of St. Andrews which he had obtained in 1570.[86] He, too, bestowed favours on an associate of Morton's, the egregious George Auchinleck of Balmanno, who received a gift of £100 per annum from the fruits of St. Andrews priory dated 11th October, 1575 which was confirmed on 5th January, 1580.[87] In addition, on 26th December, 1576, he conferred a pension of £500 per annum from the fruits of his priory on George Douglas, another natural son of the regent.[88] Bishop Gordon, an incumbent since 1545, also dispensed largesse to Morton's offspring and, on 14th April, 1574, Archibald Douglas received confirmation of a similar pension from the 'two-thirds' of the bishopric of Aberdeen.[89] This process was continued by David Cunningham, although on a less lavish scale, and on 28th October, 1578, he confirmed four previous gifts amounting to £210 altogether. Three of them were to 'servitors' of Morton's, while the other was to the 'keepare of owre soverane lordis Wardrobe'.[90] Finally, between 1576 and 1578, a dozen minor figures attached to the regent's retinue obtained small awards from the primate, Patrick Adamson.[91]

Outwith Morton's family and his followers, there was only a handful of significant awards by the members of the episcopate. One person, for instance, who clearly benefited from his ancestry was John Lindsay, parson of Menmure and son of the deceased David, earl of Crawford. On 11th July, 1576, for example, he received an annuity of £200 from archbishop Adamson.[92] So, while it must be concluded that there was no systematic plundering of the bishoprics concerned, nonetheless, particularly in the case of the archbishopric of St. Andrews where Adamson bestowed several other pensions on a variety of individuals,[93] the aggregate amount was not inconsiderable. Furthermore, as has been aptly observed, it was unlikely that the archbishop was acting throughout in a spirit of 'spontaneous generosity',[94] and was, it is more likely, yielding to pressure from his formidable patron.

The issues arising from Morton's policy towards the thirds of benefices should not obscure the fact that other procedures, such as the feuing of kirklands, the appointment of laymen as commendators, and the dilapidation of bishoprics during vacancies were also taking place and had financial implications for the kirk.

On 12th August, 1573, Alexander Hay, then clerk to the privy council and Morton's representative at the general assembly on that date, informed the members that, 'It being good reason that the ministers of the kirks should be sustained upon the rents thereof', the government intended a 'reduction of the saids fews, tacks and dispositions wherethrough the rents of the saids commons and thrids may be goodly and rightly applyed as effeirs'.[95] In actual fact, however, there was an annual average in the region of sixty charters confirming ecclesiastical feus either under the great seal or the privy seal in the period between 1574 and 1577. There was then an understandable decline in 1578 due to the disturbed nature of that year, but this was followed by a rise to over sixty such charters in 1580.[96]

Taking into account the pitfalls of any conclusion based on statistical evidence – not all such charters, for example, were necessarily registered under the great or privy seal – it still might appear that the regent had ignored his original promise. However, inspection of individual feu charters, especially those of the great seal, reveals that one of their more notable features is that many of them were originally contracted before Morton's accession, a tendency even more pronounced after 1578. A convenient example is a feu charter to Morton's natural son, Archibald, conferred by the crown on 8th February, 1574. On that date, the king ratified a charter in feu-ferm originally granted on 2nd June, 1562 by William Colthird, chaplain of St. Thomas chapel in the parish of Douglas, to James Williamson, a burgess of Dalkeith. On 23rd November, 1563, however, this had been transferred, with the consent of the burgess, to Morton's son, yet it was not until February, 1574 that the second royal confirmation was obtained.[97]

Another aspect of these charters worth bearing in mind is that a considerable proportion of them was the work of a small coterie of grantors such as Edward Maxwell, commendator of Dundrennan, Mark Ker, commendator of Newbattle, and, especially, Walter Reid, commendator of Kinloss. The last named titular abbot, for example, contrived, between 1574 and 1580 to make no fewer than fourteen such grants under the privy seal alone.[98] Clearly, then, the continuation of feuing on a fairly large scale was not quite so widespread as the statistical evidence might at first suggest.

Presumably, although some allowance must be made for lengthy delays on account of the expense and litigation involved, the greater stability of Morton's regency made some initial difference to the number of those seeking official confirmation of their feus. Similarly, the events of March, 1578 appear to have convinced other feuars that the time was opportune to seek royal approval for their possessions. But there obviously was no dramatic acceleration of feuing in the 1570s and the fact, as has been seen, that so many of the charters verified earlier covenants and were, to some extent, granted by a small group of commendators, would lend weight to the conclusion that the whole business was, for the time being, largely past its zenith.[99]

Inevitably, the kirk protested, especially over fellow members who indulged in feuing. In October, 1576, for example, the brethern resolved that, 'considering the great prejudice and hurt done to the kirk of God be beneficit persons within the Ministrie that sets fewis and taks . . . no beneficit person within the Ministrie, Bischop or utheris sall lett fewis or taks of their benefices or ecclesiastical livings, lands rents teinds and fruitis of the same . . . without the advice and consent of the General Assemblie'.[100] Indeed, by June, 1578, it had been decided that any members guilty of such an offence should be 'depryvit from thair offices and function in tyme comeing'.[101] Not unexpectedly, the setting of feus or tacks was also condemned in the second Book of Discipline.[102] On the other hand, it was not Morton who bore the brunt of the kirk's attacks so much as some of its own members, particularly if they were bishops. James Paton, bishop of Dunkeld, for example, was one prelate who had to endure the assembly's denunciation on this score. On 6th August, 1575, the members found 'great fault' with him, condemning his setting of part of his benefice in feu and his granting of a tack for nineteen years of another part to the earl of Argyll.[103] Certainly, in Paton's case, with a clutch of feus confirmed to various individuals on 12th May, 1574 alone, the assembly's concern would seem justified.[104]

In the practice of presenting laymen as commendators of abbeys, Morton's policy was no different from that of his predecessors. Undoubtedly, it was a feature of his administration and, although there would appear to be no consistent motive behind the eleven presentations which were made between 1573 and 1580, hereditary rights or claims are frequently evident.

In some instances, as with the appointment on 14th March, 1577 of Robert Forbes, son of William, lord Forbes, who replaced Alexander Forbes as commendator of Monymusk priory, the hereditary aspect was apparent as well as some concern regarding the eligibility of the candidate. Thus, Forbes was noted as being over 21 years of age, and the commissioner of the kirk gave his approval to the promotion.[105] At the same time, of course, the Forbes were noted for their hostility towards the Gordons, and their loyalty to the crown had been rewarded on a previous occasion in a somewhat different fashion. Thus, in April, 1573, the master of Forbes 'be my lord regentis grace speciall command' had received £100 from the treasurer 'for his supporte efter the feild of the Crabstane'.[106]

Again, at Beauly priory, the principle of hereditary succession would appear to have operated as, on 26th November, 1579, Thomas Fraser, second son of Hugh, lord Fraser, succeeded John Fraser who, like

Alexander Forbes, had demitted the office.[107] Indeed, as this gift was quickly accompanied by the assignation of Robert Crichton of Eliok, king's advocate, as administrator, since the 'said Thomas be nocht of perfyte age', it can also be safely assumed that the crown profited from this arrangement.[108]

Of the other presentations, the acquisition of Eccles priory on 26th March, 1575 by James Hume of Coldenknowes and of Pittenweem priory on 4th December, 1579 by James Haliburton, provost of Dundee can, up to a point, be regarded as rewards for loyal service.[109] Haliburton, for example, had been provost of Dundee since 1553, was a noted supporter of the reformation and, for many years, had played an important part in affairs of state, including acting as a commissioner for Morton in his dealings with Argyll and Atholl in October, 1578.[110] Hume of Coldenknowes, admittedly, as a border warden, was certainly a hardworking official but it is also worth noting that Eccles priory had really become a hereditary possession. This, in fact, had been the case since August, 1566 when, as a reward for faithful service to the crown, he was allowed to grant Isobel Hume, 'speciall freind to the said James, for all the dayis of hir lyftyme, all and haill the benefice of the priourie and abbay of Ecklis', as well as enjoying for himself 'all and haill the thrid of the fruits'.[111] William, lord Ruthven's position as royal treasurer would seem sufficient warranty for his son John's promotion to Scone abbey on 7th May, 1580, although it should not be forgotten that Ruthven himself had previously held this appointment.[112] In the case of Balmerino abbey, it was obtained, following the death of John Hay, by Henry Kinnear, son of John Kinnear who, as the gift under the privy seal indicates, was a philosophy student at St. Andrews university.[113] At the same time, his bequest of a pension amounting to £500 on 26th December, 1576 to Morton's son, James, would suggest that this appointment was not without its dubious aspects.[114] Ardchattan priory, on the other hand, which was in the possession of John Campbell, bishop of the Isles, but was resigned by him to Alexander Campbell on 5th June, 1580 for what might appear to be no obvious reason,[115] is yet further evidence of the strength of hereditary claims to ecclesiastical property. Alexander, it so happens, was a natural son of the bishop, and the whole procedure was merely a transference of property within a particular family. This is borne out by the further agreement made between father and son on 13th November, 1580 when it was agreed that John should receive the fruits of Ardchattan and Iona during his lifetime but demit the commends in favour of his son, Alexander.[116]

There remains Pluscarden priory and Arbroath abbey. At the former, on

6th February, 1577, Morton's son, James, replaced Alexander, son of George, lord Seton, who was dismissed for his allegedly unsound religious principles,[117] although clearly, on this occasion, the regent was also looking after the interests of his own kin. At Arbroath, however, where Esmé Stewart, in November, 1579, took over from the exiled lord John Hamilton,[118] it was palpably a question of Morton having to accept a personally unpopular choice and one which resulted from his rival's influence over the youthful monarch.

Lastly, there is the matter of vacancies among the episcopate during Morton's administration and whether the crown, by delaying appointments, took financial advantage of the situation.

In the case of Aberdeen, where bishop Gordon died on 6th August, 1577 and his successor, David Cunningham, was appointed about two months later, the crown obviously reaped no profit.[119] In the bishopric of Galloway, however, where there was a vacancy from November, 1575 until 17th September, 1578, the situation was different.[120] Here, on 16th October, 1576, Morton's son, James, acquired the obvious pecuniary advantages of the temporality and spirituality of the see until the appointment of a new bishop.[121] Similarly, in the bishopric of Ross, where Alexander Hepburn had died by 31st October, 1578, Henry, lord Methven was given the temporality on that date.[122] Since there was no subsequent appointment, he retained it for the remainder of Morton's lifetime. At St. Andrews, where archbishop Douglas died on 31st January, 1574,[123] there was a vacancy for over two years and George Auchinleck of Balmanno was the fortunate recipient of its fruits.[124] Yet, although certain pensions were also awarded out of the episcopal revenues of the see during this interval,[125] the delay does not appear to have been deliberate but rather a result of the opposition of some members of the kirk to Morton's candidate, Patrick Adamson.[126]

In short, there was some dilapidation of the bishoprics under Morton but not on an extensive scale and certainly no more so than had taken place formerly.

Morton, therefore, established greater efficiency, generally speaking, in the administration of the thirds of benefices. There is, as well, a lack of any substantial evidence to suggest excessively rapacious behaviour by the regent in his handling of the kirk's revenues, and the latter body's criticism of his financial policy was certainly muted until the year 1578.

Thus, the accounts of the collector-general were properly audited, the ministers received local assignations of the thirds, and Morton's government assumed the function of collecting such payments. In addition, state control also meant the recovery of numerous unpaid revenues (the 'new enterit benefices') as well as the more controversial re-organisation of the expanding ministry. On the other hand, the efficacy of the process of out-lawing offenders for non-payment must still be regarded as very question-able.

Again, in such matters as the granting both of remissions and pensions from the thirds, the overall impression is not one of innovation. The kirk undoubtedly still continued to receive less than it might have but, with the exception of Morton's own friends and relatives, no single faction or individual seems to have been especially favoured. Unquestionably, the awards from what were termed the 'two-thirds' of certain bishoprics were the most culpable practice.

Finally, opposition from the kirk to Morton's financial policy only became really strident on his return to power in 1578 and, even then, such protests were largely indistinguishable from the other demands of the second Book of Discipline. The treatment of one critic, John Davidson, probably acted as an effective deterrent in the earlier years, and it was the larger issue of the constitution of the kirk and its relations with the state which eventually preoccupied the minds of many members. Consequently, it is now time to examine the question of Morton and the polity of the kirk.

NOTES

1. This preface on the thirds is based on the introduction to Donaldson, *Thirds of Benefices*, vii – xxxix.
2. *Ibid*, xli. There are no accounts extant for Ayrshire, the twelfth area.
3. *BUK*, i, 263–64.
4. Donaldson, *Thirds of Benefices*, xli.
5. *R.P.C.*, ii, 227–28, 261.
6. *Ibid*, 263–64.
7. *Melrose Recs.*, iii, 146–47.
8. *R.P.C.*, ii, 286.
9. S.R.O., Thirds of Benefices, E45/8, 10, 13; *see also* Donaldson, 'The New Enterit Benefices', *S.H.R. xxxii*, 93–98.
10. *See, BUK*, i, 40, 59, 68, 70–71.
11. An abstract of the 1574 register is given in *Wodrow Misc.*, i, 396.
12. *BUK*, i, 296.
13. 'An Apologie or Defence made by Mr. Johne Davidsone for not entering the 17th Day of June, 1574 in the Tolbooth of Edinburgh, to underly the law', Calderwood, *History*, iii, 314–26.
14. *Ibid*, 324–26; McCrie, *Melville*, i, 127.
15. Calderwood, *History*, iii, 313.

16   *BUK*, i, 289–90.
17   Calderwood, *History*, iii, 312.
18   *Ibid*, 301.
19   *Ibid*, 309.
20   *BUK*, i, 290.
21   *Ibid*, 291.
22   *Ibid*, ii, 405, 419; this demand was also made in the second Book of Discipline, *ibid*, ii, 502.
23   *Ibid*, 457, 461.
24   *See*, S.R.O., Register of Assignation, E/47, 1–2; *Register of Ministers, Exhorters and Readers*, Maitland Club, 1830.
25   S.R.O., Thirds of Benefices, E45/8–14 (there is no 'discharge' for 1574, and 1575 is completely missing).
26   Donaldson, *Thirds of Benefices*, 83–91.
27   *Ibid*, 113–14; they were remitted in his favour the following year, *ibid*, 148.
28   S.R.O., Thirds of Benefices, E45/8–14.
29   *Ibid.*, E45/10, f.110r and f.110v, f.111r and f.111v.
30   Keith, *Bishops*, 131.
31   Described as James Hume of 'Sinlawis Ewest', S.R.O., Thirds of Benefices, E45/10, f.111r.
32   S.R.O., Thirds of Benefices, E45/10, f.110v; *Works Accts.*, xxvii.
33   Winram had had his thirds 'allowed' since 1563, Donaldson, *Thirds of Benefices*, 242; Brunton and Haig, *Senators of the College of Justice*, 151.
34   *Ibid*, 125.
35   S.R.O., Thirds of Benefices, E45/10, f.111v and f.111r.
36   Ibid, E45/10, f.111v.
37   For the best brief account of Balfour's chequered career, *see* Balfour, *Practicks*, xi–xxxi.
38   Donaldson, *Thirds of Benefices*, 247.
39   S.R.O., Thirds of Benefices, E45/10, f.110r, f.111r and f.111v.
40   Ibid, E45/10, f.110v.
41   *Cf.* Donaldson, *Thirds of Benefices*, 239.
42   *Ibid*, xviii.
43   S.R.O., Thirds of Benefices, E45/10, f.111r; Donaldson, *Thirds of Benefices*, 89, 241.
44   S.R.O., Thirds of Benefices, E45/13, f.104r and 104v.
45   *R.P.C.*, ii, 347.
46   Donaldson, *Thirds of Benefices*, 208; S.R.O., Thirds of Benefices, E45/11, f.112v.
47   *R.P.C.*, iii, 179.
48   *Ibid*, iii, 340–42; on 8th June, 1581, there was a royal order to repay him £40,000 of his expenses, *ibid*, 390–91.
49   S.R.O., Thirds of Benefices, E45/11, f.113r.

50. Ibid, E45/11, f.112v.
51. Ibid, E45/8, 10, 11; (the 'discharge' for 1576 includes those at the horn in 1574 and 1575).
52. Ibid, E45/11, f.124r and f.124v; Donaldson, *Thirds of Benefices,* 295.
53. S.R.O., Thirds of Benefices, E45/8, 10, 11.
54. Donaldson, *Thirds of Benefices,* xvii.
55. *R.P.C.,* ii, 310.
56. *Ibid,* 312–13.
57. *T.A.,* xii, 390.
58. *R.S.S.,* vii (1575–80), *passim.*
59. *Ibid,* Nos. 45–46, 82.
60. *See* Chap. 7, 121.
61. *BUK,* i, 339.
62. *R.P.C.,* iii, 241.
63. *R.S.S.,* vi, No. 2184.
64. *Ibid,* No. 2562.
65. *Ibid,* vii, No. 476.
66. *Ibid,* Nos. 568, 695.
67. *Ibid,* No. 861.
68. *Ibid,* No. 1070.
69. *Ibid,* No. 1253.
70. *Ibid,* Nos. 1051, 1315.
71. *Ibid,* No. 765.
72. *Ibid,* No. 2083.
73. *Ibid,* Nos. 56, 378.
74. *Ibid,* No. 2697; but *see* Robertson, *History of Scotland,* ii, 64, where it is suggested that this was simply a device by Morton to retain the support of the countess.
75. *R.S.S.,* vii, No. 1660.
76. *Ibid,* No. 1655.
77. *Ibid,* Nos. 219 and 1287; for Knox's recommendations, *see History,* ii, 288–290.
78. *R.S.S.,* vii, No. 1208.
79. *Ibid,* Nos. 1313, 1347.
80. *R.P.C.,* iii, 29–31, 35, 200–01; *A.P.S.,* iii, 149.
81. E.g. *R.S.S.,* vii, 2314, 2316.
82. *BUK,* ii, 510.
83. *R.S.S.,* vi, No. 2812.
84. *See above,* 96.
85. *R.S.S.,* vi, No. 2003.
86. Keith, *Bishops,* 215–16.
87. *R.S.S.,* vii, No. 2183.
88. *Ibid,* No. 812.

89. *Ibid*, vi, No. 2448.
90. *Ibid*, vii, Nos. 1687–1690.
91. *Ibid*, Nos. 824, 827, 862–69, 916, 941.
92. *Ibid*, No. 658.
93. *Ibid*, Nos. 1726, 1746, 2015, 2182, 2497.
94. This phrase is used by professor Donaldson in his introduction to *R.S.S.*, vii.
95. *BUK*, i, 277–279.
96. *R.M.S.*, iv, v, *passim; R.S.S.*, vi and vii, *passim*.
97. *R.M.S.*, iv, No. 2180.
98. *R.S.S.*, vii, *passim*.
99. *See* Sanderson, 'Feuars of Kirklands', *S.H.R. lii*, 117–136.
100. *BUK*, i, 373.
101. *Ibid*, ii, 413–14.
102. *Ibid*, 510.
103. *Ibid*, i, 331–32.
104. *R.M.S.*, iv, Nos. 2236–2244.
105. *R.S.S.*, vii, No. 956.
106. *T.A.*, xii, 345.
107. *R.S.S.*, vii, No. 2113.
108. *Ibid*, No. 2133.
109. *Ibid*, No. 140 (Hume), *R.M.S.*, iv, No. 2930 (Haliburton).
110. *D.N.B.*, xxiv, 127–29.
111. *R.S.S.*, v, No. 3041.
112. *Ibid*, vi, Nos. 1267, 3011.
113. *Ibid*, No. 2232; *see also St. Andrews Acta*, ii, 438–39.
114. *R.S.S.*, vii, No. 813.
115. *R.M.S.*, iv, No. 3021.
116. *Clan Campbell*, vi, 42–3.
117. *R.M.S.*, iv, No. 2640.
118. *Ibid*, No. 2920.
119. *Spalding Misc.*, ii, 46; *R.S.S.*, vii, No. 1254.
120. Keith, *Bishops*, 279; *R.S.S.*, vii, No. 1646.
121. *Ibid*, No. 730.
122. *Ibid*, No. 1693.
123. *Diurnal*, 341.
124. *R.S.S.*, vi, 2700–01.
125. *Ibid*, vii, Nos. 187, 658, 704.
126. *See* Chap. 6, 110.

6
The Polity of the Kirk

As far as the organisation of the church is concerned, Morton had been closely involved with such matters before he became regent. Indeed, it was the presentation in August, 1571 of his elderly protégé, John Douglas, rector of St. Andrews University, to the vacant archbishopric which had precipitated a serious religious controversy between the regent Mar and the kirk. Essentially, this was over the question of the kirk's right to have a voice in the selection of bishops, and eventually, after considerable debate between the two sides, it was agreed there should be a conference to settle outstanding issues.[1]

This meeting between the regent Mar's commissioners and the leaders of the kirk was held at Leith, the seat of government at that stage of the civil war, in January, 1572. The proceedings opened on Sunday, 13th January with a lengthy sermon from David Ferguson, minister of Dunfermline. He took as his text the old testament prophet, Malachi, and, eschewing the current episcopal controversy, concentrated upon the financial plight of the church which, so Mar, Morton and the others present were assured, was of such gravity that 'Tempilis (were) decaying for laik of Ministeris and uphalding and the Schulis uterlie neglectit and oversene'. The cause of all this, so Ferguson insisted, was that 'that quhilk aucht to mantene the Ministerie of the Kirk and the Pure is gevin to prophane men, flatteriers in Court, Ruffiianes and Hyrelings'. In fact, he concluded, having treated the kirk so badly, it was not surprising that the government forces had 'not prevailit aganis yone throt-cutteris and unnaturall murtheris within the Towne and Castell of Edinburgh'.[2]

Doubtless, Morton and his colleagues found Ferguson pretty insufferable but it did not prevent them from reaching agreement with the kirk's representatives. Consequently, the outcome of the Leith convention was an agreement that the exisiting diocesan boundaries should remain unaltered but, within a year of a vacancy occurring in any bishopric, the government should nominate a suitably qualified candidate. Such a nomination would, however, be followed by the approval of the chapter concerned. In addition, in the case of nominations to the commendatorships of vacant monasteries, only when proper provision for ministers out of the teinds of churches appropriated to any monastery had been obtained should appointments be made. Lastly, the powers of the new bishops were to be comparable to those of superintendents, being subject to the kirk in religious matters and to the civil powers in temporal affairs.[3]

However, another important consequence of the talks at Leith was that the kirk, which had gained succession to the lesser benefices in 1567, now obtained access to those of the higher clergy. In fact, it has been suggested that Morton hoped that, by persuading the leaders of the reformed church to accept episcopacy and consequently benefit financially from the revenues of the old church attached to the bishoprics, a solution had been found to the perennial issue of the kirk's endowment.[4] But, with so much of the wealth of the church already given away, the 1567 Act had already proved an unsatisfactory measure as far as the ministers' stipends were concerned. Furthermore, the arrangements of 1572, because of the inroads into ecclesiastical revenues, particularly by awards of pensions, did not give the bishops anything like the livings enjoyed by pre-reformation occupants. One notable example of this was the see of Galloway where the incumbent, bishop Alexander Gordon, had, by this date, whittled away much of its wealth by granting pensions to various people.[5]

In other words, the problem of finding a permanent endowment remained after 1572 and, if Morton, on his accession to the regency, did believe that the bulk of his problems within the kirk were resolved and that its members would be quiescent, he was quickly disillusioned. Actually, the general assembly in August, 1572 had made its position quite clear by accepting the Leith arrangements in principle but adding, significantly, 'that the said heids and articles agreed upon be onlie receaved as an interim till further and more perfyte order may be obtained'.[6] Although the regent helped matters by passing a statute in January, 1573 which insisted that all holders of benefices must subscribe to the confession of faith or suffer deprivation,[7] this statute operated unevenly. Admittedly, a number of deprivations are recorded in the register of the privy seal in 1573 and subsequent years. Indeed, the gift of the fruits of Pluscarden abbey to Morton's natural son, James, in February, 1577 was stated as being a consequence of the 'last pryoure thairof, for non geving of the confessioun of his faith and acknowlegeing of our said soveranis auctoritie within the space and according to the ordour appointit in the act of Parliament laitlie maid thairanent.[8] On the other hand, the act ignored those who were prepared to subscribe to the confession of faith but were not willing to serve the church, and this loophole inevitably meant that it was of limited value.

Consequently, Morton, from the outset of his regency, had to contend with the criticism of a substantial minority of ministers and their supporters. This body was determined that outstanding questions affecting endowment and polity should be answered by the government. What this radical party within the kirk lacked initially was someone to provide leadership – a deficiency remedied, however, by the return of Andrew Melville in July, 1574.

Melville, who returned to Scotland with a brilliant academic reputation acquired at Poitiers and Geneva, although offered a temporary position in Morton's household on the understanding that 'he should be honourablie advanced at the first occasion', preferred to seek a university post.[9] Thus, in October, 1574, on the special recommendation of archbishop Boyd of Glasgow and Andrew Hay, the kirk's commissioner for the west of Scotland, he was appointed principal of Glasgow University.[10] The regent, therefore, had failed in his bid to add Melville to his retinue. There were two obvious reasons for seeking to do this: in the first place, Melville was a scholar of international renown whose presence in Morton's household would have made him a prestigious acquisition; secondly, being a member of his household, it would have been more easy to muzzle a potentially dangerous religious opponent.[11] As it happened, the new principal now proceeded not only to revive the moribund university of Glasgow[12] but also to act as a catalyst to the latent disquiet among the members of the kirk.

Thus, in march, 1575, Melville replaced Alexander Arbuthnot, principal of King's college, Aberdeen, as one of the seven commissioners nominated 'to concur and reason with my lord Regents Grace his commissioners upon the jurisdiction and polity of the Kirk'.[13] Since Arbuthnot and Melville had already met and agreed on a programme of university reform,[14] this substitution was probably Arbuthnot's own suggestion. It meant that Melville became a member of the joint committee headed by the regent's chancellor, lord Glamis, who had been authorised by a recent parliamentary convention 'to convene, confer, reason and put in forme the ecclesiastical policie and ordour of the governing of the kirk'.[15]

The Glamis committee has left no record of its work but it unquestionably experienced difficulties in devising a satisfactory formula. This would explain why Glamis, about a year later, presumably with Morton's permission, sought the advice of Theodore Beza, Calvin's successor at Geneva.[16] Furthermore, in his letter to the Swiss reformer, he also remarked that 'adequate agreement has not yet been reached among us on matters of government and constitution on which men devout and right minded on all points of religion are sometimes found to differ'.[17] The contentious issues troubling the chancellor and the regent, as the dialogue with Beza reveals, included such diverse matters as the status of the bishops in a reformed church, the kirk's right to summon its own assemblies as well as the powers which these possesed, the treatment of catholics, and whether the sovereign, in the case of the kirk's patrimony, 'can appropriate the remainder so that he be free to convert it into his own or public use'.[18]

Beza's reply, on the other hand, with its anti-episcopal comments and its emphasis on the separate authority of the kirk, could hardly have appealed to Morton or his governmental colleagues.[19] Nevertheless, the correspondence can be regarded as indicative of the regent's desire to establish a *modus vivendi* with the kirk as well as further evidence of growing pressure upon him under Melville to find such a solution.

A further illustration of the impact of Melville's leadership forcing Morton to give serious consideration to a wide variety of issues affecting the kirk is provided by the forty-two questions which he submitted for the assembly's deliberation in October, 1576. Whether they emanated from the regent himself or, as Calderwood would have us believe, from the archbishop of St. Andrews, Patrick Adamson, is of little consequence.[20] What they undoubtedly did succeed in doing was to provoke discussion on such controversial topics as the powers of the assembly, the status of bishops, ecclesiastical representation in parliament, the kirk's patrimony, alterations in diocesan boundaries, reasons for deprivation, future policy regarding benefices, the judicial powers of the kirk, the permanency of the Leith arrangements as well as a number of other relevant issues. In fact, certain enquiries, like number twenty-seven, whether someone could be both a minister and also an army officer 'or a Lord or Lairds stewart, grieve, pantryman or porter', are sufficiently irreverent to suggest the influence of the regent's mordant sense of humour on some of them.[21]

Another area where Morton was likely to have become aware of Melville's more decisive authority within the kirk was the requests made either for his presence, or for one of the members of his council, at the sessions of the general assembly. Such demands, made, it has been suggested, with a view to committing the regent's government to acceptance of the policy which the kirk was busy framing,[22] were made both in October, 1576 and, with particular insistence, a year later.[23] On the latter date, Morton told the members that 'in respect of sindrie important businesses he could not have the counsell so soone convened', and suggested that a deputation from the assembly should contact him, as had happened before, about its deliberations.[24] In short, Morton had no intention of encouraging the idea once prevalent in the 1560s that the privy council, or at least part of it, should attend the general assembly. Moreover, there is every likelihood that, about this date, Morton, in conversation with Melville, made one of the more controversial comments attributed to him. Melville's party, he is supposed to have stated, 'be thair conceats, owersie dreames, imitation of Genev discipline and lawes' were a serious source of internal dissension. 'Ther will never be quyetnes in this countrey,' he allegedly told Melville, 'till halff a dissone of you be hangit or banished the countrey.'[25] Although, in a moment of exasperation, the regent could, understandably, have given vent to such an outburst – one which probably registered his innermost feelings about the Melvillians – there is no evidence that he ever seriously contemplated the unstatesmanlike solution of hanging his opponents.

On the other hand, Morton would undoubtedly have liked Melville out of the way, if only for a short period. Thus, it is quite feasible, as Calderwood avers, that, in the request made by queen Elizabeth in October, 1577 for some Scottish churchmen to attend a conference on the Augustan confession at Magdeburg, the regent saw an opportunity of being rid, if only temporarily, of Melville.[26] Certainly, Melville was one of the two delegates nominated by the government for a mission which was ultimately abandoned through 'want of expences and charges'.[27]

While Morton, despite the growing pressure from the anti-episcopal party, clearly endeavoured to establish a polity favourably inclined towards episcopacy, it would seem mistaken to regard all the criticism of bishops made in the years 1573 to 1578 as proof of a continuous campaign against them. There was also the general assembly's desire to extend its disciplinary powers to embrace all its members which brought it into conflict with particular bishops. Those most concerned were Alexander Gordon, bishop of Galloway, James Paton, bishop of Dunkeld, George Douglas, bishop of Moray, and eventually, Patrick Adamson, archbishop of St. Andrews.

Alexander Gordon, nominated to his see of Galloway in 1559, was a brother of George, fourth earl of Huntly, and a cousin of queen Mary. He had supported the reformation but lost favour with the kirk through his Marian sympathies in the civil war.[28] In March, 1573, the general assembly repeated an earlier prohibition on his exercising any spiritual functions within the kirk while, in August, 'certain heads of accusation were given in against him' regarding his behaviour during the siege of Edinburgh. Then, among other transgressions, he was alleged to have both 'taught the people most perverse and ungodlie doctrine' and encouraged them 'to rebell against our soverane lord and to joyne with manifest rebels and conjured enemies'.[29] The bishop, in reply, declared that the pacification of Perth, signed earlier that year, absolved him from any past offences, and the assembly was obliged to have recourse to Morton's arbitration.[30] The regent, although he insisted that the terms of the Perth agreement must be respected, nonetheless afforded Gordon little consolation by adding that his decision was not to be regarded as 'prejudging the privilege of the Kirk'.[31] The affair continued until August, 1575, three months before Gordon's death, when the assembly, having acted in March 'with consideration of my lord Regent's Graces request made in his favours', reduced his sentence to one of only public penance at the kirk of Holyrood house,[32] and announced that 'no fault they will find, that he will preach truly the word of God albeit he stand suspended from commission of visitation'.[33] Why Morton should have bothered to intervene on Gordon's behalf is problematical: the original sentence was that 'he should make publick repentance in sack-cloth three severall sundays ane in the Kirk of Edinburgh anotther in Holyrood-house and the thrid in the Queens Colledge for [i.e. in place of] Sanct Cuthbert's Kirk',[34] and perhaps he objected to any member of the episcopate being subjected to such a degrading punishment. For whatever reason, it did not protect Gordon from the vigilance of the regent's collector-general of thirds, lord Boyd, who, on 6th April, 1574, was given the gift under the privy seal of the escheat of Gordon's goods on account of his non-payment of pensions to Archibald Crawford, parson of Eaglesham, and Stephen Wilson, parson of Glendevon, as well as his failure 'for whatsoever years past' to contribute the thirds for either his bishopric or Inchaffray abbey, of which he was commendator once more.[35]

James Paton, nominated by the crown to Dunkeld on 8th September, 1571 to replace the Marian incumbent, Robert Crichton,[36] was charged with a variety of offences by the general assembly in August, 1573. These included accusations of inactivity against catholics, particularly John, earl of Atholl, a simoniacal agreement between himself and the earl of Argyll, and of voting in parliament contrary to the interests of the assembly.[37] By August, 1575, in addition to these shortcomings, he was being indicted for permitting the dilapidation of his benefice, non-residence and, in one instance, placing one minister in charge of several kirks.[38] At this juncture, Morton, whose council had already rebuked Paton for failing to pay ministers and readers their stipends from the thirds,[39] became involved in the proceedings. Paton argued that the controversial lease granted to the earl of Argyll had been yielded only under duress, and produced evidence that he had a promise of assistance for obtaining its reversion from the regent himself.[40] Therefore, the members of the assembly, heeding a request from Morton that 'all further process against the said bishop should be intermitted till the next assembly', postponed further action meanwhile.[41] However, at its next meeting in April, 1576, the assembly found Paton guilty of his alleged misdemeanours, and sentenced him to be permanently deprived of his office 'so farre as lyes in thair power'.[42] The regent accepted this verdict, observing that 'the kirk hath proceeded against him and deprived him worthilie for his offence, he could find no fault therein'.[43] Morton, in short, was clearly unwilling to protect a member of the episcopate who had so blatantly offended the general assembly and had the additional stigma of being a client of the earl of Atholl.

The regent displayed a similar indifference to the kirk's treatment of his kinsman, George Douglas, bishop of Moray. Douglas, a natural son of Archibald, sixth earl of Angus, and a privy council member since 1572, received royal confirmation of his appointment on 5th February, 1574.[44] The assembly in March that year immediately challenged his election on the grounds of immorality, and, although he protested that 'after admonition given him, he abstained from all cohabitation with the said woman', a committee was designated to examine the chapter which had approved his election.[45] The question of his worthiness prevailed until 1576, with the disparaged bishop twice evading a confrontation with his accusers by pleading, on one occasion, that he was unwell and, on another, the legal disability of being at the horn.[46] Clearly, Morton, in this instance, was unwilling to intervene on behalf of a prelate whose calibre, in itself a reflection on himself, the assembly had good grounds to impugn. In other words, the regent, at times, paid scant regard to the quality of some of his episcopal appointments and, consequently, to one of the terms of the Leith agreement.

Two other members of the episcopate who, in the earlier part of Morton's regency, experienced the strictures of the kirk, albeit to a lesser degree, were John Douglas, archbishop of St. Andrews between February, 1572 and July, 1574, and James Boyd, appointed archbishop of Glasgow in November, 1573. Douglas, for example, was regarded by many churchmen as unsuitable for the rigours of his task on account of his advanced years, while Boyd was criticised for allegedly neglecting some of his diocesan duties.[47] Again, the regent remained inactive, presumably because he recognised such criticism as being a regular feature of every assembly since their inception and a facet of what has been termed the 'new ecclesiastical democracy'.[48] That is to say, he was unwilling to recognise it as a general assault on the status of the bishops.

Moreover, he must have regarded the rigorous treatment of various commissioners and superintendents as confirmation of this viewpoint. Thus, at the general assembly at Edinburgh in August, 1575, to take one instance, it was not only the archbishop of Glasgow and the bishops of Dunkeld, Galloway and Moray who were the subjects of the members' attention.[49] John Erskine of Dun, superintendent of Angus and Mearns, for example, was charged with admitting an unsatisfactory minister; George Hay, commissioner for Aberdeen, was accused of permitting 'certain patron and festival dayes' and of a lack of discipline within his province; while Robert Graham, commissioner for Caithness, was indicted for defaulting on visitations and giving his consent to the controversial marriage of Barbara, divorced daughter of the earl of Caithness, and Alexander Innes of Innes.[50] Clearly, the bishops were not the only body to experience the investigative tendencies of the assembly.

In the latter part of Morton's regency, the only member of the hierarchy to feel the weight of the kirk's disapproval to any great extent was Patrick Adamson. Adamson, once an outspoken critic of his predecessor, John Douglas, had become the regent's chaplain and, on Douglas' death, his candidate for the primacy.[51] In October, 1576, the general assembly challenged Adamson's right to accept presentation to St. Andrews without first satisfying the members as to suitability and worthiness.[52] In doing so, incidentally, they were adhering to one of their own decisions, agreed upon at an earlier assembly in March, 1575, that 'no bishop be elected to a bishoprick be the Chapter before he give proof of his doctrine before the Generall Assembly'.[53] This had meant that, in March, 1575, for example, Andrew Graham, Morton's candidate for the bishopric of Dunblane, had to satisfy the assembly by preaching in front of its representatives before it approved his presentation.[54] Initially, Adamson gave the impression of acquiescing in the members' demands by stating that Morton 'had dischargeit him to proceid farther in this matter . . . and therfor he wald not midle farther'.[55] However, during a later session of the same assembly, following a complaint by the chapter of St. Andrews that 'my Lord Regents Grace hes presentit Mr. Patrick Adamson to the Bishoprick of Saint Androes', he was asked if he would 'submit himself to the tryale and examination of the Assemblie'.[56] But Adamson, probably on the regent's instructions, declined to do so and, shortly afterwards, his appointment was confirmed by the crown.[57] The assembly's reply in April, 1577 was to withhold recognition of his title and to refuse to grant him his powers of visitation.[58]

There is one further matter in these years involving the episcopate which merits consideration. This is the significance of the proposal regarding visitations of dioceses made at the assembly of April, 1576. On that occasion, so it was stated, because the bishops, superintendents and commissioners were overworked and unable to execute their supervisory duties properly, 'the whole Kirk within their bounds could not be duely overseen, [and] consequently good discipline [was] unexercised within the same for lack of visitation'. Accordingly, in an attempt to rectify this situation, it was resolved that several brethren should be nominated 'to make a proper distribution and division of the whole bounds of this realme'.[59] Consequently, the following day, a list of visitors was announced for the whole country.[60] Since only the bishops of Dunblane, Moray and Ross were included among those named, it might be thought that this is an example of the assembly seeking to extend its influence over the kingdom and, at the same time, diminish the powers of visitation possessed by the bishops. On the other hand, as has been pointed out in a recent study of these developments,[61] since the office of superintendent was becoming an anachronism in the Scottish church, all that was probably happening in 1576 was that the visitors were merging their functions with those of the superintendents.

Consequently, while many members of the kirk were clearly unhappy with the Leith arrangements, this did not mean that the bishops were under intolerable pressure while Morton remained regent. In some ways, this is unremarkable. Morton's position was much more secure than it was to become later while, conversely, Melville and the other members of the assembly were greatly preoccupied with the compilation of the second Book of Discipline. Thus, it was not until their constitution was rejected, or, more precisely, shelved, that Morton and all the episcopate had to face a really belligerent kirk.

Shortly before the *coup* of March, 1578, the committee responsible for drafting the final version of the 'Booke of Policie' presented it to the regent and fixed a date for further discussions of its contents.[62] This arrangement, however, was overtaken by Morton's demission. Therefore, acting on the assumption that there was more likelihood of effecting a change in the ecclesiastical constitution now that the royal minority had technically ended while, at the same time, concerned that, in the turmoil which prevailed, its religious recommendations might be overlooked,[63] the committee delivered its proposals and certain other requests to the new government.[64] But lord Herries and the commendator of Deer, the two commissioners representing the new administration, informed the brethren that they had no authority to discuss policy and could only refer the assembly's demand to the council.[65] Discussions between the latter and the kirk's representatives now followed, and it was agreed there should be further talks so that 'all things may be duely advised upon befor the Parliament'.[66] By this date, that is, July, 1578, Morton, as it transpired, had retrieved his position but, nonetheless, the church leaders had grounds for hoping for a successful outcome in parliament. The reason for their optimism was that, earlier in the month, when their demands were presented to the former regent, they had been received in encouraging fashion. 'Not only,' he had declared, 'would he concur with the kirk in all things that might advance the true religion presentlie professit within this realme bot also wald be a procurator for the Kirk.'[67]

Morton, at this juncture in June, 1578, was anxious to recruit as much support as possible, hence his friendly response to the kirk's delegates and, later that month, his conciliatory manner during further talks with the kirk leaders when there had been agreement on most of the articles under discussion.[68] However, in the parliament held the next month at Stirling, his influence on the kirk's behalf was conspicuous by its absence. Instead, the twelve commissioners in attendance as representatives of the kirk's interests were notified that 'the said buik being red and considerit in presence of the lords chosen upoun the articles and mony headis thairof being found of sa great wecht and consequence . . . na resolution nor determination can be presentlie gevin thairin'.[69] Consequently, yet another conference on the subject was proposed to be held at Stirling on 18th August, which was a serious blow to the kirk's envoys who seem to have believed, although this was contradicted by the archbishops of St. Andrews and Glasgow, that the meeting in June had left only four items unresolved.[70] Morton, admittedly, was willing to authorise parliament to legalise some of the proposals, but the commissioners were unwilling to accept such a piecemeal arrangement.[71] They also disagreed about the composition of the joint committee due to meet in August, and proceeded to make the rather audacious pronouncement 'that it became not the prince to prescrive on policie to the kirk and if they would appoint anie, they would not consent to it'. Not surprisingly, Morton and his colleagues 'took it in evil part' and informed the assembly's commissioners, in peremptory fashion, that 'the king might call whom he pleased and with their advice mak a law'.[72]

Thus, the kirk discovered that Morton's strategy during his latter years in office was to be one of procrastination. Obviously, the August conference never took place because of the internal dissension that month but, in December, 1578, there were further discussions at Stirling. From 22nd to 29th December, there were regular sessions at Stirling castle between a deputation from Morton's government led by Robert, earl of Buchan, and the two archbishops and one representing the kirk, consisting of Robert Pont, James Lawson, John Row and David Lindsay. While there was some measure of agreement over quite a number of articles in the second Book of Discipline, there were still important items 'referred to further reasoning', 'past over' or 'differed'. In those categories, predictably, were sections of Chapter I, 'Off Elderschippis and Assembleis and of Discipline'. In the case of Chapters VIII and IX which dealt with the diaconate and the patrimony of the kirk, it was 'Thought good to be superseded, whill the heed of the corruptions be reasouned'. Similarly, discussion on Chapter V, 'of Doctors and their office', which was particularly apposite to Melville's desire that 'doctors', like himself, should be regarded as an order in the church, was postponed 'till further reasoning'.[73]

About a year later, in November, 1579, it was agreed by parliament, in answer to a request from the general assembly in July for a resumption of the unfinished talks of the previous December, that there should be such a meeting. Accordingly, a committee headed by Morton was instructed to liaise with the kirk leaders on 11th April, 1580 at Edinburgh 'to search furth mair specealie and to consider what other special pointis or clauss sould appertene to the jurisdictioun privelege and authoritie of the said kirk'.[74] It is extremely unlikely that such a meeting ever took place and there is no reference whatsoever to it at the next general assembly in July, 1580. Indeed, on that occasion, yet another delegation was nominated for discussions with the government about a series of items including the 'Book of Policie' which, it was hoped, 'may be establischit be ane act of Privie Counsell, quhill ane Parliament be had'.[75]

The kirk's answer to Morton's vacillation was to intensify the campaign against the bishops. By October, 1578, for example, an eight-point programme of episcopal reform had been devised. Thus, bishops were required to 'be content to be pastors and ministers of ane flock'; they were inhibited from either claiming temporal titles, exercising criminal jurisdiction or voting in parliament without the permission of the kirk; they were exhorted not to live extravagantly or squander wealth which could otherwise provide stipends, assist education or relieve the poor; they were adjured not to exceed the limits of their diocesan powers either with regard to visitations or by overruling the presbyteries.[76]

In addition, as might be expected, individual prelates were also the targets for criticism. In the October, 1578 assembly, for example, there was a renewal of that harassment of the archbishop of Glasgow which, in one opinion, was partly responsible for his premature demise.[77] Boyd, on this occasion, would appear to have defended himself quite competently against various charges of 'negligence' or 'indiscipline', basing his defence, ultimately on the status of the bishops as determined by the Leith convention.[78] Then, at the next assembly in July, 1579, it was Boyd's colleague, Patrick Adamson, who, in his absence, was the object of the kirk's censure. The archbishop of St. Andrews was condemned on a number of different counts: for voting in parliament and his behaviour while attending it the previous year when he had contradicted the kirk's leaders over the decisions reached at the pre-parliamentary conference on the second Book of Discipline, for asserting his authority outwith the bounds within which the assembly thought he should be confined, and for certain other irregularities.[79] One of the latter, his intrusion of a reader into the parish of Bolton in Fife, was also the subject of a complaint by his parishioners to the members of the privy council. They, however, deferred judgment by referring the dispute to the next meeting of parliament.[80]

Predictably, in the last months of Morton's administration, as his authority distinctly declined, so the kirk's assault on episcopacy gained increasing momentum. Thus, at the assembly in July, 1580, the suspension of James Paton, bishop of Dunkeld, was renewed; Andrew Graham, bishop of Dunblane, was accused of various misdemeanours, and the bishops of Argyll, Brechin, Caithness and Orkney were all ordered to 'compeere' before the brethren.[81] This was followed by a denunciation of the office of bishop and by the issuing of instructions for synodal assemblies to be held in August at Glasgow, St. Andrews, Aberdeen and Elgin where the members of the episcopate concerned would be required 'to give obedience to the said Act'.[82]

Thus, in the years 1578-80, Morton faced a two-pronged offensive from the kirk. Initially, the members had concentrated on seeking recognition for the second Book of Discipline but, after experiencing a discouraging series of delays, they directed their energies towards a more determined attempt to undermine the bishops. Morton's answer to these tactics was to pursue a policy which was both uncertain and hesitant and in which procrastination featured prominently. Admittedly, while he was regent, he had asked the kirk to submit a detailed plan for a reformed church system but, at the same time, he obviously had no intention of accepting those controversial sections which would have established a kirk financially independent and free from civil control.

Morton's stance, it so happened, was clearly understood by Melville who, in his correspondence with Beza in 1578–79, succinctly outlined the attitude of the former regent and most of his colleagues. 'They complain,' he informed the Swiss reformer, 'that if pseudo-episcopacy be abolished, the state of the kingdom will be overturned; if presbyteries be established, the royal authority will be diminished; if the ecclesiastical goods are restored to their legitimate use, the royal treasury will be exhausted. They plead that bishops, with abbots and priors, form the third estate in parliament that all jurisdiction, ecclesiastical as well as civil, pertains solely to the king and his council and that the whole of the ecclesiastical property should go into the exchequer.'[83] Undeniably, as Melville perceived, it was Morton's intention to preserve the *status quo* and, with the support of most of the nobility as well as Patrick Adamson — one of his more inspired ecclesiastical appointments — he probably believed he could deflect most of the unacceptable proposals of his religious opponents.

Nonetheless, there is the question of how perturbed Morton was regarding the strength of the opposition emanating from the clerical party. Inevitably, although it had been serious enough when he was regent, this was a greater problem in the less stable period following his return to power. Yet this did not prevent him, on occasion, treating the members of the kirk with some asperity. There was the episode in July, 1579, for example, when he had king James exhort the assembly not to dabble in matters 'that may seeme prejudiciall to that good ordour of the government of the kirk and the ecclesiastical policie heirtofoir lang travellit in and hopeit for'. Such items, 'not concludit be our lawis or receivit in practice', the admonition continued, 'let it so rest without prejudging the same with any of your conclusions at this tyme, since our Parliament now so shortlie approaches'.[84]

Nevertheless, Morton could not have failed to be aware how influential the kirk was throughout much of the kingdom. Certainly, the Jesuit priest, John Hay, for example, on a visit to his family in 1579, was considerably impressed by the widespread powers of the protestant clergy. He, as it transpired, only avoided summary deportation through the protection of his kinsmen and the reluctance of some members of the privy council, Morton included, to be harried into precipitate action.[85] Again, if the general assembly was antagonised too much, there was always the possibility of the repercussions which took place in October, 1578 when, disgruntled with Morton, the members invited Atholl, Lindsay, Montrose and Seton, some of his most noted adversaries, to attend their sessions and sought their assistance with the king and council.[86] While these tactics produced no positive results, Lennox, astutely realising the importance of placating the kirk, made not inconsiderable efforts to convince the brethren of his religious conformity and goodwill.[87] A notable instance of this occurred in October, 1580 when he displayed considerable tact compared with Morton in his handling of the Edinburgh minister, John Durie. The latter had preached against the election to the town council of any followers of either Morton or Lennox and, while the ex-regent 'passed some bitter speech' against Durie the royal favourite was reported to have 'offered all possible kindness as well to themselves as to the advancement of their common causes'.[88]

On the other hand, the fact that Morton and the Melvillians shared, for dissimilar reasons, a preference for the English alliance should not be over-looked entirely. For Melville and his colleagues, this represented an association with the leading anti-catholic power in Europe and with a country where, at least at this stage, their co-religionists were making commendable progress. But for Morton 'to be conform with England in the Kirk's policie', as Melville's nephew acutely observed, implied 'to haiff Bischopes to rewll the Kirk and they to be answerable to the king and sa the frie preatching repressed'.[89] In fact, Morton, along with other members of his government, like Patrick Adamson, probably partly favoured retaining episcopacy in order to reserve that Anglo-Scottish amity which certainly was a cardinal feature of his foreign policy.[90]

Nevertheless, while relations between the two countries will be examined subsequently, it is as well to recognise that it is highly unlikely that foreign policy considerations exercised overmuch influence with either side when it came to matters affecting the constitution of the kirk. Thus, as far as Morton was concerned, his religious policy, like that of James VI himself in later years, was essentially a pragmatic one in which the strength or weakness of his own position determined his approach to ecclesiastical affairs. In Melville's case and that of his followers, while they might, like his nephew, commend Morton's anglophile sympathies and be prepared to concede that he was 'a man ever cast upon the best syde',[91] this, in the end, was of little consequence in their quest for a presbyterian polity.

Notes

1. Donaldson, *Scottish Reformation*, 160–63.
2. Ferguson, *Tracts*, 62–80.
3. Calderwood, *History*, ii, 172–96.
4. Macgregor, *Scottish Presbyterian Polity*, 100.
5. The largest pension was to Sir John Maxwell of Terregles, Donaldson, 'Alexander Gordon, bishop of Galloway', *T.D.G.A.S., 3rd Series*, xxiv, 113.
6. Calderwood, *History*, iii, 221.
7. *A.P.S.*, iii, 72.
8. *R.S.S.*, vii, No. 891.
9. Melvill, *Diary*, 45.
10. *Ibid*, 47–48.

11. This, according to Melville's nephew, James Melvill, was Morton's real motive, Melvill, *Diary*, 45.
12. *See* Durkan & Kirk, *The University of Glasgow, 1451–1577*, Ch. XIV.
13. *BUK*, i, 325–26.
14. Melvill, *Diary*, 53.
15. *A.P.S.*, iii, 89.
16. The date is given as probably April, 1576, Donaldson, 'Lord Chancellor Glamis and Theodore Beza', *S.H.S. Miscellany*, viii, 89–113.
17. *Ibid*, 100.
18. *Ibid*, 101–113.
19. Beza's answers are printed following each question, *ibid*, 102–112.
20. Calderwood, *History*, iii, 389.
21. BUK, i, 368–74; it is also noteworthy that it was in July, 1576 that Morton authorised the printing of a new bible, *R.P.C.*, ii, 544–46.
22. Shaw, *General Assemblies*, 55.
23. Calderwood, *History*, iii, 369, 385–86.
24. *Ibid*, 385.
25. Melvill, *Diary*, 68; Calderwood, *History*, iii, 393–94.
26. *Ibid*, 386–87.
27. George Hay, commissioner for Caithness, was the other representative, *BUK*, i, 394–95; Calderwood, *History*, iii, 387.
28. Donaldson, 'Alexander Gordon, bishop of Galloway', *T.D.G.A.S., 3rd Series*, xxiv, 111–128.
29. *BUK*, i, 261, 273–74.
30. *Ibid*, 274.
31. *Ibid*, 275.
32. *Ibid*, 319–20.
33. *Ibid*, 343.
34. *Ibid*, 277; Calderwood, *History*, iii, 293. The 'queen's colledge' mentioned was the Holy Trinity College founded by Mary of Gueldres.
35. *R.S.S.*, vi, No. 2434; he had resigned the commendatorship of Inchaffray to one of his cousins, James Drummond, in 1566, *ibid*, v, No. 2211, but resumed it on his death.
36. *Ibid*, vi, No. 2812.
37. *BUK*, i, 270.
38. *Ibid*, 331–32; Calderwood, *History*, iii, 347–48.
39. *R.P.C.*, ii, 363–64.
40. *BUK*, 340–41; Calderwood, *History*, iii, 348.
41. *BUK*, i, 341; Calderwood, *History*, iii, 348.
42. *BUK*, 350–52; Claderwood, *History*, iii, 359–61.
43. *BUK*, i, 352.
44. He succeeded Patrick Hepburn, deceased bishop of Moray, *R.S.S.*, vi, No. 2309.

45. *BUK*, i, 288.
46. *Ibid*, i, 300–02, 321, 349; Calderwood, *History*, iii, 332, 340, 359; he was at the horn for non-payment of the thirds of his bishopric, S.R.O., Thirds of Benefices, E45/10.
47. For Douglas, *see BUK*, i, 255 *et seq*; Calderwood, *History*, iii, 272 *et seq*; for Boyd, *see BUK*, i, 300 *et seq*; Calderwood, *History*, iii, 330 *et seq*.
48. The expression is used by Donaldson, 'Alexander Gordon, bishop of Galloway', *T.D.G.A.S., 3rd Series*, xxiv, 125.
49. *BUK*, i, 331; Calderwood, *History*, iii, 347.
50. *BUK*, i, 332–33; (Calderwood, *History*, iii, 349–50 omits Erskine but gives details of certain aspersions regarding John Winram, superintendent of Fife).
51. Keith, *Bishops*, 40.
52. *BUK*, i, 367.
53. *Ibid*, 326–27; Calderwood, *History*, iii, 341–42.
54. *BUK*, i, 325.
55. *Ibid*, 367.
56. *Ibid*, 376–77.
57. *R.S.S.*, vii, No. 789.
58. *BUK*, i, 385–86.
59. *Ibid*, 353; Calderwood, *History*, iii, 363.
60. *BUK*, i, 358–59.
61. Kirk, 'The Influence of Calvinism on the Scottish Reformation', *S.C.H.S., xviii*, 167–68.
62. *BUK*, ii, 404; Calderwood, *History*, iii, 399.
63. *See* Donaldson, 'The Scottish Episcopate at the Reformation', *E.H.R., lx*, 349–64.
64. *BUK*, ii, 405; Calderwood, *History*, iii, 399.
65. *BUK*, ii, 406; Calderwood, *History*, iii, 400.
66. *BUK*, ii, 408; Calderwood, *History*, iii, 402.
67. *BUK*, ii, 414.
68. Calderwood, *History*, iii, 415.
69. *A.P.S.*, iii, 105.
70. Calderwood, *History*, iii, 415.
71. *Ibid*, iii, 415.
72. *Ibid*, iii, 415–16.
73. The details of this conference are given in Calderwood, *History*, iii, 433–442.
74. *A.P.S.*, iii, 138; *BUK*, ii, 438.
75. *Ibid*, 460–61.
76. *Ibid*, 424–25.
77. W. M. Campbell, 'Robert Boyd of Trochrigg', *S.C.H.S., xii*, 220–34.
78. *BUK*, ii, 420–21; 423; Calderwood, *History*, iii, 428–30.
79. *BUK*, ii, 433; Calderwood, *History*, iii, 444–45.
80. *R.P.C.*, iii, 95–96.

81. *BUK*, ii, 451, 454; Calderwood, *History*, iii, 464–65.
82. *BUK*, ii, 453; Calderwood, *History*, iii, 469–70.
83. McCrie, *Melville*, i, 201–02; drafts of the original correspondence of 1578–79 are to be found in N.L.S. Wodrow 42, No. 3.
84. *BUK*, ii, 428–29.
85. Forbes-Leith, *Narratives*, 141–65; *R.P.C.*, iii, 204.
86. *BUK*, ii, 419.
87. E.g. Calderwood, *History*, iii, 468–69, 477.
88. *C.S.P. Scot.*, v, 520.
89. Melvill, *Diary*, 61.
90. *See* Donaldson, 'Attitude of Whitgift and Bancroft to the Scottish Church', *Trans. R. Hist. Soc. 4th Series, xxiv*, 96–97.
91. Melvill, *Diary*, 60.

7

The Administration of the Borders

If an important chapter in Morton's career undoubtedly consists of his relations with the kirk, the burden of governing the borders certainly con-
stitutes another. Indeed, this task was one of the principal concerns of his
domestic administration.

The borders had a long-established tradition of disorder which, as at
Redeswyre in 1575, could sometimes seriously affect Anglo-Scottish amity.
On such occasions, joint consultations between the respective officials on
either side were necessary, but normally the individual governments were
responsible for their own sections of the frontier. Morton's inheritance,
therefore, was a system where the central government depended for much
of the time on local officials enforcing their own brand of law and order on
their respective provinces. These comprised three districts, known as the
east, west and middle marches, each of them administered by a warden. In
addition, there was Liddesdale, technically part of the middle march, but,
in practice, a separate unit possessing its own keeper.

The border wardens

The east march, which was the smallest and least turbulent, consisted
essentially of the Merse, that is the southern and eastern sections of the
sheriffdom of Berwick. William, lord Ruthven had held the post of warden
on this march since September, 1570, having replaced the disaffected
Alexander, lord Home.[1] Morton, however, on 6th November, 1573, since
Ruthven patently could not continue to perform indefinitely the duties of
both treasurer and warden, appointed, in his place on the east march, James
Hume of Coldenknowes.[2]

The new warden was the son of John Hume of Coldenknowes who had,
in all probability, served as a deputy warden in 1561 under his kinsman,
lord Home.[3] As far as remuneration was concerned, the wardenship of the
east march, although a prestigious appointment with undoubted

opportunities for personal advancement, had been one devoid of salary since 1565.[4] The next year, a nominee of lord Home was given the nunnery of St. Bothans,[5] and presumably the revenues of that benefice served, to some extent, in lieu of a warden's pension. Similarly, under Morton, Coldenknowes' acquisition of the tack of the bailiary and chamberlainry of the earldom of March, which included a small annual fee of £20 from the rents, can be regarded as compensation for the absence of a regular salary.[6] Other comparable emoluments were the award of the escheat of the fruits of Eccles priory on 8th February, 1574 with its eventual presentation to his son, James, on 26th march, 1575,[7] and a gift of ward and nonentry shared with Sir Thomas Turnbull of Bedrule.[8]

Although Coldenknowes' career on the east march was an uneventful one with little evidence of friction between him and Morton, he was, notwithstanding, to become a prominent member of the alliance against him in the summer of 1578. While some of the reasons for this schism between Coldenknowes and the regent must remain conjectural, his conduct is by no means totally inexplicable.

In the first instance, Coldenknowes was a guarantor for the behaviour of the border family of Burnfields. In this capacity, on 28th June, 1576, he was summoned before the council and fined, along with several Burnfields, a total of £5,000 for failing to prevent a renewal of the feud between the Burnfields and the Haitlies.[9] No doubt he had taken a certain amount of umbrage at this sentence.

Another cause of resentment towards the regent was the treatment, the following year, of one of his kinsmen, Alexander Hume of Manderston, commendator of Coldingham priory. Manderston, on 2nd February, 1577, was required to submit 'the just and trow rentall of the said Pryorie of Coldinghame', since, the summons contended, 'as yit thair is not ane just and trow rentall of the Pryorie of Coldinghame gevin up, bot hes bene neglectit to be persewit for hitherto – partlie becaus the haill thrid wes gevin in the begynning to umquhile Johnne Commendatare of Coldinghame; and sen his deceis be the negligence and owersicht of the collectouris for the tyme and thair officiaris quha persewit not for ane trew rentall thairof'. Hume of Manderston now claimed, on the basis of a previous tack of the priory, that 1,000 merks was an adequate rental.[10] Morton, on the other hand, clearly felt this sum was inadequate, and the whole affair developed into a serious bone of contention between the Humes and himself. Moreover, it appears to have been a prolonged dispute, still in existence, according to Sir John Forster, warden of the English middle march, as late as September, 1580.[11]

Finally, Andrew Hume, commendator of Jedburgh and a brother of the lord Home taken prisoner after the siege of Edinburgh castle, was summoned to stand trial in October, 1576 accused of 'treasonabill Intercommowning' with James or 'Black' Ormiston of that ilk[12] who had been condemned to death in December, 1573 for his part in Darnley's murder.[13] This action against another kinsman, and resentment over lord Home's treatment when incarcerated in Edinburgh castle, could have done little to improve relations between Coldenknowes and the regent.

Certainly, Morton, once he had surmounted the obstacle presented by the opposition of the Argyll-Atholl faction, immediately dismissed Coldenknowes. This took place at the beginning of September,[14] following an interview at which, states one source, there was 'a falling out in high terms between them'.[15] However, when the 'mass of close writings' sent by Morton's border informant, John Edington in Coldingham, not to mention the award of a pension of £100 per year to him in August, 1578 are taken into account,[16] there seems every likelihood Morton was well aware of Coldenknowes' disaffection. Edington, an individual apparently not noted for either the accuracy or veracity of his reports,[17] had, at least in this instance, got his facts right.

George Hume of Wedderburn replaced Coldenknowes as warden of the east march on 6th September, 1578.[18] Wedderburn, who was a member of the oldest cadet branch of the Hume family and a future royal treasurer,[19] now occupied his first post of responsibility and clearly found it an onerous one. A council recommendation on 12th February, 1579, for example, 'to use the advice of the gudeman of Hutonhall and sic utheris as ar best experimented quhar ony difficultie appearis', indicates that Morton and his colleagues, conscious of his inexperience, were suggesting that he should utilise the knowledge of his deputies to rectify the deficiency.[20] On the other hand, although he appears to have encountered some difficulties negotiating with lord Hunsdon, his English counterpart, with the result that there was a considerable administrative backlog,[21] affairs on the east march were never a major concern of Morton's during Wedderburn's wardenship. Furthermore, Morton, even if there is no record of such a payment in the treasurer's accounts, did give instructions in 1579 that the warden of the east march should receive his warden's fee. Thus, there is an undated precept for 1579, by King James VI, for paying a warden's fee to Wedderburn who had completed the 'wardanrie of oure eist merche' for one year and was due payment of £100.[22] This in itself would confirm that the government believed he was performing his duties satisfactorily.

When Morton became regent in November, 1572, the west march, comprising the sheriffdom of Dumfries, the stewartries of Annandale and Kirkcudbright as well as part of the sheriffdom of Wigtown, had possessed no official warden for about three years.[23] The Maxwells, as the most powerful family in this area, traditionally occupied this office, and Morton, at the conclusion of the civil war, continued the policy of employing them. Thus, on 26th August, 1573, John, lord Maxwell, a young man twenty years old, whose mother was Morton's sister-in-law and whose wife was also his niece,[24] was appointed warden.[25] As it happened – and Morton was obviously prepared to overlook this – the new warden of the west march had actively supported queen Mary's cause until his marriage to the regent's niece.[26] Indeed, his nuptials had not been without incident since his ex-allies exercised a novel vengeance by seizing, on their way to Dalkeith, the wine and 'store of vennisoun and uther great provisioun' which had been ordered for the wedding celebrations.[27]

The wardenship of the west march, as its annual pension of £500 and warden's fee of £100 would imply, was regarded as a most important and onerous office. Maxwell, nevertheless, received no salary until 12th July, 1576, 'the quhilk day William Lord Ruthven, Theasaurare to oure Soverane Lord, bindis and obleissis him and his airis to content and pay to Johnne Lord Maxwell Wardane of the West Marches of this realme or his servandis in his name the sowme of auchtene hundrith pundis usuale money of Scotland and that in full and compleit payment of his fee and pension'.[28] However, this delay was not the prime cause of the division which developed between Maxwell and Morton. Its origins lay in that endemic rivalry exisiting among border families in the sixteenth century.

Maxwell, although he doubtless had some difficulty enforcing his authority in such a turbulent region, gives the impression of having been a reasonably competent official. His appointment, for example, was renewed on 4th June, 1575,[29] and lord Scrope, his opposite number, spoke very favourably of his abilities.[30] In fact, it is the English warden who provides an important hint for explaining Maxwell's subsequent resignation. 'I understand,' he wrote on 31st March, 1577 in a letter to Walsingham, 'that lord Maxwell being of late returned from Edinburgh upon certain particularities between him and the laird of Johnstone for the failing [i.e. submission] of bills minds determinately to give up his office or wardenry and no further to exercise the same . . .'[31] In other words, it was the ancient enmity between the Maxwells and Johnstones which had provoked the warden of the west march.

The first intimation of this feud during Morton's regency was a complaint by Maxwell on 28th November, 1574 against Johnstone of that ilk regarding the absence of certain of his dependants from the steward court of Annandale. Johnstone promised to rectify this and other misdemeanours while, in an effort to improve relations between the two families, it was agreed to appoint several commissioners who would meet at Edinburgh in February, 1575 'to commune and travell for away taking and componing of the saidis debaittis and contraversiis'.[32] The next recorded incident was on 19th February, 1577 when Maxwell was accused by Johnstone of wrongly presenting one of his servants, 'Jok Irving of the Sheilhill', at a day of truce the previous March.[33] The council reserved judgement until they could hear further evidence, but it would appear to have been this failure by the government to reinforce his authority as a warden which upset Maxwell and which he had confided to lord Scrope.

On 25th May, 1577, Maxwell, 'having willinglie upoun his awin motioun dimittit and geven up his office of Wardanrie of the West Marche of this realme foranent England', was instructed with his warden clerk, Herbert Anderson, 'to bring, present and exhibit all bukis, scrollis, rollis, indentis, aggrementis, bandis and utheris writtis' before the regent and his council.[34] The following day, all revenues attached to the ex-warden's stronghold of Lochmaben castle were arrested, and he was requested to hand over the fortress.[35] Shortly afterwards, he was committed to Blackness castle and, though released at the beginning of September, he was obliged to remain within the environs of St. Andrews, which he presumably did until he was released from custody in March, 1578.[36]

Sir William Fraser believed that Maxwell, as a son of a sister of Morton's wife, Elizabeth Douglas, was a victim of the claims he persisted in making to the Douglas earldom. Thus, according to Maxwell, he was entitled, as his mother's heir, to one third of the Douglas estates while, on the basis of a demission supposedly granted by Margaret, duchess of Chatelherault, another sister of Elizabeth Douglas, he claimed another third.[37] All this may have influenced the regent but it is more likely that Morton, concerned about the stability of the west march and perturbed at the friction between the Maxwells and Johnstones, decided, in an attempt at amelioration, to remove Maxwell from the borders. Moreover, a comment by Robert Bowes on 2nd August, 1577 that the former warden was under arrest 'upon suspicion of intent (to) arise troubles on the borders' tends to confirm this explanation of Morton's conduct.[38]

Maxwell's successor on the west march was Archibald, earl of Angus.[39] The new incumbent, a brother-in-law of the previous warden, had already been created lieutenant of all the marches,[40] and he undoubtedly perpetuated one feature of Maxwell's tenure, namely the cordial relationship established with lord Scrope. This was noted by the English agent, Nicholas Errington, a few weeks after Angus became warden,[41] and it is also apparent from the existing correspondence between Scrope and himself. The English warden, for example, in a letter of 7th August 1577, having given details of a number of Scottish offences, observed, 'I am the bolder herein to wryte my mynde to your lordshippe for that I am well assured of your lordshippes honourable meaning and intention to reformacion of such disorders'. Angus, in reply, reassured him of his determination to pursue the guilty culprits and promised his counterpart 'the salbe deliverit to be punist as periurd personis and sall nevir be borne with be myself nor na others of my knowledge or allowance'.[42]

Angus, on the day of his appointment to the west march, was commissioned by Morton's council to hold a justice ayre at Dumfries beginning on 10th July. In addition, the justice clerk or his deputies were ordered to proceed there a month beforehand 'to ressave dittay upoun all complaintis that sal be maid quhatsumevir personis that hes ressavit skayth or injurie within the said west March'. Finally, in order to assist these judicial proceedings, a muster was summoned to assemble at Dumfries on 2nd July.[43] Unfortunately, there is no record in the treasurer's accounts of the fines received by this court in July, 1577 but, since Morton, on the twenty-second of that month, announced plans for another expedition to the same region the following October to deal with 'a certane few nowmer purposlie maid lowse and left out', it would appear that Angus and his legal colleague, Sir Lewis Bellenden of Auchnoule, were not altogether successful.[44] Unquestionably, their task was not made any easier by the failure of several Ayrshire lairds to participate in the raid. Consequently, Fairlie of that ilk, Cunningham of Cunninghamhead and Hunter of Hunterston, for example, were all subsequently required to give sureties for their attendance before the council in Edinburgh to answer for their absence in July.[45]

Angus, as has been noted elsewhere, was dismissed by Morton's opponents in the coup of March, 1578. His successor was Maxwell who, somewhat surprisingly, considering his affinities with Argyll and Atholl, was retained by Morton once he had effected his recovery.[46] The ex-regent, however, was in a much less dominant position than formerly and probably hesitated to dismiss such an eminent member of the opposition. Nevertheless, as soon as a suitable opportunity arose, Maxwell was discarded.

Such an occasion presented itself on 21st January, 1579 when Maxwell attended a meeting of the council for discussions about the deteriorating condition of the west march where, as its warden admitted, there were over five hundred 'quhom he estemit inobeydient'.[47] Because of this situation, according to one account, the government now had serious misgivings about Maxwell's administration.[48] Maxwell and John, lord Herries who, significantly, was also present, proceeded to submit proposals for reforming the situation. Both agreed on the necessity for a company of armed light horsemen to assist the warden as well as the importance of repairing the strategically situated fortress at Annan. Where they diverged, apart from Herries' controversial suggestion that Lochmaben castle should be the warden's headquarters, was over his other proposal that members of the Johnstone family should become deputy wardens and be rewarded for their service with half the escheats taken.[49] Probably it was this recommendation which convinced Morton that he could afford to jettison Maxwell and appoint someone, namely Herries, who, being a former warden, was not only experienced but prepared to co-operate with the Johnstones, his principal rivals. Moreover, Herries was also a confederate of Argyll and Atholl, so Morton would have no need to fear repercussions over Maxwell's dismissal from that direction. Thus, the council 'deliberat to burdeyne Johnne Lord Herries with the said wardanrie'. Maxwell, who had been asked the previous day if he was willing to continue as warden and had accepted, conditionally, was understandably discomfited.[50]

Herries, a nobleman in his late sixties, had first served as warden of the west march in 1546 and had been re-appointed on several further occasions before 1579.[51] Morton, apart from his new warden's willingness to conciliate the Johnstones, seems to have found his scheme for an armed force permanently stationed on the west march, if not an original plan, at least a useful one. Certainly, it was quickly adopted and, from 1st February, 1579, there were regular monthly payments to a detachment of twenty-four horsemen and their commander which must have made some contribution towards 'the suppressing of the disordered subjects'.[52] Indeed, Herries, on 15th April, was commended for the improved condition of the west march by queen Elizabeth herself who, 'being amply advertised by lord Scrope, lord Warden of the marches, of the good offices, earnest endeavour and pains he used in the charge there committed to him in the administration of justice and repairing and punishing on his side the disorders of those that seek to disturb the peace between Scotland and England', offered her own thanks for his efforts.[53] Nevertheless, Morton, on 24th August, 1579, somewhat inexplicably, unless it was on account of his advanced years, decided to have Herries superseded by John Johnstone of that ilk.[54]

The appointment of Johnstone, head of the most powerful family on the west march after the Maxwells, undoubtedly exacerbated the hostility between these two families. Maxwell was conspicuously unco-operative, quarrelling, on one occasion, with the new warden over the custody of the fortalice of Langholm and, on another, creating difficulties with lord Scrope by his failure to hand over relevant documents.[55] By the end of September, 1580, in spite of a bond of assurance between Johnstone and Maxwell earlier that month,[56] they were so much at variance that the council suggested the earl of Angus should be offered the lieutenancy of the west march and thus have its overall supervision.[57] Morton's nephew, however, rejected the invitation, being probably reluctant to commit himself to duties in an area remote from the capital during the confused political situation which was a feature of his uncle's final months in office.[58] The earl of Argyll was given the post of lieutenant of the west march instead of Angus,[59] but the postponements of a judicial and military expedition proposed firstly for October and then November, 1580 clearly underline the indecisive nature, by this juncture, of government action in this area.[60]

Thus, Johnstone, though personally loyal to Morton – a fact emphasised by his speedy dismissal and ultimate banishment on the latter's downfall – was, in the circumstances, an infelicitous choice for a region where the Maxwells were so firmly entrenched. If Herries could not be prevailed upon to remain as warden, a more suitable candidate would have been Angus who had previously acquitted himself creditably. In this way, it might have been possible to avoid what the preamble to the proclamation of yet another expedition for 15th December described as 'the enormiteis of the thevis and brokin men'. These crimes the council rightly concluded were comitted by those who had taken advantage of 'the oversicht and sparing this lang tyme bygane' on the west march.[61]

The middle march was defined in 1581 as the 'whole shires of Roxburgh, Selkirk and Peebles',[62] and the wardenship of it was traditionally a perquisite of the Ker family. William Ker of Cessford who, by October, 1570, was recognised 'now wardane of the saidis marches'[63] (in place of his father, Walter Ker), retained the position on Morton's accession.

The fact that Cessford was the only warden to remain in office throughout Morton's career might suggest a harmonious relationship being established between him and his warden of the middle march. Certainly, Morton, in the earlier part of his regency, found him a satisfactory servant. In a letter of 5th August, 1575, for example, he congratulated Cessford for his diligence on the frontier, 'quhairin'. He added 'we pray you continew'. At the same time, however, he cautioned him against summarily executing a felon, whom he had recently apprehended, especially as it was a case in which he was personally involved.[64] Cessford, on the other hand, obviously believed he was a law unto himself since, the following year, in November, having clearly ignored Morton's admonition, he found himself summoned before the justice ayre at Roxburgh charged with 'hanging a thief called Geordie Young without an assize'.[65] Admittedly, his fine of £333.6s.8d. was remitted,[66] but it is unlikely that he enjoyed experiencing the regent's disapproval.

This episode in itself, bearing in mind the quirky temperaments of many borderers, might have been sufficient to guarantee his and his father's presence among Morton's opponents in 1578 and why they were 'most furiously bent' against him.[67] Indeed, it was a dependant of Cessford's called Tait who, in August, 1578, by being killed at a preliminary skirmish at Falkirk, achieved the unhappy distinction of being the only fatality in that affair.[68] Nevertheless, there are several other explanations to justify his behaviour.

Firstly, on 23rd September, 1577, Cessford's father complained to the privy council about what he alleged was the restarting by Walter Scott of Goldalandis of the ancient feud between the Scotts and the Kers.[69] However, the upshot of the council's investigation into the matter was unfavourable as far as the Kers were concerned. Cessford, as a result of being a signatory to an unfulfilled wedding contract of 24th March, 1564, whereby George Ker, eldest son of Andrew Ker of Fawdonside, was to have married Janet Scott, sister of the deceased William Scott of Buccleugh, was ordered to pay a fine of 1,000 merks to Scott of Goldalandis.[70] This decision, while it may have improved relations in the long term between the two families, undoubtedly, at the time, could not have pleased either Cessford senior or his son.

Secondly, on 6th August, 1577, four borderers accused of stealing 'four oxin and ane naig' from an Englishman appealed successfully to the privy council against Cessford's judgement in their case. This was doubly annoying to the warden since, shortly afterwards, he found himself liable to pay their costs as well.[71] The government's actions clearly rankled with Cessford who, in December, 1579, was still protesting about a verdict which he ultimately, by his persistence, had reversed in September, 1581.[72]

The final reason for Cessford's antipathy towards Morton undoubtedly has its origins in the reduction, around November, 1576 when the regent visited the borders,[73] of the area for which he was responsible. Under these new arrangements, Cessford was merely to be warden of the middle march 'be east the street', that is, the section east of the old Roman road known as Dere Street,[74] while the supervision of the remainder was to be in the hands, apparently, of William Douglas of Bonjedburgh, a kinsman of the regent.[75]

Cessford quickly showed his dissatisfaction with these changes by neglecting his warden duties. In no time there were complaints from his English counterparts,[76] which went unheeded since, for much of the winter of 1576–77, the disgruntled Cessford was sojourning in Edinburgh.[77]

Morton, once he had retrieved his position in 1578, decided, despite Cessford's disaffection, to retain his services in the middle march where, on the regent's resignation earlier that year, he had been speedily restored to full control including the area 'bewest the strete'.[78] Morton's decision was doubtless more a matter of expediency than preference since, with Walter Scott of Buccleugh a minor and Sir Thomas Ker of Fernihirst still in exile, there was no obvious alternative candidate.

Cessford, at least initially, would appear to have carried out his duties competently, and an English report of 31st December, 1579 spoke favourably of his administration of east Teviotdale. Nevertheless, in the same account, there was also mention of the warden of the middle march being both poorly recompensed for his efforts, and his work being hampered by the enmity prevailing between him and John Carmichael, keeper of Liddesdale.[79] Consequently, Cessford, who had never been very enthusiastic about Morton when he was regent, now, apparently, had additional grievances over pay and his relationship with Carmichael. Not surprisingly, he eventually became a staunch supporter of the earl of Lennox.[80]

As far as his warden's payments were concerned, Cessford regularly received the £100 per annum which was his official salary[81] and which, although in itself an inadequate amount, was supplemented by an annual pension of 650 merks from the fruits of Kelso abbey.[82] Forster, the English warden, however, alluded on one occasion to ill-feeling between Morton and Cessford over that abbey, and possibly he was no longer in receipt of all of this emolument.[83]

As for the question of Cessford's antagonism towards Carmichael, this sprang from the latter's attachment to Morton and the obvious possiblity that he intended, as had happened in November, 1576, a diminution of his warden's powers by utilising the services of a kinsman. As it happened, one of Morton's last significant measures was to invest Carmichael, in November, 1580, with the command of a muster at Hawick 'within the bounds of Liddesdaill and Tyndaill bewest the street'.[84] By this date, Cessford's administration of the frontier had been adversely affected and, a month before Carmichael's partial takeover, he was peremptorily ordered 'to appoint dayis of trew and keep meatingis with the opposite warden'.[85]

Liddesdale, although officially within the territory administered by Ker of Cessford, was, for much of the sixteenth century, governed either conjointly by the wardens of the middle or west march or separately by a keeper, equivalent in status to a warden. Morton appointed John Carmichael of that ilk keeper of Liddesdale, probably in November, 1573,[86] although the first reference to him as a keeper is in June, 1574.[87]

Carmichael, despite being closely involved in the Redeswyre crisis of July, 1575, survived that episode unscathed. Indeed, the expenses he incurred when sent as a scapegoat to England in September were reimbursed by Morton's government,[88] and, on his return, he was placed in charge of the arrangements to restore goods taken at Redeswyre.[89] He was temporarily dismissed in the administrative reshuffle which followed Morton's resignation in March, 1578[90] but restored once the latter's recovery had been effected.[91] Until October, 1579, his keeper's salary of £500 was provided by an annual pension, firstly from the superplus of the thirds from St. Andrews priory, and latterly, from September, 1578, from Arbroath abbey.[92] However, it seems he received nothing from this second source since, on 24th December, 1579, he complained to the council about arrears of £1,000[93] which, although allocated to him by the treasury department in October,[94] had still not been paid. In addition, Carmichael was also the recipient of that customary perquisite, escheated property,[95] although, in the turbulent conditions prevalent in the borders, how much of this he actually received must remain conjectural.

The comparative lack of references to Carmichael's territory suggests, in itself, that he was a competent official. Admittedly, he was unable to prevent some serious outrages: on 28th August, 1580, for example, there was a major disturbance involving over three hundred borderers in which certain Armstrongs, Elliots and others ambushed Walter Scott of Goldalandis and his company as they returned from a reprisal raid into England.[96] Carmichael, in addition, was also handicapped, as has been noted, by the bad blood prevailing between him and Cessford. Nevertheless, there is an overall impression of a diligent lieutenant whose devotion to Morton's cause was keenly appreciated by the latter's adversaries. Thus, when his superior fell, Carmichael was quick to follow.[97]

Government action on the borders

Although governments in Morton's period depended, to a great extent, on the efficiency of their border officials, there were certain ways in which the central authority could reinforce the powers of the local administration. One of these was for the king or regent to summon a levy of 'fencible' subjects and lead a sortie against the various criminal elements to be found on the frontier. Another was to hold a justice ayre in the centre of a disturbed region. Sometimes both tactics were employed simultaneously so that the council would order a muster of the lieges for a show of force on one of the marches while, at the same time, evacuating their headquarters at Stirling or Edinburgh to execute the law in the march concerned. Morton, when regent, normally participated personally in these enterprises and, between August, 1573 and November, 1577, he planned eight raids. One of these was postponed but he attended all but one of the others.[98] The expedition to the west march held in November and December, 1575 is a convenient example of his regime during one of its more efficient phases.

On 30th September, 1575, it was announced that the regent, because of 'sundry stowthis and utheris enorme crymes' which had been perpetrated on the west march, intended descending on Dumfries 'in quhilk journey neidfull it is that he be weill and substantiouslie accompaneit'. Consequently, there followed orders for a muster from the inhabitants of the south-western counties who were to assemble at Dumfries on 24th October 'weill bodin in feir of weir with XX dayis victuallis'.[99] A fortnight later, however, 'for certane necessairy caussis and considerationis', connected, no doubt, with events at Redeswyre, it was affirmed that Morton had decided 'to differ his passage to Dumfreis', and those to whom it concerned should 'addreis theme selfis and be in full reddiness . . . upoun sex days warning'.[100] On 28th October, a fresh date, the 16th of November, was proclaimed and all those seeking redress were advised to submit their complaints to the justice clerk or his deputies who would be at Dumfries beforehand.[101] On the prescribed day, Morton and his council proceeded to Dumfries 'at the whilk tyme many brokinmen of the borders war puneist be thair purses rather than be thair lyves'.[102] No doubt this was the case yet, compared to amounts like over £11,000 collected at Aberdeen in 1574, or even the £2,224 gathered in at Edinburgh in 1576, the sum of just under £2,000 realised at Dumfries in November, 1575 is a somewhat insubstantial total.[103] There are indications that the regent was disappointed too since, on 21st November, the privy council issued a statement denouncing the assistance given to known malefactors on both sides of the border by the local inhabitants.[104] One modest consolation, however, for a rather undistinguished judicial raid was a Scottish victory at horse-racing over their English counterparts. This success was achieved by lord Claud Hamilton who, with his brother John, was, apparently, a member of the expedition. Lord Claud, it transpired, had brought with him a horse, and this animal was 'sa weill brydlit and sa speedie' that, in a contest over the Solway sands, it had eclipsed its English challengers and 'overran thayme all'.[105]

Morton, as a result of his experiences on the west march in November, 1575, resolved to tighten up the system of taking pledges. Under the existing arrangements, established earlier in the century, prominent borderers, as a guarantee for the good behaviour of their family or dependants, were placed under a form of mild detention in households remote from the frontier, a procedure which had been used extensively by Morton previously. In September, 1573, for instance, following a foray into the middle march, numbers of pledges were dispatched to 'noblemen and utheris weill affectit to his Hienes service'.[106] A year later, after another expedition into the same territory, seventeen pledges were recorded as having been lodged in Edinburgh at the government's expense before being transferred to their custodians.[107] Morton's principal innovation in December, 1575, apart from improving the arrangements used for conveying pledges across the country, was to introduce a statutory monetary penalty of £2,000 to be imposed upon any keeper who allowed a plege under his care to escape.[108]

Initially at least, this was no meaningless piece of council legislation, as William Porterfield of Duchall, George Maxwell of Newark, Neil Montgomery of Lainshaw, Hugh Wallace of Carnell and Duncan Forbes of Monymusk discovered when, on 1st April, 1576, they were all summoned before the council to answer charges of contravening the new regulations.[109] Montgomery of Lainshaw and Wallace of Carnell, in fact, appeared before the council on 9th May where they 'confessit and grantit the letting hame of the saidis pledges' but appealed for a remission of their fines.[110] Inevitably, despite his 'greit cair and ernist travellis for quieting of the brokin men', Morton had to admit he had not solved the problem completely. Thus, his council on 22nd July, 1577, referring to conditions on the west march, observed that 'albeit thair be plegeis ressavit and liand in the Incuntre for the gude rewle of the principallis of the clannis, yit is a certane few nowmer puposlie maid lowse and left out'.[111] Nonetheless, while further judicial raids were still essential, it must have convinced a number of custodians to exercise greater surveillance over their wards.

Morton, once he retrieved the reins of power in the summer of 1578, found that the interval of provisional government had certainly not brought any improvement to the situation on the borders. On the contrary, the council, on 28th October, announced that no fewer than forty-five pledges were at liberty 'quhairthrow the Bordouris and trew subjectis of this realme ar sensyne greitlie trublit and inquietit'.[112] Accordingly, on 11th October, proclamations were ordered to be made at various market crosses giving details of three separate musters on the middle and west marches.[113] One, prepared for twenty days' service, was to assemble at Dumfries on 4th November, a second, for a similar stint and on the same date at Jedburgh, while a third 'with provisions for the space of ane moneth' was to meet at Peebles on 1st December. This was followed shortly afterwards by numerous letters to various prominent individuals such as lord Yester, Carmichael of that ilk, Coldenknowes, Ramsay of Dalhousie and Douglas of Lochleven, seeking their presence on the respective raids.[114] However, on 28th October, it was decided 'upon sindrie gude wechtie and necessarie respectis . . . to prorogat the assembling' at Dumfries and Jedburgh until 5th December.[115] This postponement, which was probably a consequence of the delicate negotiations being conducted by Morton's side and his opponents at this juncture, was followed by a change of policy in favour of 'sum ordinar force to be employed for a certane space to repress sic fugitives and outlawis'. To finance this body, it was proposed to raise £12,000 by means of a general levy on most of the population.[116] Although a similar 'stent', admittedly for only £4,000 had been demanded in 1575 for the same purpose,[117] there were strong objections, on this second occasion, to a repetition of the same financial expedient. The register of the privy council, for instance, mentions complaints which had been voiced about the unconstitutional nature of the proposed tax which some of its critics claimed was being enforced by methods 'not usit and observit conforme to the Actis of Parliament'.[118] Thus, Morton and his council appear to have abandoned the project altogether. Furthermore, there was no further conciliar action on the borders that year and it was left to lord Ruthven, in his capacity as lieutenant of the marches, to do the best he could to suppress the prevailing disorder.[119] This task, according to one source, 'he discharged with great commendation'.[120] Certainly, the details of his efforts in the council records where, despite scant assistance from some notable borderers, he appears to have been striving to tighten up the system of taking pledges and sureties for good behaviour, would substantiate this verdict.[121] However, such appointments were usually held for a short period only and Ruthven's was no exception, since he resigned from his lieutenancy in mid-January, 1579.[122]

Neither in 1579 nor 1580 did Morton authorise judicial or military expeditions to the borders although, in December, 1580, Carmichael and Johnstone, on their own initiative, undertook small-scale raids.[123] In November, 1580, there was to have been a justice ayre and a muster on both the middle and west marches but they were deferred, allegedly until talks being conducted by Alexander Hume of North Berwick with the English government were completed.[124] In fact, Hume's abortive mission was more an attempt by the supporters of Lennox to improve that nobleman's standing with Elizabeth than a serious embassy about frontier matters.[125]

Moreover, Morton's inactivity on the borders was not simply confined to his failure to conduct judicial raids in that troublesome region. In addition, despite constant English pressure throughout 1580, he failed, doubtless because of his domestic preoccupations, to make the necessary arrangements for a meeting of border commissioners from both sides. Originally, lord Herries, Mark Ker, commendator of Newbattle, and Alexander Hay, director of chancery, had been named as the Scottish representatives for such a conference which, initially, was to have been held on 20th May. It was then prorogued until 20th June.[126] This date passed without any sessions of the Anglo-Scottish commissioners and, by 14th August, when there had still been no meetings, Elizabeth was growing increasingly concerned and 'greatly marvelled that the meeting should be deferred'.[127] In fact, the only decisive action taken on the borders by Morton's government between October, 1578 and December, 1580 was the incursions on the west and middle marches undertaken by Johnstone and Carmichael on 15th December, 1580.

While Morton latterly neglected one major means of controlling the borders, he continued to employ another expedient which he had already utilised to assist his border officials in their duties. This was the provision of small companies of infantry and cavalry. These were first in action at the beginning of his regency and, over a period of three years, for example, between 1573 and 1576, there were detachments regularly employed in unruly areas.

In the first two months of 1574, a hundred infantrymen and forty lighthorsemen, commanded by captain David Hume and John Carmichael of that ilk respectively, served the government, most likely in Liddesdale or the middle march.[128] They were in action again in June and July of that year, doubtless acting as reinforcements to the raid launched on the middle march in midsummer. In the autumn, they are to be found once more on active service.[129] During the first half of 1575, Carmichael, the keeper of Liddesdale, and his small band were again carrying out regular operations[130] but, for the big judicial and military expedition to the west march later in the year, extra forces were recruited. Thus, captain David Spalding and Carmichael commanded fifty infantrymen, while captain Robert Maxwell was in charge of forty cavalrymen.[131] The earlier part of 1576 had a similar military pattern to the previous year but Carmichael's unit was the only body to assist the assault on the middle march held in November.[132] However, December of that year was the last occasion for some time when payments were made by the central government to any auxiliary forces on the borders. Presumably Morton's activity had produced some temporary improvement in conditions on the marches and he saw the opportunity for an obvious cut in governmental expenditure.

Therefore, it was not until February, 1579, shortly after it had been suggested by both lords Herries and Maxwell at the discussions held in Edinburgh in mid-January about border matters, that the practice was resumed. Thus, Herries, as newly appointed warden of the west march, now began to receive a monthly allowance for the upkeep of one captain and twenty-four men.[133] Johnstone, his successor, was given similar military assistance while, in September, Carmichael, accompanied by fifty horsemen, was once more attending to the 'retaining of good order of the borders'.[134] Clearly, it was a costly policy, and Morton, on two occasions, as has been observed, had endeavoured to defray some of the expenses by extraordinary taxation. Nevertheless, in the turbulent state of the frontier, especially in Liddesdale and the middle march, it was a commendable strategy and of value to the officials concerned.

In such manner did Morton strive to govern the border, and his endeavours, at least in the earlier part of his administration, met with considerable success. 'This regent held the contre under gret obedience and in ane establissit estait,' admitted Sir James Melville[135] who, as has been seen, was frequently unsympathetic towards him. This view was shared by the English government, certainly initially, as a letter from the privy council to Morton on 26th February, 1576 would confirm. They offered 'right hearty thanks, assuring him that they shall not fail to concur with him and desire him to continue his former care and good disposition in such causes whereof they have been advertised from the Lords Wardens of her majesty's borders and especially by lord Scrope'.[136] Moreover, in the opinion of William Davison, who was at that time a secretary attached to Killigrew's embassy in Edinburgh, Morton's sterling efforts on the borders had resulted in unparalleled good order on the frontier.[137]

Latterly, however, the English government was less enthusiastic and Bowes, in September, 1580, following his unsuccessful attempts at arranging a meeting of Anglo-Scottish commissioners to discuss border problems, wrote pessimistically that he anticipated 'slender order taken for the borders'.[138] This was scarcely surprising since Morton, after 1578, as has been shown, never exercised, with the possible exception of Liddesdale, the same control over the marches. On the east march, he had installed the comparatively inexperienced Hume of Wedderburn; on the west march, Johnstone's effectiveness was frequently blunted by the contumacious Maxwell;

while Cessford, on the middle march, was never completely reliable.

On Morton's downfall, Cessford's wardenship was renewed and he was given Liddesdale as well.[139] However, at the same time, the new council, by its detailed instructions such as those about regular quarterly sessions of the warden's court, weekly hearings of complaints, and a purge of unemployed persons in the area, provides a good indication of how unsettled the middle march had become.[140] Furthermore, as has also been noted, governmental intervention by means of judicial and military expeditions declined noticeably in the final years of Morton's administration. In short, it is quite clear that, as Morton's position at Edinburgh was undermined, so his grasp on the borders correspondingly slackened.

NOTES

1. *C.S.P. Scot.*, iii, 357.
2. *R.S.S.*, vi, No. 2176; *R.P.C.*., ii, 300.
3. Rae, *Scottish Frontier*, 238.
4. *T.A.*, xii, (1566–74).
5. *R.M.S.*, iv, No. 1716.
6. *R.S.S.*, vi, No. 2381.
7. *Ibid*, No. 2320, vii, No. 140.
8. *Ibid*, vi, No. 2369.
9. *R.P.C.*, ii, 534–37.
10. *Ibid*, 586–87; Coldingham priory's annual contribution between 1568 and 1572 of just over £222 to the collector general of the thirds was obviously based on this rental, Donaldson, *Thirds of Benefices*, 24.
11. *C.S.P., Scot.*, v, 503.
12. Pitcairn, *Trials*, i, 47–48; *T.A.*, xiii, 141.
13. *Historie & Life of King James the Sext*, 149.
14. His successor was appointed on 6th September, 1578. *R.S.S.*, vii, No. 1635.
15. Moysie, *Memoirs*, 17.
16. *T.A.*, xiii, 172–73, 261; *R.S.S.*, vii, No. 1623.
17. Chambers, *Dom. Ann.*, i, 97.
18. *R.S.S.*, vii, No. 1635.
19. *Scots Peerage*, iii, 286–87.
20. *H.M.C. Rep. (Milne-Home)*, 50.
21. *C.S.P. Scot.*, v, 341–42, 353–54.
22. *H.M.C. Rep. (Milne-Home)*, 49.
23. Rae, *Scottish Frontier*, 241.
24. Fraser, *Carlaverock*, i, 223, 228–29.
25. *R.S.S.*, vi, No. 2116.

26. Fraser, *Carlaverock*, i, 225, 229.
27. *Historie and Life of King James the Sext*, 98.
28. *R.P.C.*, ii, 543; *T.A.*, xiii, 124–25.
29. Fraser, *Carlaverock*, i, 231.
30. *C.S.P. Dom. Add.* (1566–79), 506.
31. *C.S.P. Scot.*, v, 227.
32. *R.P.C.*, ii, 421–23.
33. *Ibid*, 593.
34. *Ibid*, 613.
35. *Ibid*, 615; *T.A.*, xiii, 168–69.
36. *R.P.C.*, ii, 631, 677, 729; *T.A.*, xiii, 175, 183, 190.
37. Fraser, *Carlaverock*, i, 231–33.
38. *C.S.P. Scot.*, v, 232.
39. *R.S.S.*, vii, No. 1048; *R.P.C.*, ii, 613.
40. *Ibid*, 576.
41. *C.S.P. Scot.*, v, 230.
42. Fraser, *Douglas*, iv, 230–32.
43. *R.P.C.*, ii, 614; *T.A.*, xiii, 169.
44. *R.P.C.*, ii, 619–20; that Sir Lewis Bellenden was present is confirmed by a payment received in September, 1579 by the justice clerk of £333.6s.8d., 'in forthsetting of justice and putting order to that troubled country' at courts held by Angus and Ruthven, *T.A.*, xiii, 287.
45. *Ibid*, 181.
46. *R.S.S.*, vii, No. 1622.
47. *R.P.C.*, iii, 73.
48. Spottiswoode, *History*, ii, 260.
49. *R.P.C.*, iii, 75–84.
50. *Ibid*, 76.
51. Rae, *Scottish Frontier*, 240–41.
52. *T.A.*, xiii, 253–301, *passim*.
53. *C.S.P. Scot.*, v, 335.
54. *R.P.C.*, iii, 207; Fraser, *Annandale*, i, 40–41.
55. *R.P.C.*, iii, 286–87, 304–05, 397–99.
56. *Ibid*, 302.
57. *C.S.P. Scot.*, v, 512.
58. Bowes also advised him to turn down the offer, *ibid*, 512.
59. *Ibid*, 512.
60. *R.P.C.*, iii, 307, 310, 317, 326, 328. It was subsequently ordered for December, S.R.O. T.A., E22/4, 77R.
61. *R.P.C.*, iii, 332–33.
62. *Ibid*, 344.
63. *R.S.S.*, vi, No. 945.
64. *H.M.C. Rep. xiv*, App. pt. iii, 34–35.

65. *T.A.*, xiii, 351.
66. *Ibid*, 148.
67. *C.S.P. Scot.*, v, 317.
68. Calderwood, *History*, iii, 424.
69. *H.M.C. Rep. (Laing)*, i, 27–28.
70. *R.P.C.*, ii, 643–44, 665; Fraser, *Buccleugh*, i, 138–39, 164.
71. *R.P.C.*, ii, 622–23, 639–40.
72. *Ibid*, iii, 251, 421.
73. The privy council met at Jedburgh that month, *ibid.*, 567–73.
74. *C.S.P. Scot.*, v, 255; see also Rae, *Scottish Frontier*, 201.
75. On 21st February, 1577, for example, Forster, warden of the English middle march, addressed Bonjedburgh as 'deputy warden of West Teviotdale', Fraser, *Douglas*, iv, 215–16.
76. *Ibid*, 208–09, 211, 212–13, 216.
77. *Ibid*, 208–09, 211, 218.
78. *C.S.P. Scot.*, v, 277.
79. *Ibid*, 373.
80. *Ibid*, 502, 508, 527.
81. See *T.A.*, xiii, *passim*.
82. First awarded on 14th October, 1570 and renewed on 26th February, 1575, *R.S.S.*, vi, No. 945, vii, No. 56.
83. *C.S.P. Scot.*, v, 503.
84. *R.P.C.*, iii, 333.
85. *Ibid*, 325.
86. Rae, *Scottish Frontier*, 244.
87. *C.S.P. Scot.*, iv, 683.
88. *T.A.*, xiii, 73.
89. *R.P.C.*, ii, 498, 568.
90. *C.S.P. Scot.*, v, 277.
91. *R.P.C.*, iii, 47.
92. *R.S.S.*, vii, Nos. 378, 1657.
93. *R.P.C.*, iii, 252.
94. *T.A.*, xiii, 290.
95. E.g. *R.S.S.*, vii, Nos. 607, 955, 1080, 1468.
96. *R.P.C.*, iii, 209–10.
97. He was dismissed on 13th January, 1581, *R.P.C.*, iii, 344.
98. Rae, *Scottish Frontier*, 265–66.
99. *R.P.C.*, ii, 462; *T.A.*, xiii, 78.
100. *R.P.C.*, ii, 465.
101. *Ibid*, 467, 469; *T.A.*, xiii, 79.
102. *Historie and Life of King James the Sext*, 158; *C.S.P. Scot.*, v, 200–01.
103. *T.A.*, xiii, 16.
104. *R.P.C.*, ii, 476–77.

105. *Historie and Life of King James the Sext*, 158.
106. *R.P.C.*, ii, 275–76; *see* also *Diurnal*, 337; Pitscottie, *Historie*, ii, 309.
107. *T.A.*, xiii, 28; *C.S.P. Scot.*, v, 35.
108. *R.P.C.*, ii, 477–78.
109. *Ibid*, 514; *T.A.*, xiii, 122.
110. *R.P.C.*, ii, 525–26.
111. *Ibid*, 619–20.
112. *Ibid*, iii, 42–43.
113. *Ibid*, 38; *T.A.*, xiii, 220.
114. *Ibid*, 225; for Lochleven *see* N.L.S., Morton papers, 77, f.46; printed in *Mort. Reg.*, i, 116.
115. *R.P.C.*, iii, 41; *T.A.*, xiii, 226.
116. *R.P.C.*, iii, 46.
117. *Ibid*, ii, 467–79; *T.A.*, xiii, 107.
118. *R.P.C.*, iii, 56–57.
119. There is, however, no actual reference to Ruthven's appointment in the council minutes and he is not mentioned by name until 18th January, 1579, *ibid*, 62.
120. Spottiswoode, *History*, ii, 259–60.
121. *R.P.C.*, iii, 62–68.
122. *Ibid*, 63.
123. *Ibid*, 332–33.
124. *Ibid*, 328–29.
125. Details of Hume's mission are given in *C.S.P. Scot.*, v, 538–39.
126. *Ibid*, 392, 396, 432.
127. *Ibid*, 483.
128. *T.A.*, xii, 373–74, 377.
129. *T.A.*, xiii, 18, 23, 35, 44.
130. *Ibid*, 51, 59, 66, 69, 71, 77.
131. *Ibid*, 84.
132. *Ibid*, 91, 93, 101, 143.
133. *Ibid*, 253.
134. *Ibid*, 286.
135. Melville, *Memoirs*, 260.
136. *C.S.P. Scot.*, v, 212.
137. 'Such rare justice as has not been seen before', *C.S.P.*, *Foreign* (1575–77), 118.
138. *C.S.P. Scot.*, v, 512.
139. *R.P.C.*, iii, 345.
140. *Ibid*, 345–48.

8
Domestic Administration

Controlling the borders, while always a major concern of Morton's government, was only one of several matters requiring his attention in domestic affairs. Other important items which preoccupied him were the enforcement of justice in the rest of the country, the health of the nation's finances, including the condition of the currency itself, overseas trade and those perennial social problems, poverty and destitution.

Law and Order

Morton's judicial activities on the frontier require no further comment, but his efforts in this direction were not confined solely to that region. Thus, apart from his visit to Aberdeen in the summer of 1574, of which an account has already been given, there is further evidence of the administration of law and order both in Edinburgh itself and in the surrounding countryside. In December, 1573, for instance, following assizes at Peebles and Selkirk the month before, a justice ayre was held at Haddington in connection with offences in the sheriffdom of Edinburgh and the constabulary of Haddington.[1] Furthermore, similar legal proceedings were arranged for the same town in East Lothian a month later to deal with crimes committed within the sheriffdom of Berwick and the 'bailary' of Lauderdale.[2] In addition, between 1574 and 1578, there were three further such assizes held in Edinburgh, handling cases for the whole of south-east Scotland and including offences which ranged from 'intercommuning with rebels' and 'failing to resist thieves' to 'contravening the acts against the sale of malt' or 'destruction of the green wood'.[3] These activities, as well as similar judicial proceedings on the borders, were, doubtless, largely responsible for the observation in one account that because of 'his perpetuall policie and cullor of justice whaireby he punneist transgressors and uthers saikles the greatest part of the people fearit him and consequentlie invyit him'.[4]

Another indication of greater tranquility, generally, is the reduction in the number of those warrants for grants under the privy seal which normally imply crime of some kind or other. Accordingly, in the period from 1575 to 1580, the number of escheats, remissions and respites all fell drastically in number. Escheats during this time, for example, dropped from 650 to 450, remissions from 160 to 66 and respites from 90 to 40 compared to the years of the civil war.[5] Granted, there are some references in the privy seal to serious crime when Morton was in office. Thus, on 5th April, 1576 in Aberdeenshire, a large band of Gordons attacked 'the house and plaice of Streichin (Strichen) . . . , asseigeing of the samin be schuting culveringis, daggis and uther weirlyke persute' and, in their determination to procure the release of one of their kinsmen, killed Thomas Fraser of Strichen.[6] Again, in 1577 and 1578 at the Chanonry of Ross, as the ancient seat of the medieval bishops and canons of Ross at Fortrose in Ross and Cromarty was entitled, there unquestionably were indications of widespread anarchy in the Black Isle. Here the principal culprit was the ambitious and unruly Colin Mackenzie of Kintail whose brother Rorie had apparently been in possession of the cathedral tower since 1573 and had used this vantage point to terrorise the neighbourhood.[7] Colin's contribution to the prevailing lawlessness was his cruel treatment of Alexander Hepburn, bishop of Ross, and his wife and servants. Hepburn died in September, 1578 but his wife took up his case before the privy council. She accused Mackenzie, by his evicting her and her servants from the palace, of not only harsh behaviour to herself but also, by his actions the previous year in denying the bishop's household food and fuel, of actually hastening her husband's death.[8]

Nonetheless, these would appear to have been uncharacteristic incidents, and there are good grounds, certainly for the period of Morton's regency, for accepting the estimate of the Edinburgh burgess, Robert Birrell, that, during this period, 'he kept the country in great justice and peace'.[9] Paradoxically, it was during the more settled period of his regency that there was, allegedly, another plot on his life. Thus, on 15th June, 1577, John Sempill of Beltries, 'Dilaittit of the tressonabill conspiracie of my Lord Regentis Graceis slauchtare', was found guilty of this charge and 'the dome of forfaltour was pronunceit aganis him'.[10]

Sempill, a natural son of Robert, lord Sempill, had married Mary, daughter of Alexander, lord Livingston in March, 1565.[11] The background to the affair with Morton would appear to have been a dispute which had arisen with the regent over 'a portion of fyne ground' granted by queen Mary 'for his awin and his wyffis gude service'.[12] Morton sought to restore these lands to the crown, and Sempill, so it is stated, infuriated at such treatment, conspired with others, but notably his nephew, Adam Whiteford of Milnton, 'to kill him as he went down the street towards the palace with a harquebuss'.[13] However, as a result of certain 'rash and boasting speeches', Semphill was arrested and confessed under torture what his intentions had been.[14] He was subsequently reprieved but, meanwhile, Whiteford, whose father was fined £100 in May, 1577 for his son's absence from court in Edinburgh,[15] was apprehended later that month in Bute.[16] He, too, was tortured by the regent but apparently revealed nothing although, according to Spottiswoode, because of his maltreatment of Whiteford, 'the mouths of many opened against the regent using such rigour'.[17] Nonetheless, Whiteford's later record, with his father and himself accused along with several others of the slaughter of Patrick Maxwell of Stanelie in July, 1584,[18] would suggest he came from a turbulent family and that the earlier accusations against him were possibly well-founded.

Before we leave the incident, the question of its significance arises. Spottiswoode, for example, states that the Hamiltons were believed to be implicated.[19] Conversely, Sir James Balfour, in another seventeenth-century account of the episode, denies there was any Hamilton complicity, and dismisses the whole business as 'only a net to have catched the Hamiltons in'.[20] It is always possible Morton was contriving some devious stratagem against the Hamiltons, and Whiteford, who in May, 1579 was listed with his father among twelve individuals who gave sureties that they would not assist Claud and John Hamilton, was obviously one of their adherents.[21] Yet, January, 1576, the date when Sempill was accused of concocting his conspiracy, was just after the period when, as has been seen, the Douglases and the Hamiltons effected a reconciliation and were consequently on good terms. On the other hand, on 9th May, 1578, Sempill was rehabilitated by the provisional government which had supplanted Morton, although it was at pains to point out that 'the landis of Auchtirmowtie lyand within the erledome of Fyfe, Mekill Cumray, Lyttil Cumray and Stewartoun . . . quhilkis wes disponit to said Johnne of befoir and now is na wyise meanit to be comprehendit in this restitution, rehabilitatioun and reponing'.[22] Thus, considering how quickly he was restored, it could be argued that it was the regent's enemies, rather than the Hamiltons, who had been the instigators of Sempill's attempt and were now looking after their agent's interests. Such an explanation, especially when the chequered career of most of Morton's opponents is borne in mind, should certainly not be dismissed out of hand.

Nevertheless, it is always possible that Sempill had no links with any of

Morton's rivals and simply disliked him for the reasons given and perhaps also on account of his activities as tutor of the master of Sempill during his minority. Morton was given this commission by Robert, lord Sempill on 7th October, 1573,[23] and, since litigation in connection with this tutorship was still in progress in January, 1582, this suggests the regent had taken an active interest in it.[24]

The affair, however, does underline the precarious nature of the office of regent in sixteenth-century Scotland. Yet it was an isolated incident and in no way detracts from Morton's achievement in enforcing law and order. Moreover, before leaving this subject, it is worth noting that the regent was not only concerned about the enforcement of the existing laws but was also interested in their codification. Thus, in June, 1577, the lawyer, John Skene, was ordered 'to serve and travell with certane utheris in the revewing of the auld municipall lawis of this realme and of the registaris of the decreittis gevin be the Lordis of Counsall with the actis of Parliament . . . ' It was hoped that Skene and his committee would produce 'ane certane law be the quhilk all our soverane lordis liegis may be governit'.[25] While this did not materialise, at least, as has been recently pointed out, it did lead to the publication of several treatises on Scots law including Skene's own work entitled *Regiam Maiestatem*.[26]

Financial Administration

The supervision of the country's finances was a very different undertaking and, in any examination of Morton's financial administration, the exchequer office must feature prominently. Therefore, a brief résumé of its functions is relevant. The division of the exchequer into two offices, that of comptroller and treasurer, is a familiar feature of Scotland's financial administration in the sixteenth century. Thus, Morton's government contained a comptroller's department with a comptroller responsible for the revenues from the crown lands, burghal payments and customs duties. From this income he had to endeavour to defray the expenses of the royal household. Similarly, there was a treasury office with a treasurer in charge of all casualties. These comprised compositions, revenues from escheated property, fines, temporal fruits and revenues from vacant bishoprics as well as the profits from the royal mines and the coinage. From these sources the treasurer was expected to meet all the expenses incurred outwith the royal household.

Morton, on becoming regent, retained the services of Sir William Murray of Tullibardine as comptroller and, by 1574, this official was recording a substantial improvement in the income from this section of the exchequer. Thus, whereas the total sum collected by Murray of Tullibardine in 1573 amounted to £10,182, the following year it rose by over £8,000 to £18,932.[27] Admittedly, and this is a reflection of Morton's stronger government, a large proportion of this amount included repayment of sums outstanding for several years. Nevertheless, on the basis of the only other extant accounts, that is, those of 1579 and 1580 being just slightly less than the somewhat artificial total for 1574,[28] it is quite clear that Murray's department was operating more efficiently again. This assumption is confirmed by an examination of the available burghal and customs returns but more explicitly in the income from the various chamberlains, feu-farmers and lessees of crown lands referred to, in the exchequer accounts, as the 'ballivi ad extra'.

In 1573, when Morton's government was preoccupied for nearly half that year with the final stages of the civil war, the crown received in cash only £2,853 from these 'ballivi ad extra' but the next year, however, the figure rose to £9,758.[29] While the disparity between the two totals was undoubtedly exaggerated by William Ewart, receiver of the lordship of Galloway below the Cree, disbursing £5,909 as back payment outstanding for eleven years,[30] it is significant that, whereas only eight local officials subscribed in 1573, fourteen did so a year later.[31] Indeed, between 1575 and 1580, but excluding 1578, a notably disturbed year, out of a possible total of about twenty-five different officials who should have contributed, there were, on average, seventeen who did so.[32]

Granted, there were still omissions and irregularities as far as certain bailies were concerned. Colin, earl of Argyll, for instance, whose predecessors had apparently made no sheriff returns since 1528,[33] as chamberlain of both Bute and Cowal, rendered no contributions for Bute in 1577–78 or for Cowal from 1576 to 1578.[34] Considering the friction which, it has been seen, existed between Argyll and Morton in these years, this is scarcely surprising. On the other hand, there is no obvious reason why John, earl of Mar, in his capacity as chamberlain of Stirling, should have made no payments to the exchequer between 1574 and 1579,[35] unless it was a consequence of his friendship with the regent. Finally, there are the financial discrepancies of Sir Mathew Campbell of Loudon, sheriff of Ayr and feu-farmer of Trabboch and Terrenzean in that county, whose last payment to the comptroller was in 1575.[36] But, in Sir Mathew's case, there would appear little need for conjecture since it would seem characteristic behaviour for someone already outlawed for failing to answer charges of molesting a local laird, James Chalmers of Gaitgirth.[37] At the same time, since he had signed a bond of manrent with Morton and Angus on 6th October, 1575,[38] Sir Mathew possibly felt he could afford to be somewhat dilatory with his payments. Nevertheless, these were exceptional cases and, while it must be conceded that, in 1582, the subsequent Lennox-Arran regime has an even more impressive record,[39] Morton's administration clearly made a creditable effort at obtaining the revenues from the crown lands.

Admittedly, the crown lands were only one of the responsibilities of the comptroller. Nonetheless, although, initially, according to the exchequer records, there were large numbers of defaulters who failed 'to haif gevin compt, rakning and payment of thair intromissioun' by the prescribed date, the majority, on being admonished, obeyed Morton's government. In other words, a fine of £10 and a warning to offenders that, if their accounts were not rendered, they would be placed 'under the pane of rebellioun and putting of thame and everyane of thame to the horne', was generally sufficient warning for most of them to settle with the comptroller inside six months.[40] In 1576, for example, most of the revenues from the crown lands were still unpaid in August when the customary admonition was issued.[41] Nevertheless, by February, 1577, nearly all concerned had rendered their accounts[42] and, here again, therefore, there is further testimony of acceptance, albeit somewhat grudgingly, of the regent's authority.

Furthermore, the various individual actions taken against certain sheriffs, bailies and customs officials do not suggest a moribund administration. Thus, in 1577, for example, the provost of Ayr, with several fellow councillors, found making the journey to Edinburgh and forfeiting over £300 preferable to remaining at the horn.[43] In the same year, the burghs of Rutherglen, Lanark and Peebles were required to present their accounts for inspection,[44] while at Perth, where some of the bailies had been 'distributing the commoun gude ilkane to thair awin particular avancement', there was an enquiry into the mishandling of the town's finances.[45] Meanwhile, at Dundee, although the customs officer, James Lowell, 'offerit himself rady to mak compt, raknyng and payment of the custumes thairof sen his compt', the exchequer, clearly suspicious of Lowel's behaviour, insisted on the additional presence of his clerk of the cocket.[46] Again, at Lauder in 1577, William Woddret, bailie of that burgh, 'quhill he have maid full compt, reknyng and payment of the borrow males', was to lodge himself in custody at Edinburgh castle.[47]

Undeniably, there were a few irregularities. For instance, the customs duties of Aberdeen from 1564 to 1573, apparently given as a tack to the provost, Thomas Menzies of Pitfodellis, were not paid until 1581 despite the provost being put to the horn in March, 1575 for their non-payment.[48] In addition, the burgh of Irvine made no customs payments between 1574 and 1583, while Dumfries rendered nothing from 1560 to 1578.[49] However, in both these instances, there are explanations or extenuating circumstances. In the case of Irvine, the town had been excused payment by Morton in 1574 for a space of five years of its great customs 'for bigging, beting, and mending of the heavin and harberie';[50] as for Dumfries, the reason for the discrepancy, at least between 1567 and 1576, was that the customs in these years were leased to George Maxwell a burgess of the town, for £40 per annum.[51] Nonetheless, these deficiences, and some others, do not seriously undermine the conclusion that Morton's regime assured the comptroller's department of a much more realistic amount from the sources available to it.

However, despite a greater yield from the crown lands, the customs and the burghs, Murray of Tullibardine was unable to avoid a growing deficit by the end of Morton's career. Admittedly, in 1574, the arrears of the preceding year, which stood at £7,261, were reduced to £1,433,[52] and probably, although there are no comptroller's accounts extant for these years, they remained at a similar level until 1578. But the discord of that year produced a loss of £4,847[53] and, although there was subsequently some improvement in 1579 when the deficit fell to £3,254,[54] Morton's rule ended with Tullibardine recording a loss of £5,377.[55]

While peculation cannot be discounted – Robert Bowes, for instance, reported to his government during the course of 1580 that Morton's opponents would like to have his administration 'charged with sudden reckonings'[56] – there were mitigating circumstances which would explain Murray's predicament. In short, his failure to meet the expenses incurred by the royal household was probably due to the fact that the period of his comptrollership under Morton formed part of at least a half-century of rising and fluctuating commodity prices.[57] Evidence for such an assertion, though subject to reservations about regional variations, is provided by an examination of the prices during this period of specific items in the records of the burgh of Glasgow. Here, taking the cost of that staple commodity, bread, as a key item, it can be seen that there unquestionably was fluctuation in its price. Thus, the fourpenny loaf which, in 1574, weighed fourteen ounces, was twelve ounce in weight in 1580 and, in 1577, had been reduced to a mere ten ounces. Similarly, ale which was sixpence a pint in 1574 rose to eightpence for the same measure in 1577, falling to sevenpence per pint by 1580. Although wine and candles show less fluctuation, the former increased by twopence per pint and the latter by fourpence per pound over the same period.[58] Thus, the general rise in the cost of living, rather than the comptroller lining his own pockets by hoodwinking the royal auditors, would seem the principal reason for Murray's failure to balance his accounts and would explain why he constantly presented Morton with a deficit from his department.

The comptroller's problems, however, were of less consequence when those of William, lord Ruthven, Morton's treasurer, are considered. Ruthven's task was exceedingly onerous since, as well as defraying the innumerable regular charges arising outwith the royal household, he also had to cope with a large variety of extraordinary expenditure. One such item was debts outstanding from the years of the civil war. Here, with prominent citizens such as William Napier, Robert Gourlay and Robert Richardson all owed considerable sums by the government, the total involved amounted to nearly £4,500.[59] Then there was the siege of Edinburgh castle in 1573 which was a particularly costly affair. Some of the expenses which the treasurer had, on that occasion, included wages totalling £2,500 to the members of Berwick garrison present at the bombardment,[60] a reward of one hundred 'crownis of the sone' to the English artillerymen who, at the height of the attack, broke down Kirkcaldy of Grange's defences,[61] and £500 between four Scottish officers 'upoun considderatioun of divers sowmes auchtand to thame in the tyme of the late regent . . . and that thai wer presentlie to entir in service for asseging and enclosing of the castell of Edinburgh'.[62] In addition, there was the expensive gift to the English ambassador, Sir Henry Killigrew. This comprised 'ane ring of gold, ane basing, ane laver, thre cowpis with thair coveris and ane saltsatt with the cover all of silver graven dowbill ourgilt with gold', and it cost the treasury £680.[63]

A further charge on the treasurer were the repairs necessary, after the hostilities, to Edinburgh castle. This undertaking, an operation lasting several years, with work still in progress in the summer of 1576,[64] was one to which Morton paid considerable attention. We are told, for example, that the regent 'caussit maissons begin to red the bruisit wallis and repayrit the forewark to the forme of a bulwark, plat and brayd abone for the ressett and rynning of many cannons'.[65] The same authority also alleges that Morton not only paid the workmen with base money but had his own coat of arms ostentatiously inscribed 'upoun the new biggit part of the castell, above the lyon of Scotland'.[66] Whether he did or did not – and there is no extant evidence today that he did[67] – it does not gainsay the fact, as borne out in the treasurer's accounts,[68] that the regent devoted considerable energy to the rebuilding of the castle. Consequently, he could justifiably reflect on the occasion of his demission in March, 1578 that he had taken good care of the crown's major fortress and that, among other things, he had 'mountit all his ordynans new' and spent £10,000 on its restoration.[69]

There were two other particularly costly affairs. Firstly, there was the imbroglio at Falkirk in August, 1578 when the royal forces under Morton and Angus confronted those of the malcontents led by Argyll and Atholl. Then, the next year, there was the campaign against the Hamiltons. The Argyll-Atholl insurrection resulted in Ruthven having to disburse £5,944 to the officers commanding the king's army,[70] with, in addition, damages amounting to over £500 being paid as compensation to John Livingstone, younger of Dunipace, for 'the spulzie of his house and eating of his corn by the horsemen and others that convened at Falkirk'.[71] The persecution of the Hamiltons, on the other hand, with Morton himself being repaid the £2,474 which he had loaned the earl of Mar to pay soldiers employed in the campaign, and with nearly £3,000 being spent on transporting artillery and supplies across the country, denuded the treasury of another £8,000 or so which it could ill afford.[72]

When these facts are taken into consideration, it is scarcely surprising that Morton's treasurer found himself faced with a regular deficit and having to resort to emergency expedients. 'Be ressoun,' so he informed the royal auditors in 1574, 'the said thesaurar had nocht of the kingis majesteis geir in his handis to performe the necessar expensis and charges for furth-setting of our soverane lordis service and paying of his hienes dettis as the necessitie of the tyme requirit, it behuifit him to have recours to employ his credit at my lord regentis grace.'[73] In other words, Morton, between December, 1572 and May, 1574, loaned the treasurer a total of £57,510 and thus reduced his outstanding debt to £3,521.[74] At the same time, over this period, the regent recovered just over £45,055 of this amount from the profits of the mint and thus remained, in the treasurer's words, 'superexpendit of his awin geir debursit be him as said is in the sowme of twelf thousand foure hundreth fiftie fyve pund twenty thrie pennyis obolus'.[75] By 1576, Ruthven's deficit had fallen to £17,356 but, once again, Morton came to his rescue.[76] As before, the regent was recompensed by further profits from the mint as well as receiving £7,408 from the superplus of the thirds and £2,000 from the tax levied from the suppresion of malefactors on the borders. This left only £3,075 'to be paid by the king majesty of the readiest of his property and casualties'.[77]

The precise reason for Morton's willingness to subsidise the treasury must remain conjectural. However, there is every likelihood that the notion of the crown being indebted to him was not an unattractive proposition.

Moreover, a regent who, in 1573, had allegedly retained all the compositions collected from Marian supporters in Edinburgh instead of allotting some of the money to loyal citizens who had suffered damage to their properties during the civil war[78] must surely have realised the possibilities of profiting from his dealings with the mint. Whatever motive guided him, the practice continued after 1578, and, throughout 1579 and 1580, Morton was the recipient of regular, and frequently considerable, sums of money. Thus, beginning in December, 1578 when the treasurer's accounts contain the reference 'To the earle of Mortoun be precept to compt', £173.10.6d., there follows throughout the subsequent year a series of similar such payments, the largest being the sum of £7,204 in April, 1579.[79]

Undoubtedly, the improvement in the financial condition of the treasury, which has been noted in the middle years of his regency, owed a good deal to Morton himself. His subjugation of the borders and the north-east Scotland between 1574 and 1576, for example, yielded nearly £16,000 in fines from justice ayres.[80] His presence was felt most vividly in the city of Aberdeen where provost Menzies and his council paid dearly for their allegiance to Huntly in the civil war.[81] Although there were two other judicial hearings at Dumfries and Edinburgh, this northern circuit, undertaken in August, 1574, at which the Aberdeen council was initially fined 4,000 merks, although Morton eventually 'freely discharged' 1,000 merks of this amount,[82] accounted for approximately three-quarters of the sum collected.[83] Furthermore, four subsequent assizes shared by Jedburgh and Edinburgh between 1576 and 1578 contributed another £12,089 to the treasury.[84] Clearly, the treasury benefited from the profits of justice, and the absence of such judicial activity in the latter years of Morton's career was to its disadvanatage.

Yet Morton, at least while he was regent, would appear, by his neglect of compositions on signatures under the privy seal, to have ignored one way of increasing the royal revenue. It has been estimated, for instance, that, between March, 1573 and April, 1574, out of a total of 515 such grants, 356 were given *gratis* by the treasury, and a large number of the others were subsequently remitted.[85] Now perhaps, in this matter, the regent was perfunctory or unusually generous. This could be the explanation but, in the case of some of the larger remissions involved, the likelihood of a political motive seems distinctly possible. Take, for the sake of argument, the cases of John, lord Herries who was remitted 'by my lord regents grace precept' the composition on three signatures confirming ecclesiastical feus amounting to £474;[86] or John Johnstone of that ilk who was exonerated from a series of compositions totalling £800 affecting himself and his servants;[87] or, for that matter, John Gordon of Lochinvar who was excused payment on certain charters relating to Tongland.[88] In these instances and others of a similar nature affecting George Douglas of Bonjedburgh, William Ker of Cessford and Sir James Hume of Coldenknowes,[89] since all concerned were prominent figures in the southern half of the kingdom, Morton probably believed that their allegiance could be more effectively guaranteed by concessions of this nature. Likewise, the favour shown Andrew, earl of Errol, Alexander, lord Saltoun and William Leslie of Wardaris, all individuals of some standing in the north-eastern part of the realm who had heavy fines remitted on Morton's instructions,[90] probably had a similar objective.

Nevertheless, there is always the possibility that Morton concocted a system of exacting payments on his own account and was, in some way, bypassing the treasury. The scheme, for example, whereby he supposedly pocketed the compositions paid by certain Edinburgh citizens who had supported the losing side in the civil war, has already been noted. Moreover, it is significant that, after his recovery in 1578, the yields from compositions under the privy seal were considerably higher. Thus, between 1578 and 1580, the amount realised on compositions by the treasury was £28,000 whereas, between 1574 and 1576, it was a mere £11,000.[91] Since Morton had less control over affairs in the final years of his administration, it would seem that, reinforced by privy council and parliamentary decrees,[92] Ruthven was able to ensure that such compositions became a more substantial source of royal income. Therefore, if Morton had, as Sir James Melville would have us believe, 'set his haill study how till gather geir' when he was regent,[93] he clearly found less opportunity for such practices between 1578 and 1580.

The Currency

Undoubtedly, Ruthven's problems could not have been made any easier if the regent was defrauding the treasury in some way, nor, for that matter, by the price rise which, as has been noted, adversely affected the comptroller's department. However, the treasurer's predicament was made all the more serious by another factor – the condition of the Scottish currency.

Morton issued new coins on three occasions. In 1575, 'he causit a new pece of gold to be imprentit of the weight of ane once and ordainit to have course in the countrie for the avail of twentie punds money'.[94] This handsome piece portrayed king James VI in armour on the face side with the inscription 'In utrumque paratus', while the reverse had a crowned shield and the Virgilian lines 'parcere subiectis debellere superbos'.[95] The next issue should have been in 1578 when it was proposed to introduce a gold crown worth 40/- as well as two silver merks valued 26/8d. and 13/4d. respectively.[96] However, there was no distribution of the silver merks until the following year while, in 1580, it was decided to replace the gold crown with a golden ducat.[97]

Undoubtedly, Morton's government realised the weakness of the country's currency was caused by debasement and the circulation of innumerable foreign coins. Thus, at the convention of March, 1575, where the regent made his first attempt to repair the situation, it was announced that the roots of the problem lay partly in the quantity of false currency produced 'not allanerlie within this realme bot outwith' and now circulating within the kingdom. But, the principal reason was declared to be the 'greit quantitie of fals countirfaitit money plakkis and lyonis utherwayis callit hardheidis strikkin in cunze in the time of the government of the quene Drowarier'.[98] Morton's remedy was to order all surviving coins by the aforesaid Mary of Guise to be rendered to the mint for clipping where, in what appears to have been a device aimed at stabilising the currency, the plack and the hardhead were reduced in value. Furthermore, as from 20th November, 1575, unclipped coins became illegal tender and dealing in them an indictable offence.[99]

Reaction to the regent's measures, at least from the poor, seems to have been universally unfavourable. According to one source, the reduction of the plack from 4d. to 2d. and the hardhead from 1½d. to 1d. 'procured great envy and hatred of the commons against the Erle of Morton for the people's hands were full of that money'.[100] Indeed, so unpopular was the expedient that, as Morton and the rest of the members of the convention proceeded back and forth to Holyrood each day, they were subjected to violent abuse from the Edinburgh poor which, to quote another account, 'wes havie and lamentable to heir'.[101] If contemporary opinion regarding the 'douncrying of thair ancient pryces' produced such 'execrations and maledictions as is odious to reherse',[102] a modern viewpoint would be that Morton and those before him, by their manipulation of a coinage lacking the fixed face value of today, were pursuing 'a poverty stricken opportunist existence'.[103]

At the same time, while on the subject of Morton's unpopularity, it is worth recollecting the regent's own life style. There was, for instance, his elaborate building programme at Drochil in remote Teviotdale, not to mention his main residence, Dalkeith, externally and internally an opulent structure. In addition, there was his ambitious landscaping activities at Aberdour where, with terraced gardens reminiscent of Hampton Court or

Nonsuch Palace, there is further evidence of the impact of his earlier sojourn in England.[104] Unquestionably, such efforts in domestic architecture and gardening could lead to the belief, to quote one seventeenth-century writer, that the regent was 'making mansions with the subjects' coffers'.[105] Furthermore, if another seventeenth-century source can be believed, there was Morton's penchant for travelling, at times by coach, a rare and costly vehicle in the reign of James VI.[106] A populace adversely affected by the regent's readjustment of the currency must have found such external evidence of the trappings of affluence increasingly difficult to tolerate.

Then there is the question of what the regent did about the prevalence of forgery and the distribution of counterfeit money. This, of course, was an ancient malpractice but one towards which Morton certainly adopted a determined stance. On 5th July, 1574, for example, he was personally in attendance at the interrogation of a Bristol merchant recently apprehended at Ayr in possession of a quantity of illegal hardheads. In fact, he and another companion were only released eventually in September because, as the regent informed the English government, it was better for 'the good amity's cause' that he overlooked the affair 'than curiously and exactly to seek trial of them by law'.[107]

Morton's personal interest in the activities of the accused Englishmen might appear noteworthy but, in fact, it was neither unique nor unexpected since forgery and similar offences, as the statute book will confirm, were traditionally those which would provoke official reaction. Consequently, Morton's presence in January, 1577 at the trial of a Scottish merchant accused of importing false coins into the kingdom was presumably similarly motivated.[108] Nevertheless, his attendance in this instance, and such actions as requesting English assistance in 1574 in the matter of an Italian counterfeiter who had slipped across the border,[109] underline one clearly established feature of his regime, namely a determination to enforce the law. On the other hand, as the charges in June, 1580 of 'making, forgeing and countairfuting of certane fals and adulterat money' against George Balfour, commendator of Charterhouse and his associates testify,[110] it was always an uphill struggle.

An additional handicap facing Morton as far as the currency was concerned was the acute shortage of bullion. There was some mining of precious metals in Scotland at this period and, in 1568, the regent himself had become a member of one company organised for this purpose.[111] The principal figure in this company was a Dutchman, Cornelius de Vois, but Morton, on 29th June, 1575, 'finding his nether tending to the kingis commoditie nor weill of our cuntrie', suspended his contract.[112] Subsequently, on 18th February, 1576, and clearly in an effort to obtain a greater supply of bullion, a new agreement for 'the haill gold, silver, copper and leid mynis and mynerallis within the bounds of Crawfurdmure, Robertmure, Hendirland and ony uther partis' was signed with Abraham Peterson, another Dutchman, who had also been a member of the earlier partnership.[113] By the terms of the contract, which excluded the lead mines in Glengonar and Orkney worked by a company in which Morton's half-brother, George Douglas of Parkhead, was a member, Peterson's company was given a guaranteed price for all gold, silver, lead and copper extracted on behalf of the crown, being subject, however, to a tax 'for every hundrith unces of gold or silver that sal be found or win in the saidis gold and silver mynes . . . sex unces frelie as his Hienes just dewitie'.[114] How successful Peterson actually was must remain uncertain. One such company, for example, belonging to the earl of Atholl, exported over 125 tons of lead and ore between October, 1571 and March, 1573, paying the crown, which always exercised its royal prerogative in the production of precious metals, a total of £2,271.[115] Certainly, a subsequent deal with the master of the mint in March, 1577, and permission to introduce more foreign miners in July, 1578, would suggest that Morton was better pleased with Peterson than his predecessor.[116]

Morton undoubtedly was closely involved in these proceedings. The ubiquitous George Auchinleck of Balmanno, for example, was, with Peterson, the largest shareholder in the new venture.[117] Peterson, moreover, if the experiences of his fellow countryman, Arnold Bronckorst, can be regarded as typical, may well have discovered that Morton drove a hard bargain. Bronckorst, in partnership with the Elizabethan miniaturist, Nicholas Hilliard, also sought permission from Morton to prospect for precious metals in Scotland. However, their application was refused despite, so it has been argued, the present of a beautiful piece of tapestry,[118] and Bronckorst 'was forced to become one of his Majesties sworne servants at ordinary in Scotland, to draw all the small and great pictures for his Majesty'.[119] In fact, he was ultimately appointed 'our soverane lordis painter'[120] and had his artistic talents utilised by Morton himself, since the familiar portrait of the latter is usually attributed to this artist.[121]

Around the same time, Morton was involved in another mining venture. The arrangements for this one were concluded in November, 1577 when he ensured that his natural son, James, commendator of Pluscarden, in partnership with lord Glamis, was given an eleven-year lease of the 'leid mynes and leid ure in Conynghame, Carrik and Galloway'.[122]

Clearly, the regent, whom Sir Henry Killigrew reported on one occasion

L

in June, 1574 as having 'gone to set miners a work on Crawford Moor and make profit from it',[123] was not going to miss any opportunity for the enrichment of himself or his kin. Indeed, Stephen Atkinson, an Englishman who, in 1616, was given permission by James VI to search for gold and silver in Lanarkshire[124] and subsequently wrote a treatise about it, relates a couple of interesting, if possibly apocryphal, anecdotes about Morton. In the first, he tells of an ancient miner, whom he had once encountered, called John Gibson, who claimed that some of the gold nuggets which he had unearthed were the size of bird's eggs. Moreover, the largest of these which he had found in a burn in the Ettrick forest he had sold, so he said, for 'vis viii d. starling the ounce weight unto the Earle of Morton'.[125] In the other story, Morton is supposed to have had a basin, made by a craftsman in the Canongate, Edinburgh, from gold discovered by Peterson, and 'filled upp to the bryme with coyned peeces of gold, called unicornes', presented to the king of France.[126] There are some very obvious discrepancies here, not the least being the mention of the coins known as unicorns which had not been in circulation since James V's reign.[127] Besides, it is highly unlikely Morton ever had any such dealings with the French monarchy. Possibly, then, there is some extremely garbled reference to Morton's presentation of a basin to Killigrew after the siege of Edinburgh in 1573 but, more likely, as with other tales of tureens of gold presented to royal personages, the episode falls into the category of legend rather than fact.

Nonetheless, despite his endeavours, Morton was unable to prevent the country having a seriously inadequate supply of bullion. Moreover, as the regent certainly appreciated, the situation was undoubtedly aggravated by the practice of some Scottish merchants exporting silver overseas, hence a series of attempts by him to eliminate such transactions.

The first of these was on 13th October, 1574 when the privy council observed that, although there were existing statutes against the transport of gold and silver out of the realm, 'be a certane space bigane hes tane na effect bot hes bene planlie contravenit, partlie be misknowlege of the saidis Actis and partlie because the offendouris hes not bene punist'. Consequently, this latest measure announced that anyone convicted of the offence would forfeit not only the bullion involved but 'all the remanent of thair movabill guidis'.[128] Furthermore, Morton, as might be expected, soon showed this was no idle threat and, on 31st December of that year, a 'great multitude' of merchants was summoned before the council for bullion offences.[129] In addition to this, the following May, another batch of merchants from Kinghorn, Kirkcaldy, Dysart and Pittenweem were required to present themselves before the regent for 'away taking of gold'.[130]

Nevertheless, as subsequent proclamations testify,[131] there was still widespread evasion of these regulations, and consequently, on his return to power in 1578, Morton adopted different tactics. Accordingly, authorised by the parliament held in July 'to tak ordour how the xxx, xx and x shilling pieces with the testamentis be haldin within the realme and not transportit furth thairoff',[132] he announced, the next month, that, in order to halt the export of these coins, the government intended calling in all these denominations by 1st March, 1579. 'Lauchfull and trew cunyie', the edict stated, would be marked with a crowned thistle and they would all be raised in value: the 30/- piece was to be raised in value to 32/6d. and the others enhanced proportionally, and any 'countairfait or adulterat' money discovered would simply be clipped and returned to the owner.[133]

This operation proved a troublesome and unpopular business 'altogether mislykit', states one source, 'be the common pepill and specialie be the inhabitants of Edinburgh'.[134] The order, doubtless because of the unsettled state of the country in August, was repeated on 19th September but, in fact, there were to be two extensions before the final time limit of 20th October, 1579 was fixed.[135] These were a consequence, so the council claimed, partly of 'the stormy wether that happainit this last wyntir and springtyme' as well as of deliberate witholding by some individuals of the currency in the hope of financial profit.[136] While the sum of over £45,000, which the treasurer received from the master of the mint, underlines the profitability of this debasement,[137] its short-term nature is seen in the necessity for Morton's successors, shortly after his downfall in February, 1581, to undertake further readjustments in the gold and silver content of the nation's currency.[138]

Financial Expedients

It has been seen that both Morton's comptroller and treasurer experienced serious financial difficulties which were assisted by neither the price rise nor a currency suffering from a variety of misfortunes. The principal remedy adopted by Morton to reduce the crown's debts was to put pressure on the royal burghs, particularly the largest, Edinburgh, to contribute and thus alleviate the exchequer's position.

Consequently, on 24th July, 1574, representatives from the town council of Edinburgh were summoned before the regent's presence at Holyrood where he 'did schew unto thame that our Soverane Lord the King was detbound to certane his Hienes creditouris in the soume of xxxvi m poundis or thairby'. The solution, so they were informed, lay in their hands 'gyf thay wald glaidlie consent to bring sa mekle silver to the cunzehous without compulsioun'.[139] Eventually, following a polite rejection of his request for financial assistance from the convention of royal burghs the same month, on the grounds that they 'farther could nocht interpryse nor tak hand without the avyse of thair magistrattis',[140] twenty-one Edinburgh burgesses agreed to co-operate. This was done on the understanding that 'his Grace tak the lyke ordour with the remanent burrowis of the realme for thair help'.[141]

But this was not the end of the matter. In January, 1575, there were objections from Edinburgh to the employment for the collection of the bullion of Sir James Balfour of Pittendreich 'in respect of the iniuries done be him to the gude toune the tyme that he with his complices did withald the same from our Soverane Lord'.[142] Indeed, it would seem certain citizens voiced their complaints too vehemently for Morton's liking. As a result, on 2nd February, for opposing the regent's proposals and allegedly stating 'we haid maid his Graice and waild mismak him', William Napier, Alexander and Nicholas Udwart were imprisoned at their own expense in Dumbarton castle, Thomas Aitkenhead and Henry Nesbit in Doune and William Little and John Morrison in Linlithgow.[143] There they remained for several months despite pleas of innocences and the efforts of their relatives and colleagues to intercede on their behalf.[144]

The upshot was that the regent had to settle for a subvention from the royal burghs of £10,000 – much less than his original request.[145] However, the significance of the episode undoubtedly lies in the manner in which Morton endeavoured to impose his authority on the recalcitrant Edinburgh burgesses and the question whether the regent acted wisely in taking such draconian measures.

Certainly, his standing in the capital suffered and, when he was dislodged from office in March, 1578, 'the burghes, Edinburgh in speciall', according to Calderwood, 'were alienated from him and gave him no countenance'.[146] On the other hand, memories of his regime were not too easily effaced and, as soon as it became a possibility that he would be restored to power, the city authorities took steps to protect themselves in the event of this happening. Thus, on 21st May, 1578, the provost and his council denied in a letter to Morton's ally, the earl of Mar, that they had despatched any forces to Stirling at the time of the recent *coup d'état*.[147] Admittedly, Archibald Stewart, who, in April, had replaced George Douglas of Parkhead as provost,[148] doubtless expressed the heartfelt feelings of many burgesses by voting against Morton at the convention which restored him as head of the government[149] and by openly supporting the

Argyll-Atholl faction in the summer of 1578. Significantly, in the latter instance, according to Robert Bowes, the English ambassador, he took the precaution of protecting himself with a bodyguard in case he was assaulted by Morton's henchman, George Auchinleck of Balmanno,[150] and he paid for his audacity by being temporarily imprisoned in Doune castle on 6th August.[151] Yet, although Morton wanted him dismissed from office in September, the town council successfully resisted this move by declaring, 'thei cane nocht graunt to the diminutioun of ony pairt of thair fredomes . . . and in speciall to want the free election of thair magistrates at the tymes appointet'.[152] Morton's inability on this occasion to have his candidate, Alexander Clark of Balbirnie, installed as provost, despite exerting considerable pressure on Archibald Stewart, who was threatened with arrest unless he personally appeared at Stirling,[153] illustrates the comparatively unstable nature of his position at this juncture. Conversely, a year later, when he was more firmly established, the Edinburgh council, being instructed 'to elect and cheis Alexander Clark . . . and gif they failyeit to put thame to the horne', complied without protest.[154]

Nonetheless, all things considered, unless he really had in mind, as Killigrew has suggested, some devious scheme of taking a tough line with the wealthier Edinburgh citizens in order 'to win the goodwill generally of all the artificers in Scotland, which tends more to his strength by ten to one than the friendship of the burgesses',[155] it must remain doubtful if it was sound policy for Morton to add another source of disaffection to those already in existence. Furthermore, the financial problems of his administration could arguably have been less serious if the Edinburgh merchants had been handled more tactfully and less rigorously in 1575.

Overseas Trade

The emphasis so far has been largely on the financial condition of the country under Morton but, closely linked to this is a commercial policy apparently pursued on traditionally medieval lines. Thus, as far as overseas trade was concerned, he endeavoured to obtain as much revenue as possible from the customs, and strove to curb inflation by restricting exports of scarce commodities.

That customs returns were at least being made regularly for most ports has already been noted. However, one contribution which Morton did render towards the expansion of overseas trade was to take the lead in having the staple port for Scottish merchants established at Campveere in the Netherlands. Accordingly, at the convention of royal burghs on 12th

February, 1578, 'efter lang avisement and ressonyng with my said Lord Regentis Grace', it was decided 'that thair be electit and chosin sum speciall man ... to be sent with ampill and full commissioun to the pairtis of Flanderis sic as Antverp, Campheir, Bruges, Berry, Middelburgh and uther places neidful to enter in commoning with the principallis of the townis forsaidis tuyching the said staipill and with thir commissionis to tak with thame my said Lord Regentis Grace wrytingis in thair favouris'.[156] In this fashion, negotiations were begun which were to be completed later that year and which marked the end for Scottish merchants of a period of uncertainty about the staple which had lasted since the outbreak of the Dutch rebellion.[157]

In the matter of embargoes on exports, Morton, as soon as he became regent, placed restrictions on a number of items. Hence, parliament, in April, 1573, decreed that 'nane of the subiectis of this Realme tak upon hard to carie or transport forth of this Realme ony maner of lynning claith linget seid [i.e. lintseed] maid Candell or uther Tallow quwhatsumever eitting Butter Cheis Barkit Hydes or maid Schone'.[158] Attempts, however, to place such restraint on the export of salt posed particular difficulties for the regent. It meant that the Scottish salt industry produced insufficient quantities to satisfy home demand, but the general dislocation of European trade in the 1570s, largely caused by events in the Spanish Netherlands, made it extremely profitable for Scottish exporters to sell salt overseas and compete in a small way with the great salt entrepreneurs of the Bay of Biscay.

Morton's first legislation against such practices was also in the April, 1573 parliament where it was stated that 'forasmekle as it is understand the great and exorbitant prices the small salt is laitlie rissin to', a three-year ban was accordingly being placed on its export by all merchants except 'strangeris of Norway and utheris of the Eist partis' who provided Scotland with timber.[159] However, in August that year, the council announced changes in the laws affecting salt so that there was now to be no export of that commodity until the demand in Scotland had been satisfied and it was only to be sold at a price fixed by the council. On the other hand, 'the rest of the salt mair nor sall satisfie the subiectis of this realme' could be taken abroad providing those transporting it paid to the master of the mint 'sex uncès of silver for every chalder contenit in thair cokquett'.[160] Just over a year later, on 20th September, 1574, there was a further change when, on account of a shortage of salt and its high price, the government revoked all existing export agreements.[161] But this proved to be only a temporary measure since, following objections from several ports, burghs such as

Prestonpans, Bo'ness, Culross and Fordell were granted exemptions.[162] Indeed, the principle of awarding dispensations to export salt and the necessity of obtaining permission 'under the signet and subscription of the regent's grace' became established policy, being confirmed by the parliamentary convention of March, 1575 and repeated in a privy council statement shortly thereafter.[163]

Henceforth, the control of the salt industry operated more satisfactorily. Nevertheless, it could have given Morton another opportunity to indulge in questionable financial dealings similar to those in which, so several authorities aver, he participated regarding licences for, among others, importing wine and corn, or eating flesh at Lent. Thus, according to one account, 'he maid lawis that na merchand sould bring wynis from France without his licence, Bot how dere cost war these licences to the merchands, I report me to thair pursis'.[164] Again, in a report to the English government in 1575, the regent's issuing of wine licences was described as one 'wherein he is noted for corruption', while his insistence that merchants paid in silver for the privilege of exporting herring and coal was regarded as 'redounding greatly and only to his particular commodity'.[165] Nor are these the only references to dubious practices by Morton. Hume of Godscroft, for instance, mentions certain Edinburgh butchers, arrested for forestalling victuals, who were promptly released on payment to the regent;[166] Calderwood, to give another example, tells of the prosperous Edinburgh merchant, Robert Gourlay, who, when threatened by the kirk for contravening the legislation affecting the export of corn, protested that he had obtained a special licence to act thus from the regent.[167] In short, when these and other such allegations, like the one that lord Somerville bribed him in 1577 to ensure success in his litigation against another relative, are taken into account,[168] it would seem irrefutable that Morton was not above reproach in some aspects of his domestic policy.

Social Policy

Finally, Morton's government had the social problems presented by the poor. For a regent who strove to establish law and order, he was, not unexpectedly, distinctly concerned about the existence of large numbers of impoverished individuals and their potential threat to authority. Accordingly, the convention of 1575 recommended that sturdy beggars should be 'scurgeit and burnt throw the girssill if the right eare with ane het Irne to the compass of ane inche about'. Conversely, what were regarded as the deserving poor were to benefit from a system of relief administered by church elders and deacons, who were to 'considder quhat thair neidful sustentatioun will extend to in the owlk' and provide for the impoverished members of their parish by taxing 'the haill inhabitants within the prochyn according to the estimatioun of thair substance'.[169] A later statute of 1579 differed substantially from the act of 1575 only in the manner of collecting poor relief. Thus, it was now the duty of 'provestis, baillies and Jugeis . . . to taxt and stent the haill inhabitatis within the parochyne according to the estimatioun of thair substance . . . to sic ouklie charge and contributioun as sal be thocht expedient'.[170]

That these measures were effective seems unlikely. Indeed, by July, 1580, the royal burghs were already complaining about the neglect of the enactments of the previous November which, they protested, were so blatantly ignored that it was impossible for the burghs 'to tak ordour thairanent being oppressit with ane greit and infinit nomber of strang and extraordinar beggeris nocht born nor bred within the saidis burrowis'.[171] This is a clear indication of the difficulty Morton's government experienced in enforcing its poor law.

There remains Morton's personal attitude to the less fortunate. Admittedly, the impression given so far of his domestic administration is hardly that of a benevolent figure. In fact, by his manipulations of the currency, it has been seen that he allegedly caused considerable distress among the poor. Nevertheless, Morton could occasionally appear to display some concern in this direction. Hence, at Aberdeen, for example, during his visit in August-September, 1574, the council was left in no uncertainty about the regent's intentions. Thus, he commanded that 'the organis with all expeditioun be removed out of the kirk and maid proffite of to the use and support of the pure'. Furthermore, there were instructions that 'the pure be not defraudit of the almus collectit at the kirk dur', that the Greyfriars building 'be roupit to the maist avale and settin few heretabillie to sic as will gif maist yearlie dewtie thairfore and the same to be fully applyit to the use and sustentatioun of the pure', and that the leper house, which had fallen into disrepair, should be restored and its occupants given assistance. Lastly, the council had £1,000 of the fine imposed upon it remitted on condition that there was built 'ane Hospitall within our said burgh for the harbring and ressett of the puyr and impotent personis of the same'.[172]

However, it would obviously be unwise to place too much emphasis on Morton's behaviour at Aberdeen since it might well have been more a desire to embarrass a council which had annoyed him by its support for his adversaries in the civil war than a genuine interest in the condition of

Aberdeen's paupers. Similarly, the remission regularly given in the accounts of the collector of thirds to 'the puir beid men being four in number of the maison dieu in Elgin in almonis at my lord regent's command', which might appear, albeit on a minor scale, to be evidence of Morton's generosity, on closer scrutiny assumes a different complexion.[173] In fact, in 1567, the preceptory of this hospital at Elgin, with an obligation for sustaining the poor therein, had been given to Robert, son of Henry Douglas of Drumgarland.[174] The regent, therefore, for reasons best known to himself, was in a small way once again looking after the interests of a kinsman rather than specially assisting four indigent members of the community.

The conclusion must be that, when it suited his purpose, as at Aberdeen, or when it seemed in the interest of a kinsman, as with Robert Douglas of Drumgarland, or perhaps when he felt obliged to, as in the case of certain wounded English soldiers whom he ensured were paid their outstanding wages in 1573,[175] only then did Morton display a personal concern for those in the lower ranks of society.

Thus, Morton, as far as his record in domestic government is concerned, emerges as someone comparatively successful in some aspects but decidedly less so in others. Undoubtedly, there was greater respect for royal authority. Moreover, both departments of the exchequer operated more efficiently, benefiting from such features of the regent's more determined rule as increased returns from the crown lands and the customs, his subjugation of the borders, and his financial impositions, especially on the city of Aberdeen. Firm action too was taken, in an effort to protect the currency, against forgery and the illegal export of silver. In addition, the establishment of the staple on a permanent footing at Campveere was undoubtedly of considerable assistance to Scottish merchants.

On the other hand, Morton, even if he was temporarily able to effect some reduction in the amount involved, could not prevent both exchequer departments having a constant deficit. Shortly after his final overthrow in 1580, the treasurer, for example, reported a loss of £36,000 'or thereby'.[176] Nor, for that matter, could the remedies he adopted – debasement and manipulation of the currency as well as a demand for a compulsory contribution from the royal burghs – be considered solutions to a problem no doubt acerbated by inflation. Furthermore, his poor law legislation, while well-intentioned, at least for those regarded as the deserving poor, was never properly enforced. As for his economic policy, the only notable item, apart from his commendable efforts with the staple, was his restraint of the salt trade. In this he may have been relatively successful, although the practice of issuing licences raises the question of his integrity in such matters.

Indeed, it is this very question of his venality that Morton seems most open to criticism. Clearly, if not surprisingly, he, at times, took care of his own kin – hence the grant in partnership with Glamis to his own son, James, commendator of Pluscarden, of the leadmines in Ayrshire and Galloway, or, at a humbler level, the favour conferred on Robert Douglas, preceptor of the hospital at Elgin. Moreover, from his own involvement in the mining industry, the dubious business of lending the crown large sums of money and recouping himself from the profits of the mint, as well as his curious neglect of compositions, it can justifiably be concluded he took good care of his own interests as well.

Nevertheless, none of this seems too exceptional when the widespread nature of corruption in sixteenth-century Scotland and England is borne in mind. What seems more significant is that, although he undoubtedly dominated affairs by his forceful personality, yet, despite his authority, the exchequer remained in deficit, the currency continued as unstable as ever, and the poor law legislation was largely ignored. In short, there were distinct limitations to Morton's achievements in his domestic administration.

NOTES

1. *T.A.*, xii, 272.
2. *Ibid*, 272.
3. *Ibid*, xiii, 16, 123, 329–48, 382–83.
4. *Historie and Life of King James the Sext*, 160–61.
5. The figures are given in *R.S.S.*, vii, v (introduction).
6. *Ibid*, No. 735.
7. *R.P.C.*, ii, 276–77.
8. *Ibid*, iii, 88–91; *see also R.S.S.*, vii, No. 2090.
9. Dalyell, *Fragments*, 21.
10. Pitcairn, *Trials*, i, pt. iii, 72–73.
11. *Scots Peerage*, vii, 548.
12. *Historie and Life of King James the Sext*, 161; Spottiswoode, *History*, ii, 203.
13. *Ibid*, 204; Gabriel Sempill, younger of Cathcart, is also mentioned as involved, *R.S.S.*, vii, No. 1536.
14. Spottiswoode, *History*, ii, 203–204.
15. Pitcairn, *Trials*, i, pt. iii, 70–71.
16. *R.S.S.*, vii, No. 1025; *T.A.*, xiii, 166–67.

17. Spottiswoode, *History*, ii, 204–05.
18. Pitcairn, *Trials*, i, pt. iii, 133.
19. Spottiswoode, *History*, ii, 203.
20. Balfour, *Annales*, i, 364.
21. *R.P.C.*, iii, 172.
22. *R.S.S.*, vii, No. 1536.
23. S.R.O., Morton papers, GD 150/2282; *see also, ibid,* GD 150/1769.
24. S.R.O., R.S.S., xlviii, PS 1/48, f. 92r.
25. *R.S.S.*, vii, No. 1070.
26. Williamson, *Scottish National Consciousness,* 65.
27. *E.R.*, xx, 118, 179.
28. The total for 1579 was £17,379 and, for 1580, £18,166, *ibid*, 342; xxi, 128.
29. *Ibid*, xx, 115, 176.
30. *Ibid*, 176.
31. *Ibid*, 104–112, 158–171.
32. *Ibid*, xx and xxi, *passim*.
33. Murray, 'Procedure of the Scottish Exchequer in the 16th C.', *S.H.R.*, xl, 98.
34. *E.R.*, xx, 258–70, 284–92, 305–07.
35. *See E.R.*, xx, accounts of the *ballivi ad extra*.
36. *E.R.*, xx, 230.
37. *R.P.C.*, ii, 464–65.
38. S.R.O., Morton papers, GD 150/457.
39. *E.R.*, xxi, 182–201.
40. E.g. *E.R.*, xx, 447, 503–04, 518–19, 547–48.
41. *Ibid*, 503–04.
42. *Ibid*, 258–70.
43. *Ayr Accts.*, 140–41.
44. *E.R.*, xx, 517–20.
45. *Ibid*, 517; *R.P.C.*, ii, 627–29.
46. *E.R.*, xx, 517–18.
47. *Ibid*, 517.
48. *Ibid*, 467–68; xxi, 162.
49. *See, ibid*, xix, xx, xxi, *passim*.
50. *R.P.C.*, iii, 196.
51. Murray, 'Customs Accounts of Dumfries and Kirkcudbright (1560–1660)', *T.D.G.A.S.*, 3rd Series, xlii, 114.
52. *E.R.*, xx, 145, 205.
53. This figure is based on the 'superexpenditure' from the previous year shown in the account of 1579, *ibid*, 342.
54. *Ibid*, 362.
55. *Ibid*, xxi, 155.
56. *C.S.P. Scot.*, v, 418.

57. *See* Devine and Lythe, 'Economy of Scotland under James VI', *S.H.R.*, l, 94.
58. *Glas. Recs.*, i, 22–82 *passim*.
59. *T.A.*, xii, 363.
60. *Ibid*, 350.
61. *Ibid*, 350.
62. *Ibid*, 334.
63. *Ibid*, 350.
64. *Works Accts.*, i, 299–301.
65. *Historie and Life of King James the Sext*, 145.
66. *Ibid*, 152; this is the famous halfmoon battery.
67. *See, R.C.A.H.M. (Edinburgh)*, 15–18.
68. There are frequent references in the Treasurer's Accounts, e.g. *T.A.*, xii, 387; *T.A.*, xiii, 17, 23, 29, 33, 36, 40.
69. *Warrender Papers*, i, 135–36.
70. *T.A.*, xiii, 215, 218.
71. *Ibid*, 253.
72. *Ibid*, 265–72.
73. *T.A.*, xii, 392.
74. *Ibid*, 393–94.
75. *Ibid*, 394.
76. *Ibid*, xiii, 106.
77. *Ibid*, 107.
78. *Diurnal*, 336; *Historie and Life of King James the Sext*, 148.
79. *T.A.*, xiii, 387–408 *passim*; *T.A.*, (MSS), E22/4, 81v.
80. *T.A.*, xiii, 16.
81. *R.P.C.*, II, 394–96, 402–03.
82. *Abdn. Counc.*, 11–16.
83. *T.A.*, xiii, 16.
84. *Ibid*, 123.
85. *T.A.*, xii (introduction), xxiv.
86. *T.A.*, xiii, 140.
87. *Ibid*, 153.
88. *Ibid*, 151.
89. *Ibid*, 27, 148, 165.
90. *Ibid*, 27–28, 53.
91. *Ibid*, 6–14, 241–48.
92. E.g. *R.P.C.*, ii, 683; iii, 285, 326; *A.P.S.*, iii, 149.
93. Melville, *Memoirs*, 259.
94. *Historie and Life of King James the Sext*, 158.
95. *See* Stewart, *Scottish Coinage*, 92–94.
96. *A.P.S.*, iii, 108, 150; *R.P.C.*, iii, 31–32.
97. *Ibid*, 283, 287.

98. *A.P.S.*, iii, 92.
99. *Ibid*, 92–93; *C.S.P. Scot.*, v, 97–98.
100. Calderwood, *History*, iii, 302.
101. *Diurnal*, 345.
102. *Historie and Life of King James the Sext*, 152.
103. Lythe, *Economy of Scotland*, 103.
104. *See*, Dept. of Environment, *Aberdour Castle*, 1980.
105. *Scotia Rediviva*, i, 388.
106. The only reference to Morton using a coach is in Somerville, *Memorie of the Somervilles*, i, 449–55.
107. *C.S.P. Scot.*, v, 21, 60–61.
108. Pitcairn, *Trials*, i, pt. iii, 66.
109. *C.S.P. Scot.*, iv, 666.
110. *R.P.C.*, iii, 294; *T.A.*, xiii, 281.
111. Atkinson, *History of the Gold Mines*, 19–20.
112. *H.M.C. (Laing)*, i, 25–26.
113. *R.P.C.*, ii, 506–13.
114. *Ibid*, 507.
115. *T.A.*, xii, 273.
116. *R.P.C.*, ii, 598; iii, 2.
117. *Ibid*, ii, 510.
118. Subsequently known as the Morton tapestry, Warrack, *Domestic Life in Scotland*, 91–97.
119. Atkinson, *History of the Gold Mines*, 35.
120. Quoted in 'Painters in Scotland, 1301–1700', *S.R.S.*, New Series, vii, 31.
121. Thomson, *Painting in Scotland, 1570–1650*, 22–24; see also 'Painters in Scotland 1301–1700', *S.R.S.*, New Series, vii, 31. The portrait would tend to confirm Hume of Godscroft's statement that Morton was stockily built and had reddish hair, Hume, *History*, ii, 138.
122. *R.S.S.*, vii, No. 1271.
123. *C.S.P. Scot.*, v, 5.
124. *R.P.C.*, x, 531–33.
125. Atkinson, *History of the Gold Mines*, 21.
126. *Ibid*, 22.
127. Stewart, *Scottish Coinage*, 75.
128. *R.P.C.*, ii, 410–11.
129. *T.A.*, xiii, 46.
130. *Ibid*, 68.
131. *R.P.C.*, ii, 554–55, 615.
132. *A.P.S.*, iii, 108.
133. *R.P.C.*, iii, 17–18.
134. Moysie, *Memoirs*, 18.

135. *R.P.C.*, iii, 32–33, 100, 158–59, 196.
136. *Ibid*, 159.
137. The exact amount was £45,457.15.9d., *T.A.*, xiii, 249.
138. *A.P.S.*, iii, 191.
139. *Edin. Recs.* (1573–89), 18.
140. *R.C.R.B.*, i, 28.
141. *Edin. Recs.* (1573–89), 20–21.
142. *Ibid*, 35.
143. *Ibid.*, 40–41; *Diurnal*, 343; *Historie and Life of King James the Sext*, 151.
144. *C.S.P. Scot.*, v, 180; *Edin. Recs.* (1573–89), 37.
145. *R.C.R.B.*, i, 42–43.
146. Calderwood, *History*, iii, 396.
147. *H.M.C. (Mar & Kellie)*, i, 31; the reinforcements concerned would appear to have been ordered by a section of the privy council, N.L.S. Advocates MSS, 29.2.6, No. 140.
148. *Edin. Recs.* (1573–89), 71.
149. *C.S.P. Scot.*, v, 296.
150. *H.M.C. (Hastings)*, i, 14.
151. *R.P.C.*, iii, 19–20.
152. *Edin. Recs.* (1573–89), 84–85.
153. Moysie, *Memoirs*, 18–19.
154. *R.P.C.*, iii, 226.
155. *C.S.P. Scot.*, v, 180.
156. *R.C.R.B.*, i, 51–52.
157. *Ibid*, 53–65; Davidson and Gray, *Scottish Staple*, 177–82.
158. *A.P.S.*, iii, 83.
159. *Ibid*, 82.
160. *R.P.C.*, ii, 264–65.
161. *Ibid*, 406–07.
162. *Ibid*, 424–25.
163. *A.P.S.*, iii, 93; *R.P.C.*, ii, 442–43.
164. *Historie and Life of King James the Sext*, 150.
165. *C.S.P.*, v, 157.
166. Hume, *History*, ii, 243.
167. Calderwood, *History*, iii, 328; nonetheless, Gourlay, on this occasion, still had to submit himself to the judgment of the kirk, *Maitland Misc.*, i, 101.
168. Somerville, *Memorie of the Somervilles*, i, 449–55.
169. *A.P.S.*, iii, 86–89.
170. *Ibid*, 139–42.
171. *R.C.R.B.*, i, 102.
172. *R.P.C.*, ii, 391, 402–03; *Abdn. Counc.*, 12–13.

173. E.g. S.R.O., Thirds of Benefices, E45/11, f. 111v.
174. *R.S.S.*, vi, No. 23; Cowan & Easson, *Medieval Religious Houses*, 179.
175. *T.A.*, xii, 361, 363.
176. *R.P.C.*, iii, 340.

9

Foreign Policy

Morton's foreign policy is essentially a survey of Anglo-Scottish relations during this period. Admittedly, France still exercised some influence in Scottish affairs, particularly at the beginning of his regency, but, while the regent on various occasions might hint at a possible revival of the 'auld alliance', this, in fact, was highly unlikely. French support of Mary and her followers in Scotland, not to mention the religious differences and the unstable political condition of France, effectively ensured that a *rapprochement* of some kind or another was never seriously contemplated. Again, as far as other European powers were concerned, dealings with them were notably infrequent. Granted there was some correspondence with Sweden and the Netherlands about the recruitment of Scottish mercenaries for service in these countries,[1] and a certain amount of letters also passed between the royal courts of Scotland and Denmark. In the latter instance, however, the subject matter was mainly either about the fate of the earl of Bothwell or, somewhat ironically, one of his enemies, captain John Clerk, who was also incarcerated at Dragsholm during the 1570s.[2] In short, the keynote to the regent's attitude to foreign affairs was his desire for amity with England.

Anglo-Scottish relations under Morton fall conveniently into four phases. Firstly, there is the period from his accession in November, 1572 to the downfall of the Marian forces within Edinburgh castle in May, 1573 when both sides ultimately combined against the common foe. Then there is a largely uneventful interval between the surrender of the castle and the regent's own deposition in March, 1578, during which Morton unsuccessfully sought a formal alliance with England. However, there did occur, in July, 1575, the Redeswyre crisis which, at least temporarily, endangered the concord between the two countries. Thirdly, following Morton's recovery, there is the pacification of the Argyll-Atholl faction in August, 1578, an episode in which Robert Bowes, the English ambassador, played a not inconsiderable part. Finally, there is English reaction to the presence of Esmé Stewart at the court of James VI and the renewed efforts by Morton to obtain a categorical guarantee of English support.

Morton, on the death of the regent Mar on 28th October, 1572, could not only depend on the support of his own followers for his nomination as regent but had the additional advantage of being the candidate preferred by the English government. Thus, queen Elizabeth, on hearing of Mar's demise, observed, as she proffered her condolences, that she was 'comforted by the trust that he will follow herein the footsteps which he had begun'.[3] In other words, she was confident that Morton's well-established predilection for England, observed in his earlier career, would prevail now that he had reached the pinnacle of it. Certainly, the new regent, who informed the earl of Huntingdon on 1st December that 'there shall be no lack in him in that which may continue the good intelligence with England',[4] clearly had no intention of severing his ties with his neighbour.

As it happened, there were several good reasons on both sides why Morton and Elizabeth should endeavour to remain on good terms. In the first place, when he became regent, there were only a few weeks left before the truce or 'abstinence', which had halted the civil war between the supporters of queen Mary and the government of king James VI, was scheduled to end. This had been arranged by the Anglo-French commissioners, Davison and du Croc, and was originally supposed to last two months but had eventually been extended to 31st December, 1572.[5] Furthermore, by this date, although the allegiance of several important nobelemen was still ambiguous, the most active Marians were those within Edinburgh castle. Here, within that fortress, commanded by Kirkcaldy of Grange, they confidently awaited French assistance.[6] To some extent, their confidence was not entirely misplaced since previously, in August, 1572, a French agent had been dispatched with money for Grange and the promise of more if he could retain the castle for the Marian cause.[7] Morton, therefore, as leader of the king's party, required English assistance if he was to defeat the Marians and establish himself as the undisputed head of state. Moreover, he was well aware of the inadequacy of his own resources and, as he confided to Burghley shortly after his accession, 'The knowledge of her majesty's meaning has chiefly moved me to accept the charge, resting in assured hope of her favourable protection and maintenance'.[8] Thus, the regent, as head of an impecunious and militarily vulnerable state, looked towards England for succour. His principal task in the first months he was in office was to convince Elizabeth of the necessity of direct intervention on his behalf against his enemies.

From an English standpoint, Mary was now their prisoner but, as long as her supporters flourished in Scotland and were the recipients of foreign aid, there was always a threat to English security and Elizabeth's crown. Accordingly, it was the continued presence of Mary's adherents in the northern kingdom and especially their retention of the principal stronghold of that country which had caused Elizabeth to regard Morton's predicament with increasing disquiet. Her attitude was aptly summarised by a government memorandum of September, 1572 which declared that 'The Scottish Queen's party in Scotland seek to set up her that seeks to throw down the Queen's majesty and the King's party seek the suppression of her that seeks to suppress the Queen's majesty. It is therefor manifest,' it concluded, 'that the overthrow of the Scottish Queen's party is the overthrow of her and the surety of the Queen and the overthrow of the King's party is the peril of the Queen's majesty and the way to set up her greatest enemy . . . '[9] In short, just as the Huguenots, based at their great fortress of La Rochelle, were presenting serious difficulties to Charles IX of France, so for England there was an equivalent situation in Scotland.

Morton, on 1st January, 1573, when he resumed hostilities against the defenders of Edinburgh castle, having failed so far to obtain any definite guarantee of English support or even any material assistance, obviously renewed the struggle suffering certain disadvantages. Possessing, for example, only two large pieces of artillery, neither of them in the capital, and a few smaller guns, he patently lacked effective firepower.[10] Furthermore, although he had asked Sir Henry Killigrew, Elizabeth's ambassador, for financial aid 'for the present payment of our men of war their bypast wages',[11] this money had not been forthcoming. By 24th January, this had clearly become a serious issue since, on that date, the privy council received a complaint about outstanding wages from several officers. However, they were apparently placated by an assurance from Morton's government that it would 'mak full and compleit payment of the saidis thre monthis wageis to the saidis capitanis and their companyis . . . betwix the dait heirof and the first day of June nixtocuum'.[12]

That Morton was perturbed about the strength of the castle compared with his limited resources is underlined in a request, that month, to Sir William Drury, marshall of Berwick, for some 'auld experimentit captainis with a mynour'.[13] Drury sent two experts who, apart from demonstrating the proper construction of trenches, concluded that mining was impracticable but that, if a sufficient supply of ordnance was mounted, the castle could be taken within three weeks.[14]

Meanwhile, most of February was taken up with neutralising the Hamilton-Huntly faction, a task in which, as has been seen, Killigrew played a prominent part. However, by the time the Perth agreement was concluded, it would appear that Elizabeth was at last considering a more forward policy in Scotland. Thus, Killigrew, on 25th February, while Morton's guest at Aberdour, could reassure him 'of her majesty's good meaning to assist the Regent for the recovery of the castle'.[15] Moreover, by this juncture, Drury had also been notified that he would command any English expeditionary force raised for a Scottish campaign.[16]

At the same time, Morton was occasionally not averse to putting pressure on the English government by dark threats of changing his allegiance or abdicating his post. Thus, on one occasion, for instance, he warned Killigrew that 'should he be in danger to be left in the mire he would surely quit the regiment'.[17] But while such talk doubtless alarmed Elizabeth, it was the realisation that the regent was unable to take the castle single-handed and the menace to England of the continued presence of a French-subsidised party in Scotland which finally converted her. Nevertheless, Morton was clearly also indebted directly or indirectly to various English officials for their advocacy of his cause. Chief among these, apart from Sir Henry Killigrew, were the earl of Huntingdon, president of the council of the north, Sir Thomas Smith, Burghley's secretarial colleague, and Francis Walsingham, at that moment English ambassador in Paris.[18] Walsingham, for instance, during January, sent reports of a number of disturbing rumours which he had picked up of which the most serious was that the French government had decided to seek a settlement, for the time being, with the Huguenots in order to intervene more effectively in Scotland.[19] Moreover, and this was probably the viewpoint which swayed Elizabeth, lord Burghley, her principal counsellor, favoured immediate action on behalf of Morton. Thus, in a memorandum about the siege, he noted in cryptic fashion: 'Delay – The Scots power shall withdraw. The castle shall wax the stronger. The foreign aid shall come thither in time. The expense of one pound now will cost £5 within a month or two. Therefore – a present attempt should be made.'[20]

The first indication that Elizabeth really meant to intervene was the commission issued to Drury on 12th March. Thereby, if Morton produced evidence 'of any that shall detain any castle of the King's or shall levy any forces against the King thereby seeking to renew the civil war or to bring strangers into Scotland for that purpose' or if, in addition, 'he shall require aid of him to concur with the King's forces for the reduction of such disordered persons to obedience', then this should be the task of 'such forces as are there in her pay and with any others that shall be sent thither or may be levied by him and with such munitions, artillery and other things thereto belonging . . . '[21] In addition, on 17th March, the English commander received a warrant for the treasurer of Berwick, Sir Valentine Browne, 'to imprest such sums as shall seem requisite to him for the service of Sir William Drury and others for extraordinary service in Scotland'.[22] However, it was not until 25th March, following further instructions, and by which time his preparations were well under way, that Drury forwarded these details to Morton.[23] Consequently, it was nearly the end of March before the regent could be absolutely certain that English reinforcements were a reality and he could confirm arrangements for the reception of the English army as well as the dispatch of the requisite number of Scottish hostages.[24]

As far as the latter were concerned, Morton had originally thought that six was an adequate number. However, he eventually agreed to ten hostages, including the son of his own cousin, the laird of Kilspindie, as well as representatives of other leading noblemen, being 'intertenit within Ingland in Northumberland, the bischoprik of Durehame, or Yorkschyre at thair ressonabill expenssis'.[25] However, it was to be over a fortnight before the hostages departed and, although Morton would have preferred awaiting the arrival of the English forces and then storming the castle, which enterprise, according to Killigrew, he was prepared to lead himself,[26] there was, on 5th April, yet another unsuccessful attempt to negotiate with Grange. The breakdown of these discussions, at which the earl of Rothes represented Morton's government, led to the decision that this would be the last offer until Drury's forces were actually assembled.[27]

Eventually, on 17th April, at Lamberton church in Berwickshire, lord Ruthven handed over the Scottish hostages and signed the appropriate articles of agreement, on behalf of the Scottish government, with Drury. The terms included guarantees that neither side would seek an independent settlement with the occupants of the castle and that the ringleaders 'sa far as may be sal be reservit to be justifiit be the lawis of Scotland, quhairin hir Majesteis advise sal be usit'. Additionally, there was provision that 'in cais the said Castell sall not utherwayis be recoverit than be force . . . all ordinance, munitionis, royall plate, jewellis, wardrop and houshald stuff with the registers and recordis belongand' would be surrendered to Morton's government. Finally, *apropos* the hostages, it was agreed that 'the number of ten remane in England during the tyme that the saidis forces and ordnance sall remane in Scotland and for sauf returning of the same'.[28]

Once the English commander and his troops had arrived at Edinburgh, the final stages of the siege proceeded as Morton desired. The garrison ignored a final opportunity to surrender, and, on 17th May, the allied bombardment commenced, lasting until 28th May when the castle surrendered unconditionally.[29] The rank and file were allowed their freedom, but Grange, Lethington and certain other prisoners were eventually handed over, in accordance with the previous agreement.

This marked the end of a successful combined operation during which Morton's forces had co-operated effectively with Drury's to overcome the small but resolutely commanded garrison within the castle. For Morton, it meant the elimination of the last threat, at least for the present, to his position, whereas, for Elizabeth, it signalled the collapse of the active pro-French, Marian party in Scotland who, as Killigrew observed, were 'now very thin sown'.[30] Moreover, although Drury's activities provoked a sharp diplomatic protest from the French ambassador in London,[31] this, as it materialised, was to be the limit of French reaction. Nevertheless, Morton and his English allies were perhaps fortunate that the Huguenots at La Rochelle, with clandestine English and Dutch assistance, resisted all attacks upon them until it was too late for French intervention in Scotland.

The only discordant note in the proceedings was struck by Morton himself in his relationship with the English general, Sir William Drury. Consequently, while Killigrew was receiving, as a reward for his outstanding services, a basin, a laver and three cups 'all in silver . . . by his grace command',[32] Drury was being subjected to considerable criticism for his alleged 'slender gudewill and furthwartnes'.[33]

The first occasion when there would appear to have been any friction between the two of them was in connection with an application by Grange for the release from the castle of his sister. The latter had become unwell during the siege, but Grange's entreaty that she be allowed into the town in order to receive proper medical attention was rejected by Morton.[34] On the other hand, Drury's comment in a despatch to Burghley that 'because the same [i.e. Grange's application] is mislike of the regent he will not grant to such request' suggests that he thought the petition should have been allowed.[35] However, this matter was apparently smoothed over by Killigrew who, on 12th May, wrote to Burghley that 'By his conference old friendship, somewhat shaken was renewed'[36] and, although one contemporary source does allude to ill-feeling between Morton and Drury over the latter's negotiating with Grange unbeknown to the regent,[37] there is no reference to this in any of the inter-governmental correspondence. Thus, the primary reason for Morton's displeasure would seem to have been Drury's sympathetic attitude towards his prisoners, particularly Grange, once the castle had been taken. Indeed, in one communiqué, Drury commented 'on the good conformity grown to with the Castilians',[38] and he is also supposed to have interceded with his government in an effort to save Grange's life.[39]

It is understandable that Morton should have disapproved of Drury's attitude towards Grange. At the same time, while there admittedly was also the question of certain royal jewels given by Grange to Drury, it does seem unfortunate that the regent allowed their differences to become the basis for, on his part, a rather squalid personal vendetta. In June, for example, in a letter to the countess of Lennox, the regent was warning her 'to be war and circumspect with the Marshall of Berwick's information for that he is undoubtedly the secret friend of our enemies'. Moreover, he even suggested to the countess that she should try to arrange Drury's dismissal from his post at Berwick,[40] a consummation, in the prevailing circumstances, highly unlikely. In fact, the marshall of Berwick was subsequently rewarded for his stalwart service on the frontier by being appointed president of Munster and, shortly before his death in October, 1579, lord justice of Ireland.[41] However, the significant point about all this is surely that it reveals an unattractive facet of Morton's character and shows him capable of behaviour which can only be described as unworthy and ungenerous.

With his immediate internal problems resolved, Morton could now consider long-term defensive arrangements with England. Accordingly, Killigrew, on his departure on 26th June, was given a lengthy description of the type of agreement between the two kingdoms which the regent was to seek intermittently until his deposition in March, 1578. Such a pact, it was suggested, might have the same format as the earlier treaty of Berwick signed between the two countries in 1560 but might also incorporate a clause guaranteeing 'the maintenance and defence of the true religion against the Council of Trent'.[42] In short, what the regent envisaged was an alliance which protected the protestant faith in both states and also ensured that, in the event of foreign attack, each country would come to the other's aid.

However, it was another ten months before Killigrew returned to Edinburgh and meanwhile, following the cool reception given to Morton's request in November, 1573 for financial assistance and a supply of gunpowder,[43] it appeared, at least to the English government, that the regent's allegiance was wavering. This was the reason, therefore, for Killigrew's mission in the summer of 1574 with instructions 'to diligently search out what alteration has happened since your last being there in particular whether the Regent continues constant in his affection towards us'. In addition, the English ambassador was to endeavour to ascertain 'whether there hath not been any lately sent out to France to practice underhand any alteration in that state'.[44] Nonetheless, Killigrew was advised to proceed very cautiously in any discussions with Morton regarding 'a league between our two realms for mutual defence against foreign invasion'. While the prospect of a compact between other protestant powers in Europe, including Scotland, was not to be discouraged, and negotiations with the Palatinate could be cited as proof of Elizabeth's intentions in this direction, this should be the limit of his commitment. Moreover, he should emphasise to the regent that such a protestant league would make a formal alliance with England superfluous. In any case, the Scottish leader should be reminded that the English government had never neglected his welfare in the past. Finally, as far as his official instructions were concerned, Killigrew was to avoid any promise of financial support either to Morton himself or any of his colleagues, and, if Morton proved persistent, then the English ambassador should procrastinate by declaring he was referring the matter to his government.[45]

However, there was one other topic not mentioned in his government's memorandum which Killigrew clearly had authority to discuss. This was the question of queen Mary's return to Scotland or, as it was cryptically referred to in the official correspondence, 'the great matter'. The possibility of Mary being handed over to the Scottish government had been raised in Killigrew's embassy of September, 1572 during Mar's regency,[46] but the latter's death caused a postponement which lasted until the English ambassador's present mission. In the event there were some deliberations between Morton and Killigrew on this subject and, in July, 1574, the possibility of Mary returning to Scotland 'if he [i.e. Morton] will take upon him the safe-keeping of the Queen of Scots with such conditions as were propounded' was again raised by the English government.[47] However, there were no further developments; perhaps the improved international situation made Elizabeth less anxious to unburden herself of her cousin, especially as it would have meant transferring her to a government highly unlikely to have spared her life; Morton, conversely, may well have believed that Mary's repatriation would only cause trouble for his administration by exacerbating relations between him and her former supporters in the kingdom.

Meanwhile, Killigrew had arrived in Edinburgh to find there was what he termed some 'practicing for France', although he could not determine whether or not the regent leaned in that direction.[48] Certainly, despite being well looked after by the latter, he detected Morton's manner as distinctly less cordial than formerly.[49] Nevertheless, he was reassured by Sir James Balfour that this 'marvellous alteration' was partly a reaction to unremitting English piracy against Scottish ships, not to mention the failure of the English government to curb it, and disappointment that no agreement had been made regarding an alliance.[50] Consequently, Killigrew was adamant that a treaty with Morton's government was imperative unless 'want thereof, by appearance will endanger the loss of their good affections', and, in addition, he strongly recommended about £2,000 being allocated annually as pensions for Morton and the leading members of his council.[51]

Nevertheless, there is every likelihood that the regent played on English fears of France, since he must have been well aware that therein lay his strongest card in any bid for a closer alignment with England. Undoubtedly, at this stage, the French did have certain designs on Scotland although their activities seem to have been confined to the second half of 1574. Thus, in July, for example, Catherine de Medicis exhorted her ambassador in London to promote French interests in Scotland,[52] while, in October, she sent advance notice of the arrival of one of her agents on a mission, supposedly 'pour la conservation de la bonne et ancienne amitie'.[53] But Morton was clearly unimpressed by these French overtures. In September, for instance, he warned Elizabeth of Catherine's stratagems and, two months later, in connection with the visit of her ambassador, he confided to Walsingham that he hoped the recent outbreak of plague in Edinburgh would make him have second thoughts about leaving France.[54]

Although Catherine's emissary never did come to Scotland, the question of Morton's allegiance was again a matter of some concern to Elizabeth's government in the earlier months of 1575, and Killigrew found himself once more in Edinburgh.[55] On this occasion, however, he was instructed to convey to Morton his mistress' regret that the league of protestant princes was no longer feasible 'since the said Princes are not so willing to enter therein as she looked for'. At the same time, the regent was to be consoled with reassurances of English assistance whenever the situation warranted it and to reiterate England's favourable record in recent years in this connection.[56] However, at the beginning of July, before Killigrew could make a significant impact, friendly relations between the two countries were suddenly dramatically threatened by an incident at Redeswyre on the English middle march.

If there are conflicting versions of some aspects of the Redeswyre affair, the main details, nonetheless, are relatively uncomplicated. On 7th July, Sir John Forster, warden of the English middle march, and Sir John Carmichael of that ilk, keeper of Liddesdale, both accompanied by a motley collection of followers, assembled at Redeswyre, just inside the English boundary, 'for the execution of justice only'. Admittedly, in the early stages, the meeting seems to have proceeded harmoniously, although the drinking in which both sides participated would probably, in the circumstances, have been better avoided. Ultimately, however, a dispute arose between Forster and Carmichael over the delivery to the latter of an Englishman whom he wished to prosecute. Harsh words ensued and, with their henchmen joining in, were followed by an exchange of blows in which the Scottish party was apparently coming off worse until the welcome arrival of reinforcements from Jedburgh. Thereupon, several Englishmen, including the deputy warden, Sir George Heron, a brother-in-law of Forster's, were slain. Carmichael, allegedly a reluctant participant, now, at this point, arrested the English warden and another deputy, Cuthbert Collingwood, taking them, with a large number of their adherents, to Jedburgh to await Morton's instructions.[57]

The reaction of both Morton and Elizabeth's leading ministers was to endeavour to defuse the situation. The regent, for example, immediately contacted Walsingham regarding 'the unhappy accident fallen at the middle march' and sought English advice 'for eschewing further breach and mischief that hereon may grow'.[58] His next step was to summon 'such of the Council of Scotland as then could be had together most readily'; this body decided that, considering 'the nature of the said Warden, his disadvantage so freshly received, the recent slaughter of his brother-in-law and the multitude of broken men and disordered people under his rule', it would be in the interests of peace on the borders that 'he should be a little while stayed'.[59] Accordingly, Forster and certain others were brought to the regent's own residence at Dalkeith. Meanwhile, Morton, by the issue of proclamations and strict instructions to his wardens about the need to preserve law and order, strove to maintain peace on the marches. Subsequently, after about a fortnight's custody, Forster and his colleagues, on indicating that 'their tarry was somewhat scaithful to them', were released on condition that they promised to return if required to do so.[60]

As far as Walsingham was concerned, while he was somewhat disconcerted about the death of the deputy warden and the treatment of Sir John Forster, he was reluctant to ask for too severe measures against Carmichael on account of his strong ties with the regent. Instead, he suggested in a note to him that the solution lay in a joint commission 'who may without partiality examine how the disorder grew'.[61] In fact, the only person on either side to adopt a really intransigent attitude was the queen herself. Indeed, Elizabeth's annoyance at the arrest of an English warden was so intense that Walsingham, writing to Burghley on 3rd August, described her as 'so seasoned with choler that he thinks they may take their leave of the amity of Scotland'.[62]

Morton, however, had no intention of permitting a border skirmish to endanger the accord between the two nations permanently, and recommended that Elizabeth should suspend judgement until discussions had taken place between her representative, the earl of Huntingdon, and himself.[63] These talks, during which Huntingdon, according to his biographer, 'found a Scot he could unreservedly admire',[64] began on the boundary of the middle march in mid-August and eventually produced, on 6th September, a declaration by Morton wherein, though suitably placatory, he stressed the fact that he was confident that Elizabeth would, on reflection, 'esteem him to have done that thing which most probably and apparently serves to keep quietness for continuance of the peace, deserving her good allowance and thanks in that respect'.[65] This testimony was followed a week later by the signature at Foulden, Berwickshire, of a mutual agreement formally resolving the whole incident. The Scottish signatories were Morton, Patrick, lord Lindsay, Robert Pitcairn, commendator of Dunfermline, Mark Ker, commendator of Newbattle, Sir James Hume of Coldenknowes and John Sharpe, advocate, and, by its terms, amicable relations were officially restored and a joint commission appointed to bring the principal offenders to justice. In addition, 'since it appears that her highness esteems her honour herein offended, for further saisfaction of her highness and declaration that the regent will leave nothing undone that in honour and reason may satisfy her', it was also agreed that eight hostages would be sent to Berwick to remain there or wherever the queen should transfer them and that Carmichael would be delivered 'to abide simply such punishment as her majesty shall determine'.[66]

Undoubtedly, in the summer of 1575, the Redeswyre affair seemed of great consequence, and Morton and his border officials were certainly alarmed about its possible repercussions. On July 26th, for example, lord Maxwell, warden of the west march, wrote to Sir Patrick Vaus of Barnbarroch notifying him of a day of truce on 10th August and also observing that, because of 'the laitt cummeris on the middill bordouris', lord Scrope, his opposite number, intended to be present in force at this meeting. Therefore, Maxwell, who was to issue similar instructions to Vaus about another day of truce in September, recommended on this occasion that Barnbarroch should ensure his own warden was adequately protected.[67] In another instance, on 5th August, the regent himself advised William Ker of Cessford, warden of the middle march, to stand 'as far on your guard until we see what success matters take'.[68]

Nevertheless, on reflection, Redeswyre was never much more than yet another chapter in the troubled history of the Anglo-Scottish frontier. Moreover, the main reason for its prominence was indisputably queen Elizabeth's imperious reaction to it. Her warden, Sir John Forster, was a man of very questionable character, aptly described in one recent history of the borders as 'neck-deep in deals and arrangements with law breakers'.[69] Moreover, he was subsequently to be involved, about ten years afterwards, in another incident similar to Redeswyre which was to lead to a government investigation of his administration.[70] Yet Elizabeth could describe the arrest of this unscrupulous rogue as a matter which could 'in no ways be excused' and could threaten 'prosecuting that just revenge that she is provoked to'.[71] Incontrovertibly, this was a distinctly overbearing and irascible stand to adopt.

Morton, on the other hand, undoubtedly handled the affair in a more statesmanlike manner. In the first instance, there patently was an inflammable situation on the middle march which Forster's precipitate release could have worsened. Furthermore, he was conciliatory and prepared to negotiate over an event which Elizabeth chose, perversely, to regard as a diplomatic insult, but which, as her own officials recognised, was essentially a consequence of the turbulent condition of the borders. As Huntingdon remarked, 'if the said feuds had not been so many and great amongst the people assembled on both sides, those stirs and slaughters had not been done'.[72]

Nonetheless, Elizabeth's high-handed manner serves to illustrate one point, namely her estimate, in the prevailing international political climate, of Scotland's value as an ally. In other words, when there was no danger of her neighbour being utilised as a *point d'appui* by France or Spain for attacking England, she obviously regarded Scotland as an unimportant minor power and treated her regent accordingly. In short – and the complaisant behaviour of the Scottish delegation who, in September, 1575 were said by Huntingdon to be prepared 'to seek peace on their knees' rather than provoke hostilities with England substantiates this conclusion[73] – Scotland, at times, was no more than a client state of England's and the Redeswyre episode simply another example of what has been termed 'satellite diplomacy'.[74]

The interval between the settlement of the Redeswyre crisis and Morton's dismissal in March, 1578 has been fairly accurately described as 'practically a blank page'.[75] Thus, there was little diplomatic activity apart from some talk in February, 1577 of reviving the idea of 'a general combination between all Princes of the religion'[76] and, the following September, as a result of growing English concern about the deterioration in relations between Morton and the nobility, a brief visit by Robert Bowes, treasurer of Berwick.[77]

However, early in 1578, largely because of Morton's unstable position within Scotland and unfavourable developments in the Netherlands, there were indications of a greater English initiative. Thus, on 30th January, Thomas Randolph was instructed to join Bowes at Berwick before they both proceeded to Edinburgh. Randolph, moreover, had authority to discuss a 'mutual contract of amity' and, in a postscript, added significantly after the news of the Dutch defeat by Spanish forces at Gembloux had reached England, was given an assurance that 'her majesty will not stick at money, considering how much it stands her upon to assure Scotland to her'.[78] Whether Morton, at this juncture, could have obtained his long-awaited alliance with England would still seem doubtful, especially when the essentially devious nature of Elizabeth's policy is borne in mind. However, the possibility did not arise, since the upheaval of 8th March saw him excluded from public affairs. As the ex-regent in temporary retirement observed shortly afterwards to Burghley, 'There rests not now in me that ability to do good whereunto I was always disposed and inclined during the while that I bore the charge'.[79]

Morton, once he had effected his restoration, wasted no time in renewing the quest for closer links with England. Thus, on 17th June, Robert Pitcairn, commendator of Dunfermline, was given his instructions for a mission in which border matters, piracy and the king's claim to the estate of the recently deceased countess of Lennox were included but whose principal object was 'the ratification and confirmation of the peace and amity contracted in the first year of her reign'.[80]

On Friday, 25th July, Pitcairn had his first audience with the queen and her council where he raised the various considerations within his remit as well as, it would appear, the question of English financial assistance towards the provision of a bodyguard for king James VI.[81] He was given a cordial reception, perhaps assisted by the fact that Morton, in the hope of affecting the queen's decision, had taken the precaution beforehand of contacting certain influential councillors and sympathisers including Walsingham himself.[82] In addition, he had written to Sir Ralph Sadler, who previously had served on many missions to Scotland and was well acquainted with the ex-regent, requesting him 'to continew as he have worthelie done heirtofore and be a gude meane unto our said dearrest sister upoun the hering of our trustie and weil belovit counselar, Robert'.[83] Nonetheless, Pitcairn returned empty-handed. Elizabeth, while welcoming Scottish assurances of friendship and reciprocating them, had studiously avoided what the French ambassador, always an interested party, described as 'une ligue offensive et defensive entre l'Ecosse at l'Angleterre'.[84]

On the other hand, Morton's anglophile attitude stood him in good stead during his confrontation with the Argyll-Atholl faction in August, 1578. At the height of the emergency, for example, he had the knowledge that English forces, at Elizabeth's express command, were stationed on the border poised to attack, if necessary, the territories of Cessford and Coldenknowes, the border allies of his adversaries.[85] Moreover, at Falkirk, when the rival armies actually faced each other and seemed about to commence fighting, it was owing largely to the diplomatic ability of Robert Bowes, Elizabeth's ambassador, that a bloody and probably disastrous conflict, as far as Morton was concerned, was averted.[86]

The persecution of the Hamiltons during 1579 certainly produced some repercussions on Anglo-Scottish relations, and Elizabeth complained on several occasions that the retrospective punishment of the Hamiltons contravened the Perth agreement and arrangements previously made with her.[87] Indeed, in a letter written to king James in November, 1579, she pointedly reminded him that Morton, in June, 1573, 'by a writing under his hand', had specifically guaranteed that her suggestions regarding the Hamiltons 'should be followed and fulfilled'.[88] Nonetheless, it was the impact on Scottish affairs of Esmé Stewart, subsequently earl of Lennox, which dominated the final part of Morton's administration. By April, 1580, both he and Elizabeth were displaying a mutual concern about the Frenchman's ascendancy.

Lennox, in Morton's view, presented a serious threat to his supremacy and was all the more dangerous on account of his supposed connections with France. However, although Morton could allege that, as a result of the influence of this contender for royal favour, the adolescent monarch had been persuaded 'to commend and to be contented to hear the practices of France beyond his accustomed manner',[89] just how deeply Lennox was actually involved in the tangled skein of European political intrigue must remain problematical. In fact, it would seem much more likely his affinities lay with the house of Guise and its ally, Philip of Spain. Certainly, shortly after Morton's downfall, the French ambassador in London acquainted his master, king Henry III, with information concerning Spanish involvement in Scotland, and, significantly, linked Lennox with this activity.[90]

For Elizabeth, the arrival and promotion of a French nobleman in Scotland was an unpleasant development fraught with all manner of sinister possibilities. Accounts of interviews before he left France with the former archbishop of Glasgow, James Beaton, and, equally incriminating, the Duke of Guise, bred instant suspicion.[91] Eventually, by the summer of 1580, he was being branded by Walsingham as both a papal emissary and 'a man especially chosen by the French . . . to bring in that nation to the utter overthrow of Scotland and the disquiet of England'.[92] Consequently, Elizabeth, on 17th April, following a plea from Morton 'for the expedition of her help' as well as further unfavourable reports from her agent, Nicholas Errington, ordered Robert Bowes to undertake another mission to Scotland.[93]

Bowes, once he contacted Morton, discovered that he and his supporters had certain suggestions to offer as a remedy to their problems. They recommended, in the first place, that Elizabeth should make a general statement about her intention to protect the protestant religion in Scotland. Presumably this was intended to be both a warning to Lennox should he attempt any religious alterations and a guarantee to Morton and his associates of English intervention in such an eventuality. Their second proposal was that, in order to obtain greater influence over king James 'and thereby more readily stop the way of foreign practices and of discontented subjects', the English government should provide loans or subsidies to the Scottish crown. Finally, it was suggested that 'two young men in whom the king will have pleasure' – Angus and Mar were mentioned specifically – should always accompany him. In addition, there should also be 'one well chosen and wise counsellor', who should remain in court, 'to reduce things to the former course'. Not surprisingly, Morton himself was nominated for this latter position for which, as with that of royal companions, it was recommended there should be appropriate remuneration.[94]

These proposals, therefore, were apparently what Morton regarded as the basis for a solution to his current difficulties, and he believed if they were adopted by England, Lennox's attempt to supplant him could be thwarted. Such a conclusion may have been well-founded but, although Bowes disbursed some money which was sent by his government, apparently amounting to about £500,[95] Morton's suggestions, to all intents and purposes, were ignored. Consequently, as has been observed elsewhere, he toyed fleetingly with the possibility of reaching some agreement with his rival.

However, on 31st August, the vacillating policy of the English government took yet another turn when, alarmed at the implications of Lennox's custody of Dumbarton castle, Bowes, who had retired to Berwick in June, was commanded to return to Scotland.[96] The English privy council was now of the opinion, so it informed its ambassador, that, if Lennox were permitted to retain such authority as he now possessed, he would destroy the pro-English party in Scotland, cause widespread and costly damage on the borders and, in all probability, arrange either a French marriage for James or one equally hostile to English interests.[97] With Elizabeth's councillors in such a mood and still bitterly divided among themselves about the possibility of their own queen marrying the duc d'Alençon, brother of Henry III, Morton could be excused for imagining his earlier proposals were about to be implemented. Moreover, Bowes' recommendation that 'it was time he was well satisfied'[98] must have reinforced such a conclusion.

On the other hand, while Bowes was unquestionably sympathetic to Morton's interests, there is every likelihood that one of his communiqués shortly afterwards actually ensured that no English aid was forthcoming and that Morton would be left to his own devices. This was a letter he wrote to his government on 27th September in which he recounted a recent conversation with the Scottish treasurer, lord Ruthven. The gist of his interview with this important nobleman, who had recently deserted Morton, was his assurance that Lennox was powerless without the backing of the nobility and that, if the latter perceived 'any purpose in him to practise anything against the religion or amity with her majesty [they] would soon leave him alone and withstand his practices'. In the same bulletin, Bowes reported a similar conference with Robert Melville, Sir James Melville's brother and former 'castilian', in which he also insisted that support for Lennox did not necessarily imply any antipathy towards Elizabeth or the English alliance.[99] Clearly, although Bowes, in another report shortly afterwards, was anxious lest Morton should feel he was being surrendered 'as it were a prey to Lennox and his faction',[100] there was much less need for concern by England about developments in Scotland. Morton was probably unaware of Bowes' assessment of the situation or, for that matter, the response of his government. Nonetheless, in the last weeks of 1580, as Lennox consolidated his position even further, he undoubtedly must have regarded with increased misgivings the reluctance of the English government to commit itself further on his behalf.

For Morton, the essence of his foreign policy was patently the maintenance of harmonious relations with England, and, if possible, a permanent treaty with that country. Clearly, there was little alternative to this, and certainly, on two occasions when interests seemingly inimical to England were proving awkward, that is at the siege of Edinburgh castle in 1573 and in his struggle with the party of Argyll and Atholl in 1578, his friendship with England was invaluable. Yet, as witness the abortive mission of the commendator of Dunfermline in July, 1578, he was unable to persuade Elizabeth either to compromise her country by some league of mutual defence or even, as her various ambassadors frequently suggested, to furnish adequate financial subsidies. Therefore, the inevitable conclusion must be that such an alliance between the two nations was much more desirable and advantageous to Morton, especially once his influence waned, than it was to Elizabeth. 'A poor and unimportant kingdom well out of the mainstream of European politics', while a modern assessment of Scotland's significance in the second half of the sixteenth century,[101] is one which Elizabeth would also have endorsed. Her imperious treatment of the regent, for example, over the Redeswyre affair in 1575 is just one illustration of this attitude. Admittedly, there could be a flurry of ambassadorial activity by England if, as in 1574 and 1575 or even 1580, it was suspected that Morton was veering towards France or his position was in some jeopardy. However, once it was perceived that some of Lennox's adherents were anglophile in outlook, Elizabeth obviously regarded the threat from that direction as much less menacing and virtually abandoned her ally. Furthermore, her reluctance to commit herself fully to Morton's cause was to prevail when, as will shortly be seen, he was overthrown by his enemies.

NOTES

1. *R.P.C.*, ii, 235–38, 641–43; Berg and Lagercrantz, *Scots in Sweden*, 14–17.
2. *R.P.C.*, ii, 310–12, 412; *Public records*, (1885), App. II, pt. iv.
3. *C.S.P. Scot.*, iv, 430.
4. *C.S.P. Foreign* (1572–74), 210.
5. *C.S.P. Scot.*, iv, 363–64, 443.
6. *Ibid*, 454.
7. Fénélon, *Correspondence*, vii, 327; Grange admitted he had received 2,000 crowns from this source in December, *C.S.P. Scot.*, iv, 443.
8. *Ibid*, 441.
9. *Ibid*, 394.
10. *Ibid*, 452.
11. *Ibid*, 453.
12. *R.P.C.*, ii, 176–77.
13. *C.S.P. Scot.*, iv, 460.
14. *C.S.P. Foreign* (1572–74), 242–43, 269–70; *Bannatyne Misc.*, ii, 69–71. The advice about mining was later disregarded and a large mine was subsequently dug under the part of the castle known as the 'Spur', *C.S.P. Scot.*, iv, 565.
15. *C.S.P. Scot.*, iv, 503.
16. *Ibid*, 504.
17. *Ibid*, 457.

18. For Huntingdon and Smith, *see ibid*, 488–89 and *C.S.P. Foreign* (1572–74), 268–69.
19. *Ibid*, 233, 235–36.
20. *H.M.C. (Salisbury MSS)*, ii, 67.
21. *C.S.P. Scot.*, iv, 514.
22. *Ibid*, 520.
23. *Ibid*, 525.
24. *Ibid*, 529–30.
25. *R.P.C.*, ii, 218; *C.S.P. Scot.*, iv, 549–50.
26. *Ibid*, 552–53.
27. *Ibid*, 537, 539–40, 544.
28. *R.P.C.*, ii, 216–19.
29. *C.S.P. Scot.*, iv, 552–54, 564.
30. *Ibid*, 587.
31. Fénélon, *Correspondence*, v, 322.
32. *T.A.*, xii, 350.
33. *C.S.P. Scot.*, iv, 590.
34. *Ibid*, 559.
35. *Ibid*, 561.
36. *Ibid*, 562.
37. *Diurnal*, 333.
38. *C.S.P. Foreign* (1572–74), 348.
39. Melville, *Memoirs*, 255.
40. *C.S.P. Scot.*, iv, 595.
41. *D.N.B.*, xvi, 60–62.
42. *C.S.P. Scot.*, iv, 593–94.
43. *Ibid*, 625, 638.
44. *Ibid*, 663–64.
45. *Ibid*, 664.
46. Murdin, *State Papers*, 224–25.
47. *C.S.P. Scot.*, v, 33; *see also, ibid*, iv, 679, 682, v, 6, 25, 28.
48. *Ibid*, iv, 673.
49. *Ibid*, 679, 682.
50. *Ibid*, 679.
51. *Ibid*, v, 7.
52. Catherine de Medicis, *Lettres*, v, 63.
53. *Ibid*, 93.
54. *C.S.P. Scot.*, v, 60, 67.
55. *Ibid*, 83, 112–113.
56. *Ibid*, 152–54.
57. The most reliable account is provided by the earl of Huntingdon in *C.S.P. Foreign* (1575–77), 103–05; Forster's own version is given briefly in *H.M.C. (Salisbury MSS)*, ii, 101.

53. *C.S.P. Scot.,* v, 166.
59. *Ibid,* 186; since the date given for this meeting in the privy council register is 26th July, Morton presumably took the decision at an emergency session and had it endorsed later, *R.P.C.,* ii, 459.
60. *C.S.P. Scot.,* v, 186–87.
61. *Ibid,* 166–67.
62. *Ibid,* 170–71.
63. *Ibid,* 173.
64. Cross, *The Puritan Earl,* 204.
65. 'The Regent Morton's declaration to the earl of Huntingdon', *C.S.P. Scot.,* v, 185–88.
66. *Ibid,* 188–90.
67. Vaus, *Correspondence,* i, 96–97, 184–85.
68. *H.M.C. Rep. xiv,* App. part iii, 34–35.
69. Fraser, *Steel Bonnets,* 268.
70. *C.S.P. Border,* i, 232.
71. *C.S.P. Scot.,* v, 184.
72. *C.S.P. Foreign* (1575–77), 105.
73. *C.S.P. Scot.,* v, 175.
74. Lee, 'The Fall of the Regent Morton', *Journal of Mod. Hist.,* xxviii, 1956.
75. Read, *Walsingham,* ii, 140.
76. *C.S.P. Scot.,* v, 226–27.
77. *C.S.P. Foreign* (1577–78), 144–46.
78. *C.S.P. Scot.,* v, 268–70, 271.
79. *Ibid,* 285.
80. *Ibid,* 297–300; *R.P.C.,* ii, 707–08.
81. *C.S.P. Scot.,* v, 309, 312–13.
82. *Ibid,* 302.
83. Sadler, *Papers,* ii, 343–44.
84. Teulet, *Papiers,* ii, 382.
85. *C.S.P. Foreign* (1578–79), 138; Bowes, *Correspondence,* 11.
86. *C.S.P. Scot.,* v, 317–18.
87. E.g. *ibid,* 349–50, 358–59, 381–82.
88. *Ibid,* 359.
89. *Ibid,* 412.
90. Teulet, *Papiers,* ii, 443–44.
91. *C.S.P. Foreign* (1579–80), 50; *C.S.P. Scot.,* v, 356.
92. *Ibid,* 493.
93. *Ibid,* 388–89, 396–98.
94. *Ibid,* 424.
95. *Ibid,* 443.
96. *Ibid,* 492–93.
97. *Ibid,* 504.

98. *Ibid*, 514.
99. *Ibid*, 514–16.
100. *Ibid*, 524.
101. Smith, *Reign of James VI & I*, 8.

10

The Final Months

Morton's administration officially ended with his arrest and imprisonment on 31st December, 1580. Initially, after a brief spell in Holyrood, he was incarcerated in Edinburgh castle but, on the afternoon of Wednesday, 18th January, he was transferred, on the orders of the privy council, to the Lennox stronghold of Dumbarton castle.[1] On this journey he was accompanied by a guard which included the earl of Glencairn, lords Robert Stewart and Seton and the lairds of Coldenknowes, Drumquhassill and Manderston as well as an armed detachment of a hundred men from the city council.[2] This development, which had been rumoured the previous week,[3] was clearly a precautionary measure by the new government which obviously hoped that, with Morton removed from the capital, there would be less likelihood of his being freed by his supporters. Thus, on 22nd January, king James VI, in conversation with Randolph, the English ambassador, confided that Morton had been shifted to Dumbarton because his council was concerned 'what practices his friends would use either to give him intelligence or to carry him away'.[4] However, no doubt his opponents also appreciated that, with Morton well out of the way, they could concentrate on consolidating their position within the country. Furthermore, since Morton had not been executed immediately, it is clear that Lennox and his followers were disappointed with the information provided by Sir James Balfour of Pittendreich who had returned from France about the same time as Morton's arrest. Obviously, he had come back without any really incriminating evidence of his part in the Darnley murder.[5] Presumably, the Lennox faction now had some misgivings about its own strength and the repercussions which might occur, both within and without Scotland, should Morton be eliminated too hastily.

Morton, as has been seen, had been unable to prevent Lennox establishing an impressively large faction and, when his overthrow did take place, the bulk of his support lay largely among his own relatives and kinsmen. Unquestionably, the most important member of this group was his nephew, Archibald, earl of Angus. He, for example, shortly before his uncle was taken from Edinburgh, was reported to be active in Fife rallying support for him and, by the date of his departure for Dumbarton, he had, by one account, 'convocat together about two thousand hors'. However, since Morton's escort warned him that his life was only secure provided his friends made no effort to rescue him, any plans to liberate him en route to his new gaol were abandoned 'least his life sould be in hazard'.[6]

Unfortunately, for both Angus and Morton, time was not on their side, as the new regime had already taken steps to lessen the possibility of a successful counter-revolution. Thus, on 13th January, the anti-Morton Ker of Cessford, warden of the middle march, was additionally appointed keeper of Liddesdale in place of John Carmichael of that ilk, a noted adherent of Morton.[7] Furthermore, the day before Morton was to be transported to Dumbarton, as a precaution against any possible rescue attempts a proclamation was issued ordering certain specified relatives and friends of Morton's as well as 'all utheris the said Erlis servantis and propir dependors' to return home and 'on na wyse to repair to his Hienes presence and court or to the burgh of Edinburgh or to ony uther place quhair they sall understand his Majestie to be for the tyme quhill the said triall be done or that they have his Hienes express licence with avise of his Counsale to the contrary'. Among those named were Morton's natural sons, James and Archibald, his half-brother, George Douglas of Parkhead, Malcolm Douglas of Mains, George Auchinleck of Balmanno and his two brothers, and Archibald Douglas, formerly constable of Edinburgh castle.[8] In fact, according to Calderwood, Angus and Douglas of Lochleven were also meant to be included on this list but, on James VI's orders, their names were 'scraipped out'.[9] In addition to these individuals, the notorious Archibald Douglas, parson of Glasgow and senator of the college of justice, had already been denounced and had his property forfeited.[10]

The next significant measure undertaken by Lennox was to have the privy council on 7th February announce, allegedly on account of 'divers incursiones, stowthis, reiffis and depredationes', a general levy of the whole realm for service on the borders. However, since this proclamation also referred to the fact that queen Elizabeth 'for the terrour of the saidis thevis and brokin men and saulftie of hir peciable and gude subiectis intendis to place sum forces upoun the Bourdouris', Lennox patently was making preliminary preparations to tackle his other main threat – Morton's English allies.[11]

As far as the English government was concerned, the news of Morton's deposition was decidedly unwelcome and provoked a prompt reaction. Hence, on 6th January, the veteran diplomat, Thomas Randolph, had been dispatched northwards with instructions to convey his queen's displeasure at recent events, especially the part played in them by Lennox who was only in Scotland, so it was stated, 'to breed some alteration in the State, however it be dissembled in the meantime and to turn him [i.e. James VI] away from the true service of God and to establish in that realm the Romish religion'. If, so Randolph was instructed, he was unable to convince king James of Lennox's real intentions, he should instead 'enter into conference with the party which you shall find and know to wish well to the king and have a desire to have the practices of D'Aubigny encountered'. Randolph, moreover, in order to assist this body, was, if necessary, to utilise certain forces which would be placed on the borders under the command of the earl of Huntingdon, president of the council of the north.[12]

Accordingly, just over a week later, the English privy council, because 'the Queen of England has been given to understand of the disorderly proceedings in Scotland', ordered Huntingdon to raise two thousand infantry and five hundred cavalry for service on the frontier.[13] In charge of these units was lord Hunsdon, governor of Berwick, who, like certain members of the privy council such as Francis Walsingham and the earl of Leicester, was a powerful advocate of English intervention on behalf of Morton.[14] Thus, on 29th January, for example, in a letter to Randolph, Walsingham reminded him that, by the terms of his military appointment, he was given 'full power to invade any part of Scotland as often as the Earl of Huntingdon, he or the rest of the Council of the north shall think expedient'.[15]

However, on 8th February, the English ambassador submitted a particularly pessimistic appraisal of Morton's position. In his opinion, only Angus and the earl of Mar of the leading noblemen could be regarded as definitely on Morton's side, whereas Lennox could certainly count on Argyll, Ruthven and Montrose, and probably Rothes and Lindsay. In addition, both Edinburgh and Perth supported the new administration and, although James Haliburton, provost of Dundee, remained loyal to Morton, his fellow councillors were 'so given to peace and particularities that hardly for any cause would they be moved'.[16]

Hunsdon, on the other hand, insisted that the situation was nothing like so gloomy as that outlined by Randolph and that Angus could almost certainly depend on the earls of Montrose, Mar, Glencairn and Rothes. In addition to these noblemen, so Hunsdon asserted, there were also lords Boyd and Cathcart, and possibly Lindsay and Ruthven, not to mention the powerful laird of Lochleven.[17] Doubtless this impression was formed as a result of conversations with the egregious Archibald Douglas who seems to have been able to influence the opinion not only of the governor of Berwick but also his colleagues, the earl of Huntingdon and Robert Bowes. Indeed, Randolph was later to observe, somewhat scathingly, that Bowes' assessment of developments in Edinburgh was largely based on his being 'led thereunto by Mr. A. Douglas – not the best instrument to appease troubles'.[18]

Understandably, Randolph's efforts at diplomacy were sometimes criticised not only by Huntingdon and the English privy council as well;[19] nonetheless, he was in the best position to gauge the political mood of the country. Consequently, his estimate of the situation seems infinitely more realistic than that of the governor of Berwick. The latter may have been right about Boyd at this juncture, and certainly he was correct in his assessment of the laird of Lochleven. Nevertheless, Montrose, whose illicit relationship with Angus's wife was soon to be uncovered,[20] was hardly an ally of Morton's nephew – a fact underlined by his subsequent appointment as commander of the royal army.[21] Likewise, Glencairn, that is, the son of the former ally of the regent, although he might have favoured the English alliance and, in March, 1581, was reported by Randolph as being one of the few noblemen favourably disposed towards England,[22] regarded himself as 'hardly dealt with' by Morton, and consequently must be looked upon as a very doubtful partisan.[23] Finally, if Lindsay and Ruthven are regarded as of uncertain allegiance, there is lord Cathcart whose disposition is also less easy to determine. Certainly, his attendance at the privy council in the first half of 1581 was conspicuously infrequent and, apart from attendance at the convention of estates in February, he was present on only one occasion between January and June, 1581.[24] It is possible, therefore, that he was awaiting the outcome of events before committing himself.

Meanwhile, Lennox, following his general mobilisation for duty on the borders, now called a convention of the estates for 20th February.[25] By so doing, he could request the money which had to be raised in taxation to pay any royal army while, at the same time, by studying the attitudes of those present he could assess the remaining extent of support, if any, for Morton. Accordingly, at this meeting of the estates, it was decided that, 'Forasmekle as the Kingis Majestie being informit of the preparationes making for armes in sindrie partis of Europe and that his dearest sister and cousine the quene of England . . . hes raisit sum forces and draivin thame towards the frontiers of the realme', the sum of £40,000 should be raised for the nation's defence.[26] Lennox, moreover, obviously convinced by this stage of his own ascendancy, permitted Randolph to make what turned out to be a polemical attack against him to the convention wherein he outlined the insidious nature of his role in the universal papal conspiracy against protestantism. This remarkable outburst was concluded by the English ambassador's assuring the members of the estates[27] that 'If the greatness of Monsierr D'Aubigny shall seem to terrify or stay them from reformation of him', they could depend on his government to overthrow him and 'procure that the earl of Morton may be recovered from D'Aubigny's possession to be openly tried by the laws of Scotland'.[28]

If Lennox now felt, as seems likely, that the defeat of his opponents was within sight, Angus, conversely, must have realised that any likelihood of dislodging him was becoming increasingly remote and that a final desperate effort on behalf of his uncle was imperative. Consequently, as soon as he had left the convention, departing, in fact, before it was over,[29] he was frantically contacting a number of noblemen and lairds whom he hoped would favour the Douglas cause. He began, apparently, by endeavouring to raise support from among his own followers on the borders and then, in company with the earl of Mar, made overtures to such possible allies as the latter's uncles, the commendators of Cambuskenneth and Dryburgh, as well as Boyd, Glencairn and Douglas of Lochleven.[30] Thus, Mar, for example, in a letter to the laird of Lochleven seeking his co-operation, urged Morton's cousin 'to keip the apoyntit day tharof in this toune for sic causis as I haif ado quhilkis ar of gret Importance and can nocht tak guid effect at the presence of my freindis of quhilk number I esteme zow ane of the speciallis and tharfor I vill luik for na excuse of zow at the forsaid day'.[31]

About the same time, the feasibility of a direct assault on Dumbarton castle was also considered but, probably on Morton's own recommendation, the project was abandoned as being too hazardous. The reason for this decision would appear to have been that both Angus and Morton feared that the custodian of the fortress would use the occasion of an attack on the castle as a pretext for putting him to death.[32]

At this stage, clearly discomfited by the extent of support for Morton which could be guaranteed within Scotland, and with the loyalty of Boyd, for example, regarded as distinctly uncertain,[33] Angus and Mar appealed to lord Hunsdon for English assistance. Unquestionably, he and Huntingdon were both very sympathetic and, if the Spanish ambassador in London can be believed, at one stage they actually suggested a bogus attack by some of the followers of Angus on English property as an excuse for an incursion by him across the border.[34] However, Hunsdon was also a realist and he reluctantly informed Morton's allies that English aid was not forthcoming because 'their party was neither sufficient nor so to be trusted as in such a cause was to be looked for [and] it was not thought good to hazard Her Majesty's force without better assurance'.[35]

In this fashion, the possibility of English intervention on Morton's behalf evaporated. Shortly afterwards, Randolph, having narrowly escaped an assassination attempt in which a couple of shots fired by an unknown assailant struck the window immediately above where he was writing, left Edinburgh and retired to Berwick.[36] Whereupon, his government, disbanding its border levies, suggested a joint commission to discuss Anglo-Scottish relations and resolve outstanding problems.[37]

Meanwhile, Lennox stepped up his campaign against his adversaries by having certain of Morton's kinsmen and servants arrested. Thus, during the course of March, William Douglas of Whittinghame, George Auchinleck of Balmanno, William Hume, younger of Spott, as well as Alexander Nesbit and Alexander Jardine, two chamberlains attending Morton at Dumbarton, were summoned for interrogation.[38] Obviously, Lennox hoped that, either by threats of torture or its actual application, Morton's confidants would divulge information about the intentions of Angus or damning evidence to incriminate Morton himself when he was brought to trial. Accordingly, George Auchinleck, whom the granting of an early remission and the gift of an escheat would suggest was quite prepared to desert Morton and ingratiate himself with the new regime,[39] supposedly confessed that Morton 'was privy to the poisoning of the earl of Atholl'.[40] As for Douglas of Whittinghame, he apparently required little persuasion before allegedly providing his inquisitors with startling revelations of a plot concocted by Angus for the elimination of Lennox, Montrose and Argyll, and the removal of king James to England. In addition, he was also supposed to have declared that a letter between James Beaton, former archbishop of Glasgow, and Lennox, which had been used by Randolph to compromise the royal favourite, was, in fact, a forgery perpetrated by Archibald Douglas.[41]

While the second allegation of Douglas of Whittinghame may have been well-founded, the story of the assassination plot and the seizure of the king is decidedly questionable. Indeed, that Whittinghame ever made such a statement was subsequently contradicted by someone present at his interrogation, and Hunsdon, the recipient of this information, recalling a similar earlier scare in 1580 involving king James, acutely observed that, on that occasion, Argyll was believed to be the author of the rumour.[42] In short, Whittinghame, as his speedy remission for involvement with Morton emphasises,[43] undoubtedly assisted the enquiries of Lennox and his party but just to what extent is open to question.

Nevertheless, under the circumstances, Lennox undoubtedly believed he had sufficient grounds to justify concerted action against Morton's followers. Thus, on 14th March, 1581, James and Archibald, his two natural sons, John Carmichael younger of that ilk, Malcolm Douglas of Mains and William Douglas of Lochleven were ordered to appear before the privy council 'to answer to sic things as sal be inquirit of them'.[44] The same day, Angus, 'for the suretie of his Hienes maist noble person, eschewing of truble, furthering of justice and certaine utheris ressonable caussis', was commanded to enter ward within six days beyond the river Spey.[45] A few days later, there followed another edict prohibiting any communication with him since, so it was stated, 'the King and Council ar credibilie informit that divers his Hienes subjectis hes bene movit of lait be Archibald, Erll of Angus and utheris on his behalf to ryse and tak armes for purposes suspitious'.[46]

Angus, however, still hopeful of English support, ignored these privy council warnings and, by his retention of such fortresses as Tantallon, Cockburnspath and Douglas, continued to pose a minor threat to Lennox's security. Consequently, on 27th March, the previous ban against him and his followers was repeated and, with those in charge of these garrisons, he was commanded, under pain of treason, to surrender them within forty-eight hours.[47] One of those affected by a similar prohibition was George Douglas of Parkhead[48] who, as a consequence of retaining 'ye toure, fortalice and castell of Torthorwall and tressonabill withalding of ye same', subsequently forfeited his lease of lead mines in Orkney.[49]

But, by this date, Lennox, in fact, was on the verge of total victory while his opponents, conversely, were about to disintegrate completely. A significant development contributing towards this outcome and also occurring on 27th March was the renunciation by ten border lairds of 'all and quhatsomevir bandis of manrent or service made and subscrivit be thame in ony tyme by gane for the service of Archibald Erll of Angus, lord Douglas and Abirnethie or any utheris'.[50] This meant, for example, that Andrew Rutherford of Hundalee, John Rutherford of Hunthill and Thomas Turnbull of Bedrule, who had signed bonds of manrent with Angus quite recently, were now forsaking him.[51] Similarly, George Douglas, younger of Bonjedburgh, whose father, as has been seen, owed his promotion to joint warden of the middle march between December, 1576 and March, 1578 to Morton, was giving notice that he at least had changed his allegiance.

Lennox, not unexpectedly, took advantage of these defections from the Angus camp by almost immediately instructing Douglas of Lochleven to place himself in exile by 8th April 'beyond the wattir of Cromartie'.[52] At the same time, pressure was being exerted on the earl of Mar by his uncle, Alexander Erskine, who warned his nephew of the dire consequences ensuing 'gif he consent or follow furth the evill and desperat course of the Earl of Angus'.[53] The youthful earl heeded his uncle's admonition and, in this manner, Angus lost both Stirling castle, which was controlled by Mar, and a valuable confederate. Finally, on 22nd April, John Johnstone of that ilk, one of the most loyal Douglas partisans, joined the others on the list of rebels and, one week later, his wardenship was transferred to his great rival, John, lord Maxwell, a prominent supporter of Lennox.[54]

Lennox's triumph meant that Angus, with the remnant of his followers, must seek refuge in England. Thus, on 16th May, Robert Bowes, treasurer of Berwick, reported that Angus, 'seeing the end of toleration to approach and distrusting to find the king's favour without his submission to unreasonable conditions', intended applying for shelter in England.[55] On 8th June, Morton's nephew, accompanied by James and Archibald Douglas, James Carmichael, younger of that ilk, Malcolm Douglas of Mains and a number of servants, arrived at Carlisle where they were taken under the protection of Henry, lord Scrope, governor of that city and warden of the west march.[56]

Angus's bid to save Morton failed for a number of reasons. In the first instance, Lennox was in a very strong position, having complete control over king James VI who automatically approved all his decisions. Further-more, the great majority of the privy council was on his side. Indeed, of the thirty or so official members of that body, possibly only Cathcart, Herries and Lindsay, at least on the basis of their poor attendance at the council, could be regarded as in any way sympathetic towards Morton. Moreover, albeit Lennox's taxation proposals 'took no execution' and another conven-tion for the purpose of raising money proved necessary in April,[57] his action in summoning the estates proved decisive in that it gave him the authority to recruit a royal army. This force, even if it was, in Randolph's view, a non-descript one,[58] nonetheless afforded some protection in the event of a possible English invasion and also meant that Lennox could concentrate on the task of having Angus and his associates proscribed.

Angus, conversely, found only meagre support for his uncle within Scotland. Admittedly, much of the responsibility for this poor response can be attributed to Morton's own latter-day unpopularity. Nevertheless, there is every chance that there would have been a stronger reaction on his behalf if queen Elizabeth and her government had acted differently. Elizabeth, it has been seen, having initially mobilised her forces on the borders and sent her ambassador to Edinburgh, proceeded to recall and disband her levies just at the moment when Angus's predicament was most critical. Granted, the English government was preoccupied, as has been emphasised in one modern analysis of Morton's downfall,[59] with the marriage negotiations still in the offing between Elizabeth and the duke d'Alençon, and was consequently reluctant to offend the French by any incursions into Scotland. Unquestionably, this was the case although, considering that, in February, 1581, Henry III of France was being informed by his ambasador in London that Lennox was in league with his rival, the king of Spain, it would appear that Elizabeth laid too much stress on the consequences of an aggressive policy towards Scotland.[60] Indeed, this argument is strengthened by the reply of Henry III two months later to a complaint by the former archbishop of Glasgow about Elizabeth's support for Morton and the presence of Huntingdon on the Scottish frontier. On that occasion, the French king told Beaton that he would not 'deal in anything that might impeach their entire amity'.[61]

On the other hand, it is possible that, on Morton's arrest, Elizabeth initially acted out the pique at this maltreatment of her principal supporter in Scotland. However, once she had reflected on recent Spanish success in Portugal and Philip's recovery in the Netherlands, as well as his utilisation of disaffection in Ireland, she may have regretted her original impetuosity. Such additional considerations as the cost of a Scottish expeditionary force and the poor condition of her border levies were further incentives for restraint. In other words, as the advantages of nearness to France became increasingly attractive, so events in Scotland became correspondingly less significant. Besides, there were Ruthven's fairly recent assurances that, despite Lennox's ascendancy, most Scottish noblemen still held her in high regard. This was another good reason for allowing her anger, genuine or otherwise, to subside.

Whatever the reasons for Elizabeth's vacillation, the consequences for Morton's party of her ineffectual policy were twofold. Firstly it gave Lennox a pretext for mobilising a Scottish army, and this was, in Morton's case, as Sir James Melville correctly opined, 'rather the cause to haist his wrak'.[62] Secondly, by failing to intervene openly, Elizabeth presented Angus with a well-nigh impossible undertaking since, without visible signs of English assistance, support for Morton was inevitably confined to his friends and kinsmen.

Lennox, once Angus was rendered impotent, with his dwindling band of supporters confined to a few Douglas strongholds, could, with his accomplice, the earl of Arran,[63] tackle the question of Morton's fate.

Accordingly, a meeting of the leading members of the council to discuss this topic was held at Dalkeith, Morton's old residence, on 3rd May.[64] At this conference, it was decided to offer an ultimatum to Morton and his family, to Angus and to Archibald Douglas. This consisted of a series of humiliating conditions which were required to be accepted in return for Morton's life, though not his freedom. Thus, the former regent was expected to surrender to the crown Dalkeith and Blackness, the latter stronghold being under Morton's control as sheriff of Linlithgow; he was, in addition, to renounce his heritable sheriffdoms of Linlithgow and Lothian as well as his post of high admiral. James Douglas was to lose his commendatorship of Pluscarden, and Archibald his pension from Balmerino in favour of lord Seton's sons, while their other pensions from the bishoprics of St. Andrews and Aberdeen were to be rendered to the crown. In addition, 'The whole charges of the soldiers levied and the extraordinary charge that the King has been at since the last of December', as well as certain bullion which he had 'caused to be coined', were to be repaid by Morton. As for his kinsman, Archibald Douglas, he was to continue to forfeit his parsonage of Glasgow and his position as a senator of the college of justice.[65]

Presumably these were the terms which Angus referred to as 'unreasonable conditions' when he had applied for permission to enter England. Moreover, his adversaries doubtless calculated that they would be rejected and that they then would be justified in arranging for Morton to stand trial for his life. Certainly this was what now followed.

Trial and Execution

On Tuesday, 23rd May, Montrose and Arran were instructed to bring Morton from Dumbarton[66] to Edinburgh, where he duly arrived four days later, and was confined in the house of his Edinburgh merchant friend, Robert Gourlay.[67] At this point, certain rumours began to circulate in the capital alleging that Morton, as well as being tried for his complicity in the Darnley affair, was to 'be burdynnit and accusit of sic thingis as wer done and execute in oure Soverane lordis name for the furthsetting of his authoritie and service alsweill during the tyme that the said Erll of Mortoun wes Regent . . .'[68] However, a proclamation quickly appeared denying such 'seditious and sclanderous bruittis', which obviously must have alarmed numerous prominent individuals,[69] and, on Thursday, 1st June, Morton was taken to the tolbooth to stand trial.[70]

Originally there was a lengthy indictment against him consisting of about twenty charges. Calderwood, for example, quotes nineteen accusations against Morton including involvement in the Chaseabout raid, 'conspiracie preceeding the murther of the king's father and concealing the same', consenting to and supporting Bothwell's marriage to queen Mary, the 'abstracting of the king's casualties', certain currency offences at the time of his deposition in March, 1578, and collusion, thereafter, with the Erskines in the Stirling castle *putsch*. In addition, there was participation in a conspiracy to seize the king at Doune in April, 1580, as well as being implicated in plots the same year on the life of Lennox, planning to escape while being transported from Edinburgh to Dumbarton, and transferring the bulk of his wealth to his natural son, James Douglas, who was alleged to have employed it for 'the maintenance of the King's rebels and furnishing of the English forces'. Finally, there were the charges that he had accepted English pensions and had been 'traffiquing with forrane princes specialle the Queene of England and States of Flanders'.[71]

It is interesting to note that there is no reference here to the poisoning of the earl of Atholl, one of the most serious allegations against Morton, and this would confirm that, despite intensive enquiries, there was still insufficient evidence available. Nonetheless, there undoubtedly was considerable substance to many of these accusations. Morton, for example, had temporarily supported Bothwell in 1567 at the time of the Darnley conspiracy and his subsequent marriage to queen Mary; as regent, he could quite easily have devised various means of denuding the royal treasury, not to mention, on his dismissal in 1578, proceeding to issue coins illegally; it is quite likely that he plotted Lennox's overthrow in 1580, and he certainly did consider escaping from custody while *en route* to Dumbarton. As for his wealth, if Melville is to be believed, his son James and a servant carried off 'his gould and silver . . . and eftervat hid in some secret partis'.[72] On the other hand, according to Calderwood, the whereabouts of his treasure, both at Dalkeith and Aberdour, were revealed under torture by George Auckinleck.[73] Finally, in matters of foreign affairs, he unquestionably did pursue an anglophile policy, thus laying himself open to the charge of shady dealings with England.

Nevertheless, the Lennox administration decided to 'slippe from the rest' and merely accuse Morton of complicity in the Darnley murder.[74] The reasons for so doing are fairly obvious. Apart from any delay which detailed examination of all these charges would have entailed, there was the undeniable fact that several of Lennox's existing government had served under Morton, and to continue with the original indictment must inevitably have produced embarrassing revelations as far as they were concerned. Indeed, the proclamation issued the day before Morton's trial was especially designed to allay such fears. In other words, royal servants such as Ruthven, Sir William Murray of Tullibardine, Robert Pitcairn, commendator of Dunfermline, Alexander Hay, clerk register, David Borthwick of Lochill, royal advocate, and Argyll, who had latterly been chancellor in Morton's government, had no desire to rake up the immediate past.

Morton's opponents, once they had decided how they would present their case, had then to ensure that they obtained the requisite verdict. This was done by selecting a jury which largely consisted of adherents of the Stewarts or of the ex-regent's enemies.[75] Thus, ignoring the earls of Argyll, Montrose and Glencairn, as well as lords Maxwell and Seton whose sentiments have been discussed already, there was on the jury Alexander, earl of Sutherland, a member of the Gordon family who doubtless regarded his kinsman Adam Gordon of Auchindoun as harshly treated by Morton. Certainly, like another member of the jury, James Stewart, lord Innermeath, he was, in contemporary opinion, 'matched with the houses of Lennox, Atholl and Arrol'.[76] Lord Ogilvie, it has been seen, had been imprisoned by Morton between 1576 and 1578, and his pro-Lennox sympathies were underlined by the appointment of his son as a gentleman of the king's bedchamber in October, 1580.[77] Then there was the master of Livingston, another gentleman of the king's bedchamber who came from a family with distinctly Marian tendencies, and who was so devoted to Lennox that he later accompanied him to France in 1583.[78] In short, of the jurymen present of noble extraction, only three, namely the earls of Eglinton and Rothes and lord Somerville, had no obvious allegiance to the Lennox faction. As for the other members of the jury, Sir William Livingston was a kinsman of the Livingstons and another gentleman of the king's bedchamber;[79] Sir Patrick Learmonth of Dairsie was provost of St. Andrews and a kinsman of Kirkcaldy of Grange's widow, Margaret Learmonth, whose interests he had recently been looking after;[80] Hepburn of Waughton, the remaining juryman, was also linked with Grange, having served with him in France, and Morton had specifically protested against his inclusion.[81] Unquestionably, with such a jury, the odds were stacked very strongly against the defendant.

On Thursday, 1st June, Morton's trial began in the Tolbooth, Edinburgh where, as James Melvill was to observe, 'oftentymes during his government he haid wrysted and throwin judgment partlie for gean wharto he was gein and partlie for particular favour'.[82] The verdict, of course, was a foregone conclusion and, after only a brief hearing, the earl of Montrose was able to announce, on behalf of the court, that they had unanimously found the ex-regent guilty of 'airt, pairt, foir knowledge and conceling of the treasonable and unnatural murthow foirsaid'.[83] At this point in the proceedings, there was a characteristic flash of the old Morton as he banged his staff on the courtroom floor and shouted indignantly, 'Art and part! Art and part! God knoweth the contrary'.[84] Indeed, if Calderwood is correct, he had every right to feel aggrieved since the jury had initially only found him guilty of concealing the conspiracy against Darnley. It had been Arran and Montrose, to give greater weight to the verdict and imply his actual participation in and direction of the events of February, 1567, who, allegedly, had insisted on the insertion of the damning phrase 'art and part'.[85] Not surprisingly, Morton's protest went unheeded and the court dempster proceeded to deliver the grim sentence of death. 'The said James Erll of Mortoun,' he announced, 'suld be had to ane geibbett beside the mercatt-croce of the said burgh of Edinburgh, and thair hangit quhill he wer dead; and thairefter drawin, quartarit and demanit as ane tratour.'[86]

This sentence, quickly mitigated by king James to one of execution,[87] was to be carried out the following day but, in the interval before this happened, Morton had a lengthy disquisition with several stalwart representatives of the kirk. Those who took part were Walter Balcanquhall, John Brand, James Carmichael, John Durie, David Fergusson, James Lawson and the moderator for that year, Robert Pont. Also in attendance at one point or another was Morton's old religious protagonist, John Davidson, minister of Liberton since 1579, and David Lindsay, minister for South Leith, who had interceded, unsuccessfully, with the regent on behalf of Kirkcaldy of Grange when the latter had requested him to do so in 1573. Moreover, 'the some of all the conference . . . and the chiefe thinges which they can remember' was subsequently recorded by Balcanquhall and Durie to become known as Morton's 'confession'.[88]

Unfortunately, Morton's answers to this interrogation by the clergy on the morning of his execution sheds little additional light on the more controversial aspects of his career. Thus, it began with a refutation of any complicity in the Darnley murder, although there was the admission that he had not discouraged his kinsman, Archibald Douglas, from participation. The explanation given for this oversight was the dangerous situation in which he was placed at the time and the fact that his kinsman was 'a depender of the erle Bothvel, making count for himself rather than a depender of myne'. Next, there was a vehement denial of any involvement in the Atholl poisoning, accompanied by the memorable rejoinder, 'Ffye, thair is overmeikle filthines in Scotland alreadie: God forbid that that vile practise of poysoning sould enter amonges us'. This statement was followed by the rejection of such allegations as having planned the Stirling *coup* of 1578, having plotted against Lennox, having been a pensioner of England or having conspired to take king James to that country and of having 'furnishit the queine of Englandis shuldeouris now last upoun the Borderis'. As for the kirk, while he admitted, perhaps not surprisingly considering his several illegitimate progeny, that he had been 'a filthie abusare of my body in the pleasures of the flesh', he refused to agree that he had been 'a grit hinderer of the materis of the kirke and authoritare of the bischopes'. On the contrary, in his opinion, he had always had the kirk's interests at heart and, if he had erred in his handling of church matters, it was done 'of ignorance and for laike of better knowledge' rather than from 'contempt or malice'. Finally, there was a justification of the imprisonment of the Edinburgh citizens arrested for contravening the bullion legislation, and an account of his deathbed conversation with John Knox and the advice to Angus that he should seek a reconciliation with king James. There was also a warning, which the ex-regent hoped the clegymen present would convey to his majesty, that his opponents sought to encompass more than his death and that they had 'sum other purpose in hand'. To put it bluntly, with the king surrounded by those 'knowin to be papistis and suspect to be enemies to the religione', the danger to protestantism was manifest. Indeed, in his estimation, 'the estait of the religion in this cuntrey appeired never to be in sic danger'.

This dialogue between Morton and the clergy was followed by prayers after which he handed over a small religious treatise written by the English reformer, John Bradford. This, apparently, had been given to him by lady Ormiston, wife of a prominent protestant laird in East Lothian, at the outset of his imprisonment, and he requested that it should now be returned to her. After breakfast, he was rejoined by the brethren, and this would seem to have been the first occasion when John Davidson was present since the pair of them were now reconciled. Morton, on his part, avowed he had never meant any harm to this critic of his religious policy, while the emotional Davidson responded by bursting into tears.

About two in the afternoon, Morton was given his last meal. At this point a delegation for the clergy, in order to contradict various rumours already circulating about his statements to them, departed forthwith to king James at Holyrood to furnish him with a true account of the interview. No sooner had they returned than Morton was being summoned by the executioner. However, just as he left Robert Gourlay's apartments, there was one final incident when one of his most bitter opponents, the earl of Arran, appeared demanding a written and signed confession. But this request the ex-regent absolutely refused to consider. 'I pray you truble me no moir with thea

P

thingis,' he told Arran, 'for now I have ane uther thing to advise upoun, that is, to prepair me for my God.' This seems to have satisfied his adversary since, before he set out again for the scaffold, the pair of them had forgiven each other. As Morton aptly commented. 'It is na tyme now to remember upoun querrallis'.[89]

It was four o'clock in the afternoon of Friday, 2nd June, 1581 when Morton reached the scene of his execution beside the Cross in Edinburgh's High Street. Among the crowd present to hear his final words and witness his execution was his old border antagonist, Ker of Ferniehirst, who was standing at the open window of a house adjacent to the scaffold 'with his large ruffes, delyting in this spectacle'. Another group in attendance were lord Seton and two of his sons who were watching from a stairway nearby, doubtless rejoicing in the proceedings just as much as Ferniehirst.[90] Morton, after making the customary protestation of condemned royal ministers that 'the king shall lose a guid servant this day', delivered a speech in similar vein to his conversations with the clergy but with the references to his kinsman, Archibald Douglas, omitted.[91] The oratory over, he took up position beside the instrument of execution known as 'the maiden'. This was a machine, similar to that later invention the guillotine, which Morton, accrding to Hume of Godscroft, had previously seen in operation in England and which he himself had introduced into Scotland.[92] Then there followed a short prayer by the minister of St. Giles, James Lawson, after which various individuals came forward for a final word of reconciliation with the ex-regent. The latter's last action was to place his head on the block. As he awaited sentence to be carried out by the hangman, who was resplendent in a new uniform specially purchased 'for honour of the towne', he cried out, 'Lord Jesus receave my soule! In thi handis, Lord I committ my spreit! Lord Jesus receave my soule'. And, still uttering these pious sentiments, his life was abruptly terminated.[93]

Morton's body lay on the scaffold covered only by a cloak until sunset, when it was removed to the Tolbooth to be buried thereafter in the course of the evening in Greyfriars churchyard.[94] His head, on the other hand, was 'sett upon a prick in the highest stone of the gavell of the Tolbuith towards the publict street',[95] where it remained until December, 1582. On the 14th of that month, with Angus back in favour as a result of the Ruthven Raid, king James ordered the town council to remove Morton's head from its position of prominence, and his nephew, assisted by the faithful Carmichael of that ilk, organised a decent interment. In this manner, Morton's last, if decaying, remains were 'layed in a fyne cloath, convoyed honorabilie and layed in the kist where his bodie was buried'.[96]

The Aftermath

While Morton's death may have been regarded by some of his countrymen as merely the realisation of an old prophecy about the Douglases suffering at the hands of the earls of Arran,[97] there can be no gainsaying the fact that he did not have a fair trial. Indeed, as he remarked to the members of the kirk on the day of his execution, 'It had been all alike to me gif I had bene as innocent as Sanct Stevin as gif I had been als guiltie as Judas, for I perceivit plainlie that there was nothing but my life sought . . .'.[98] Clearly, therefore, he was beheaded because the Lennox administration still feared him and the possibility that he might repeat his performance of 1578 and retrieve his position yet again. At the same time, there was the additional attraction of the numerous possessions in his hands, and those of his supporters, which would come the way of his adversaries if he was eliminated and his followers outlawed. Not unexpectedly, no time was wasted in redistributing these spoils.

Thus, Lennox himself did especially well, amassing, among other rewards, the lordship, regality and barony of Dalkeith and the baronies of Aberdour, Mordington and Whittinghame.[99] Over and above this, he obtained for himself gifts of escheat of the property of Malcolm Douglas of Mains and certain debts owing to Morton by Robert, earl of Buchan, William Douglas of Whittinghame and Robert Colville of Cleische as well as 'all sowmes of money auchtand to the said James erle of Morton be quhatsumevir persone or persons'.[100] In addition, his daughter, Henrietta, received a gift of escheat of a marriage, which had formerly been in the hands of Angus.[101]

Another individual who benefited handsomely was the earl of Arran. He had acquired, while still captain James Stewart, the pension of £500 per year from Balmerino abbey, previously a perquisite of James Douglas, commendator of Pluscarden, as well as a gift of escheat of a marriage also belonging to this natural son of Morton.[102] Moreover, on 13th June, 1581, the tack of the leadmines held by George Douglas of Parkhead also fell into his possession.[103] Furthermore, while one of his brothers, William Stewart of Monkton, received the lease of the teind sheaves of Lanark, forfeited by Angus,[104] another brother, Henry Stewart, gained possession of Morton's lands at Nether Gogar near Edinburgh.[105] Even one of his domestics benefited by being granted certain teind sheaves surrendered by Angus.[106]

Another member of the Stewarts who profited was James Stewart, son of Sir James Stewart of Doune. He was awarded the pension of £500 from the bishopric of Aberdeen which had once been the prerogative of another natural son of Morton's, Archibald Douglas, as well as the escheat of a tack formerly held by the regent himself.[107] Yet another Stewart beneficiary was Francis Stewart, nephew of Bothwell and subsequently the holder of that earldom himself. He acquired a lengthy catalogue of Douglas territories including Morton's sheriffdom of Edinburgh and Haddington, his office of high admiral and Angus's sheriffdom of Berwick and 'bailiary' of Lauderdale.[108]

Apart from the Stewarts, the other main recipients of the generosity of the Lennox administration were its faithful adherents, and in this category John, lord Maxwell undoubtedly features very prominently. Indeed, this nobleman, before Morton's trial had actually taken place, had come to an arrangement with Lennox whereby, on the former regent's being convicted, he would receive his earldom.[109] Accordingly, on 5th June, 1581, by a charter under the geat seal, Maxwell was appointed to the earldom of Morton, receiving the title about a fortnight later.[110] Thus, in this fashion, the Maxwells, at least for the time being, supplanted the Douglases.

Excluding Maxwell, there were others, such as the Campbells, Setons and Humes, who all profited from Morton's downfall. Thus, Argyll assumed Morton's office of sheriff of Linlithgow,[111] while his kinsman, James Campbell of Ardkinglas, 'be resson of escheit throw the proceis and dome of forfaltour', obtained two not inconsiderable sureties which Argyll himself had once been obliged to guarantee to pay Morton.[112] In the case of the Setons, it was Alexander, son of lord Seton, who benefited by recovering for his family the commendatorship of Pluscarden.[113] Finally, Alexander Hume of Manderston, an inveterate foe of Morton's gained possession of certain lands in Haddington which had been the property of James Douglas,[114] Alexander, lord Home received the escheat of a tack held by Angus,[115] while Patrick Hume of Polwarth had bestowed on him the lands and barony of Bonkle and Bothwell.[116]

Outwith the Stewarts and their close allies, one family particularly favoured was the Ruthvens. The treasurer himself, for instance, was the recipient of several substantial awards. Thus, he obtained the escheat of a gift of marriage forfeited by the commendator of Pluscarden as well as certain lands appertaining to Angus.[117] Additionally, he came by the sum of £10,000 which had once been an obligation made by John, lord Glamis to Morton in return for gifts of marriage and ward involving the Cassillis family,[118] not to mention another 4,000 merks, the legacy of an act of caution made with Morton by the master of the mint and an Edinburgh burgess.[119] Two further donations to his brothers Alexander and James Ruthven[120] only serve to underline the importance the new regime attached to the allegiance of its powerful treasurer and his kinsmen.

In this manner the Douglases were stripped of their possessions and perquisites by their triumphant foes. However, Lennox and the others were soon to discover that their redistribution of the spoils of victory afforded them only a brief taste of power. In just over a year after the execution of Morton, they too were overthrown and replaced by another faction led by lord Ruthven, now earl of Gowrie, and the earl of Mar. Moreover, the Ruthven Raid was also a signal for Angus to return from exile and, ultimately, have his uncle's earldom completely restored to him in 1587.[121]

Conclusion

In the final analysis, Morton's record, both as regent and particularly when he occupied 'first rowme and place', can only be described as an uneven one. Unquestionably, for much of the time, he handled the nobility adroitly, yet he allowed himself at one stage to become embroiled in a bitter quarrel with Argyll, and also failed to prevent a formidable alliance combining against him in March, 1578. Hence, in his relations with Argyll and Atholl, he revealed a lack of political acumen. In other words, his strategy should either have been their total subjugation to his rule or, alternatively, realising the magnitude of the task, he should have endeavoured to reconcile them. Moreover, his subsequent campaign against the Hamiltons, his principal means of diverting his adversaries, was a questionable policy to pursue. Again, in 1580, his failure to take decisive action against the Lennox-Arran faction was the main reason for his ultimate deposition. Indeed, his maladroit behaviour in 1580 is one of the more enigmatic aspects of his whole career. However, it should always be borne in mind that, by this date, Morton was no longer in his prime and, by sixteenth-century standards, was well advanced in years. Consequently, he was all the more likely to regard the burdens of office with growing distaste and disenchantment. In fact, in 1579, because of the necessity to seek a cure for his 'disesis and infirmiteis', he had obtained permission 'to depairt and pas furth of this realme to the pairtis of Almany beyond sey . . '.[122] However, during 1580 he never seems to have considered utilising this means of eluding his enemies, partly, no doubt, because having savoured power for so long, he was reluctant to recognise Lennox's ascendancy. At the same time, there would appear to be every likelihood that his 'grit aige', to quote the licence to go overseas, was now seriously impairing his judgment. It was to be his misfortune that the indecision and irresolution which he displayed in these months was the most serious miscalculation of his life.

As to the kirk, while he probably has been unjustly criticised regarding his reorganisation of the parishes and ministers, he undoubtedly, by the favours bestowed on his family and the pensions granted to numerous individuals, continued the dilapidation of its resources. Over the vexed question of the kirk's constitution, it seems improbable that he had any permanent or acceptable solution to offer, and what is remarkable is the comparatively favourable opinion presbyterian writers formed of him. This reputation, however, of being 'one of the chief instruments of the reformation of religion'[123] or one of its 'most stout and valiant advengers and defenders'[124] would seem unlikely to have remained had he continued in office much longer.

His foreign policy, with its dependence on England, was clearly the right one for someone in the political position which he occupied although, since the diplomatic tune was called by the stronger partner, he never realised the permanent alliance which he sought. At the end of the day, his eventual desertion by Elizabeth in 1581 must surely have come as no surprise to someone with Morton's long experience of Elizabethan diplomacy.

In domestic affairs, his administration of the borders provides the clearest evidence of the dichotomy which is such an obvious feature of his career. Thus, until his dismissal in 1578, with his frequent judicial excursions, innovations in the pledge system, extensive fining of malefactors and his stationing of small military detachments on the borders to assist the wardens, Morton displayed the characteristic signs of an efficient regime. On the other hand, after his restoration in 1578, there was an unsatisactory situation on the west march, no governmental incursions on the borders and not even the meeting of Anglo-Scottish commissioners sought by the English authorities. In other aspects of his domestic administration, apart from his success regarding the staple at Campveere in the Netherlands, there was, admittedly, some improvement in the condition of the exchequer, a consequence mainly of his firmer rule. But the impact of events in 1578 ultimately produced deleterious results and, in his final years, the deficits of both treasurer and comptroller departments were rising steadily. Again, there was some legislation passed dealing with the poor, but their problems as a whole remained insuperable. Apart from this, in his handling of such matters as licences, compositions or loans to the treasury, there is always a strong whiff of venality. Admittedly, his cupidity is difficult to prove conclusively[125] but, nonetheless, Archbishop Spottiswoode, when he observed that Morton was 'inclined to covetousness',[126] probably summed up his behaviour reasonably well.

Moreover, Morton's rapacity is only one of several rather unattractive features of his character. Clearly, by his employment, at times, of expedients such as arbitrary arrest and torture he could be harsh and cruel. Furthermore, in his disputes with Argyll or, for that matter, Sir William Drury, he showed a stubborn and vindictive streak which did him little credit. As for his persecution of the Hamiltons in 1579, this was undertaken, in his case, from motives which can only be described as ruthless and cold-blooded. His private life too was not above reproach, although Hume of Godscroft insists that it was his wife's insanity from about 1559 which caused him 'to loose the reins to others' and father four illegitimate sons and a daughter.[127]

Clearly, therefore, neither in public nor private life was Morton a paragon of virtue. Nonetheless, he did possess one really outstanding quality, namely his powerful personality. Who else among the Scottish nobility, for instance, could have survived for eight years in the hazardous position which he occupied? Lennox, for example, was to remain in office for just over a year after Morton's execution, while his succesor, lord Ruthven, lasted for less than twelve months. Even Arran, an abler figure than Lennox or Ruthven, eventually had his position undermined by conspiracy after about two-and-a-half years. Again, while he was regent in the 1570s, no one emerged who could be seriously regarded as his rival or successor. Certainly, neither the irascible earl of Argyll nor the irresolute earl of Atholl ever displayed any signs of incipient statesmanship. In other words, while there were some unpleasant aspects to Morton's character, he was unquestionably the best person to govern Scotland during the royal minority. For eight years, he brought the country comparatively strong, effective government and respect for royal authority. This, in the circumstances, was no mean achievement and is undoubtedly the one for which he best deserves to be remembered.

NOTES

1. *R.P.C.*, iii, 350.
2. Calderwood, *History*, iii, 484–85; Moysie, *Memoirs*, 29; *Edin. Recs.* (1573–89), 192.
3. *C.S.P. Scot.*, v, 580.
4. *Ibid*, 589.
5. Balfour, *Practicks*, i, introduction, xxix; *C.S.P. Scot.*, v, 586–87.
6. *Ibid*, 586; Calderwood, *History*, iii, 485.
7. *R.P.C.*, iii, 344–45.
8. *Ibid*, 348.

9. Calderwood, *History*, iii, 484.
10. *Ibid.*, 481–82; S.R.O., R.S.S., xlvii, PS1/47, f. 66v.
11. *R.P.C.*, iii, 355–56.
12. *C.S.P. Scot.*, v, 572–74.
13. *Ibid*, 585.
14. *H.M.C. (Hastings)*, ii, 16–17.
15. *C.S.P. Scot.*, v, 595–96.
16. *Ibid*, 623–24.
17. *Ibid*, 625.
18. *Ibid*, 655.
19. E.g. *Ibid*, 592–93, 606, 629–30.
20. *C.S.P. Scot.*, v, 645–46.
21. *R.P.C.*, iii, 393.
22. *C.S.P. Scot.*, v, 688.
23. *Ibid*, 632.
24. *R.P.C.*, iii, 340–89.
25. *C.S.P. Scot.*, v, 628.
26. *A.P.S.*, iii, 189.
27. If Calderwood is correct, the commissioners of the burghs were dismissed before Randolph's speech, presumably lest his allegations caused them to have second thoughts about assenting to the proposed taxation, *History*, iii, 488.
28. *C.S.P. Scot.*, v, 638.
29. Calderwood, *History*, iii, 487–88.
30. *C.S.P. Scot.*, v, 649, 695.
31. N.L.S. Morton papers, 77, F.58; printed in *Mort. Reg.*, i, 126.
32. *C.S.P. Scot.*, v, 677–78.
33. *Ibid*, 693.
34. *C.S.P. Spanish*, (1580–86), 85.
35. *C.S.P. Scot.*, v, 696.
36. *Ibid*, 680.
37. *Ibid*, 681–83.
38. *Ibid*, 663, 670, 679; Moysie, *Memoirs*, 31.
39. S.R.O., R.S.S., xlviii, PS1/48, f. 44v and f. 105r.
40. *C.S.P. Scot.*, v, 663.
41. *Ibid*, 670–71, 673.
42. *Ibid*, 673, 675.
43. S.R.O., R.S.S., xlviii, PS1/48, f. 124r.
44. *R.P.C.*, iii, 364–65.
45. *Ibid*, 365.
46. *Ibid*, 365.
47. *Ibid*, 367.
48. *Sheriff Court Book of Dumfries, T.D.G.A.S.*, 3rd Series, xii, 175–76.

49. S.R.O., R.S.S., xlviii, PS1/48, f. 7r.
50. *R.P.C.*, iii, 368.
51. Fraser, *Douglas*, iii, 266–68.
52. N.L.S. Morton papers, 77, f. 60; printed in *Mort. Reg.*, i, 127.
53. *H.M.C. (Mar and Kellie)*, i, 33–34.
54. *R.P.C.*, iii, 374–76.
55. *C.S.P. Scot.*, vi, 11.
56. *Ibid*, 24, 28.
57. *A.P.S.*, iii, 192; *R.P.C.*, iii, 369–70.
58. *C.S.P. Scot.*, v, 650.
59. Lee, 'The Fall of the Regent Morton', *Journal of Mod. Hist.*, xxviii, 111–30.
60. Teulet, *Papiers*, ii, 443–44.
61. Reported on 20th April, 1581 by Cobham, English ambassador in Paris, *C.S.P. Foreign*, (1579–81), 122–23.
62. Melville, *Memoirs*, 266.
63. Captain James Stewart was elevated to this title on 22nd April, 1581; *R.M.S.*, v, 167.
64. Calderwood, *History*, iii, 556.
65. *C.S.P. Scot.*, vi, 10–11.
66. *R.P.C.*, iii, 387.
67. Calderwood, *History*, iii, 556.
68. *R.P.C.*, iii, 388.
69. *Ibid*, 388.
70. Calderwood, *History*, iii, 557.
71. *Ibid*, 557–58; Sir John Seton in a letter to Walsingham on 4th June, 1581 listed twenty-two charges against Morton, *C.S.P. Scot.*, vi, 23.
72. Melville, *Memoirs*, 267.
73. Calderwood, *History*, iii, 506–07.
74. *Ibid*, 557; *C.S.P. Scot.*, vi, 26.
75. Pitcairn, *Trials*, i, pt. 3, 114.
76. 'An Estimate of the Scottish Nobility during the minority of James VI', *T.R.H. Soc.*, ii, 231, 238.
77. *R.P.C.*, iii, 323.
78. *Scots Peerage*, v, 443.
79. *Ibid*, v, 188–89.
80. *R.P.C.*, iii, 98.
81. *C.S.P. Scot.*, iv, 276; vi, 18–19.
82. Melvill, *Diary*, 83.
83. Pitcairn, *Trials*, i, pt. 3, 115.
84. Spottiswoode, *History*, ii, 277.
85. Calderwood, *History*, iii, 559.
86. Pitcairn, *Trials*, i, pt. 3, 115.
87. Spottiswoode, *History*, ii, 278.

83. Bannatyne, *Memoriales*, 317–32; Calderwood, *History*, iii, 559–75; *C.S.P. Scot.*, vi, 14–23; *see also* Scott, *Fasti*, i, *passim*.
89. Bannatyne, *Memoriales*, 317–32.
90. Calderwood, *History*, iii, 575.
91. Bannatyne, *Memoriales*, 331.
92. Hume of Godscroft, *History*, ii, 284; the first near-contemporary reference to the actual employment of this means of execution is in Row, *History*, ii, 86.
93. Bannatyne, *Memoriales*, 331–32; *Edin. Recs.* (1573–89), 209.
94. Calderwood, *History*, iii, 575; Hume of Godscroft, *History*, ii, 285; Spottiswoode, *History*, ii, 279.
95. Calderwood, *History*, iii, 575.
96. *Ibid*, 692; *Edin. Recs.* (1573–89), 262.
97. Chambers, *Domestic Annals*, i, 145; Spottiswoode, *History*, ii, 276.
98. Bannatyne, *Memoriales*, 324.
99. *R.M.S.*, v, No. 198.
100. S.R.O., R.S.S., xlvii, PS1/47, f. 106v; f. 131v.
101. Ibid, xlviii, PS1/48, f. 19r.
102. Ibid, xlvii, PS1/47, f. 117v, and f. 107r.
103. Ibid, xlviii, PS1/48, f. 7r.
104. Ibid, f. 22r.
105. *R.M.S.*, v, No. 204.
106. S.R.O., R.S.S., xlvii, PS1/47, f. 141r.
107. Ibid, f. 113v, f. 130v.
108. *R.M.S.*, v, No. 218.
109. Fraser, *Carlaverock*, i, 252.
110. *R.M.S.*, v, No. 203; Fraser, *Carlaverlock*, i, 252.
111. *R.M.S.*, V, No. 199.
112. S.R.O., R.S.S., xlvii, PS1/47, f. 124r.
113. S.R.O., Lordship of Urquhart, GD94, No. 16; confirmed by act of Parliament in November, 1581, *A.P.S.*, iii, 276, cf. *Clan Campbell*, vi, 39–40.
114. *Melrose Recs.*, iii, 304.
115. S.R.O., R.S.S., xlvii, PS1/47, f.135v.
116. Ibid, xlviii, PS1/48, f. 40r.
117. Ibid, xlvii, PS1/47, f. 106v, f. 137r.
118. Ibid, f. 131r.
119. Ibid, f. 131r.
120. Ibid, f. 126r; xlviii, PS1/48, f. 6r.
121. *A.P.S.*, iii, 472; *Mort. Reg.*, ii, 316–18.
122. *R.S.S.*, vii, No. 2093; a similar licence had been granted previously in September, 1578, *ibid*, No. 1640.
123 Calderwood, *History*, iii, 575.
124 Melvill, *Diary*, 161.

125. Pitscottie aptly commented, 'there were many writings cassin in upon the regent of his greediness bot nocht avowit', *Historie*, ii, 313.
126. Spottiswoode, *Historie*, ii, 197.
127. Hume of Godscroft, *History*, ii, 137; Fraser, *Douglas,* ii, 321. Neither Hume nor Fraser mentions a natural daughter, but apparently there was one called Jean, *see R.M.S.*, iv, No. 1877 and *R.S.S.*, vi, Nos. 713–14.

Bibliography

Note: Only sources cited in the text have been included.

1 *MANUSCRIPT SOURCES*

Scottish Record Office
Accounts of the Collectors of Thirds of Benefices, E45/8–13.
Register of Assignations, E47/1–2.
Register of the Privy Seal, Vols. xlvii–xlviii, PS1/47–48.
Accounts of the Treasurer of Scotland, 1580, E22/4.
Airlie Muniments, Vol. ii.
Johnstone of Westerhall papers.
Moray Muniments, Vol. i.
Morton Papers.
Lordship of Urquhart Papers.

National Library of Scotland
MS 74–(Morton Royal Letters).
MS 75–(Morton Letters).
MS 76–(Morton Documents, 1476–1570).
MS 77–(Morton Documents, 1571–1618).
MS 3157–(Earl of Atholl).
Advocates MSS   29.2.6 (Balcarres MS).
                 29.2.7 (St. Andrews University)

National Register of Archives
Argyll Muniments (N.R.A. 6).
Douglas-Home Papers (N.R.A. 859).

2 *PRINTED WORKS*

A. *Primary*

Abbotsford Misc.   *Miscellany of the Abbotsford Club*, (Abbotsford Club, 1837).

Abdn. Counc.	*Extracts from the Council Register of the Burgh of Aberdeen* (Spalding Club, 1844–48).
A.P.S.	*The Acts of the Parliaments of Scotland*, edd. T. Thomson and C. Innes (Edinburgh 1814–75).
Les Affaires du Conte de Boduel	*Les Affaires du Conte de Boduel* (Bannatyne Club, 1829).
Argyll Letters	*Letters to the Argyll Family*, ed. A. MacDonald (Maitland Club, 1839).
Atkinson, *History of the Gold Mines*	Stephen Atkinson, *The Discoverie and Historie of the Gold Mines in Scotland* (Bannatyne Club, 1825).
Ayr Accts.	*Ayr Burgh Accounts, 1534–1624*, ed. G.S. Pryde, (Scottish History Society, 1937).
Balcarres Papers	*Foreign Correspondence with Marie de Lorraine, Queen of Scotland from the originals in the Balcarres Papers* (Scottish History Society, 1923).
Balfour, *Practicks*	*The Practicks of Sir James Balfour of Pittendreich*, ed. P.G.B. McNeill, (Stair Society, 1962).
Bannatyne, *Memoriales*	Richard Bannatyne, *Memorials of Transactions in Scotland, 1569–73*, (Bannatyne Club, 1836).
Bannatyne Misc.	*The Bannatyne Miscellany* (Bannatyne Club, 1827–55).
Bowes, *Correspondence*	*Correspondence of Robert Bowes*, ed. J. Stevenson, (Surtees Society, 1842).
B.U.K.	*Acts and Proceedings of the General Assemblies of the Kirk of Scotland*, (Bannatyne and Maitland Clubs, 1839–40).
C.S.P. Border	*Calendar of Letters and Papers relating to the affairs of the Borders of England and Scotland*, Vol. i, ed. J. Bain, (Edinburgh, 1894).
C.S.P. Dom. Add. (1566–79)	*Calendar of State Papers, Domestic Series of the reign of Elizabeth, Addenda, 1566–79*, ed. M.A. Green, (London, 1871).
C.S.P. Foreign	*Calendar of State Papers, Foreign Series (1572–82)*, ed. A.J. Crosby, (London, 1876–1909).
C.S.P. Scot.	*Calendar of State Papers relating to Scotland and Mary Queen of Scots, 1547–1603*, edd. J. Bain and others, (Edinburgh, 1898).
C.S.P. Spanish	*Calendar of Letters and State Papers relating to English Affairs, Vols. ii and iii*, ed. M.A.S. Hume, (London, 1894–98).
Calderwood, *History*	David Calderwood, *History of the Kirk of Scotland*, (Wodrow Society, 1843).

Clan Campbell — Abstracts of entries relating to the Campbells in the Books of Council and Session and Register of Deed, 1554–1660, Vol. vi, ed. H. Paton, (Edinburgh, 1918).

Chronicle of the Kings of Scotland — A Chronicle of the Kings of Scotland, ed. J. Mackenzie, (Maitland Club, 1830).

Cowan & Easson, Medieval Religious Houses — I. Cowan and D. Easson, Medieval Religious Houses, (Edinburgh, 1977).

Dalyell, Fragments — Fragments of Scottish History, ed. J.G. Dalyell, (Edinburgh, 1798).

Diurnal — A Diurnal of Remarkable Occurrents that have passed within the country of Scotland since the death of King James the Fourth till the year 1575, (Maitland Club, 1830).

Donaldson, Thirds of Benefices — Accounts of the Thirds of the Benefices, 1561–72, ed. Gordon Donaldson, (Scottish History Society, 1949).

Edin. Recs. — Extracts from the Records of the Burgh of Edinburgh, (Scottish Burgh Record Society, 1809–92).

E.R. — The Exchequer Rolls of Scotland, edd. J. Stuart and others, (Edinburgh, 1878–1908).

Fasti — Fasti Ecclesiae Scoticanae Medii Aevi, ed. D. Watt, (Scottish Record Society, 1969).

Fénélon, Correspondence — Correspondence Diplomatique de Bertrand de Salignac de la Mothe Fénélon, (Bannatyne Club, 1840).

Fergusson, Tracts — D. Fergusson, Tracts, (Bannatyne Club, 1860).

Forbes-Leith, Narratives — Narratives of Scottish Catholics under Mary Stuart and James VI, ed. W. Forbes-Leith, (Edinburgh, 1885).

Fraser, Annandale — W. Fraser, The Annandale Family Book, (Edinburgh, 1894).

Fraser, Buccleugh — W. Fraser, The Scotts of Buccleugh, (Edinburgh, 1878).

Fraser, Carlaverock — W. Fraser, The Book of Carlaverock, (Edinburgh, 1873).

Fraser, Douglas — W. Fraser, The Douglas Book, (Edinburgh, 1885).

Fraser, Grant — W. Fraser, The Chiefs of Grant, (Edinburgh, 1883).

Fraser, Lennox — W. Fraser, The Lennox, (Edinburgh, 1874).

Fraser, Melville — W. Fraser, The Melvilles Earls of Melville and the Leslies Earls of Leven, (Edinburgh, 1890).

Glas. Rec. — Extracts from the Records of the Burgh of Glasgow (1574–1642), ed. J. Marwick, (Glasgow, 1876).

Hamilton Papers — The Hamilton Papers, ed. J. Bain (Edinburgh, 1890–92).

H.M.C.	Reports of the Royal Commission on Historical Manuscripts, (London, 1870–).
H.M.C. Salisbury	Calendar of the Manuscripts of the Marquis of Salisbury, Vol. ii, (London, 1888).
H.M.C. Hastings	Report of the Historical Manuscripts Commission on the Hastings Manuscripts, Vol. ii, (London, 1930).
H.M.C. Laing	Report of the Historical Manuscripts Commission on the Laing Manuscripts preserved in Edinburgh University, Vol. i.
H.M.C. Mar & Kellie	Report of the Historical Manuscripts Commission on the Manuscripts of the Earl of Mar and Kellie, (London, 1904).
H.M.C. Milne Home	Report of the Historical Manuscripts Commission on the Manuscripts of Colonel David Milne Home, (London, 1902).
Historie and Life of King James the Sext	The Historie and life of King James the Sext, (Bannatyne Club, 1825).
Hume of Godscroft, History	David Hume of Godscroft, The History of the House and Race of Douglas and Angus, (Edinburgh, 1743).
Keith, Bishops	R. Keith, An Historical Catalogue of the Scottish Bishops, ed. M. Russell, (Edinburgh, 1824).
Keith, History	Keith, R., The History of the Affairs of Church and State in Scotland, ed. J.P. Lawson, (Spottiswoode Society, 1844–50).
Knox, History	John Knox's History of the Reformation in Scotland, ed. W.C. Dickinson, (Edinburgh, 1949).
Laing Chrs.	Calendar of the Laing Charters 854–1837, ed. J. Anderson, (Edinburgh, 1899).
Maidment, Analecta	Analecta Scotica, ed. J. Maidment, (Edinburgh, 1834–37).
Maitland Misc.	Miscellany of the Maitland Club, (Maitland Club, 1833–47).
Catherine de Medicis, Lettres	Lettres de Catherine de Medicis, Vol. v, ed. H. de la Ferrière, (Paris, 1895).
Melrose Recs.	Selections from the Records of the Regality of Melrose, (Scottish History Society, 1914–17).
Melvill, Diary	The Autobiography and Diary of Mr. James Melvill, ed. R. Pitcairn, (Wodrow Society, 1842).
Melville, Memoirs	Sir James Melville of Halhill, Memoirs of His Own Life, (Maitland Club, 1827).
Mort. Reg.	Registrum Honoris de Morton, (Bannatyne Club, 1853).

Moysie, *Memoirs*   David Moysie, *Memoirs of the Affairs of Scotland*, (Maitland Club, 1830).

Murdin, *State Papers*   S. Hayes and W. Murdin, *State Papers*, (London, 1740–59).

Oppressions of the Sixteenth Century on the Island of Orkney and Shetland   *Oppressions of the Sixteenth Century on the Island of Orkney and Shetland*, ed. D. Balfour, (Maitland Club, 1859).

Pitcairn, *Trials*   *Ancient Criminal Trials in Scotland*, ed. R. Pitcairn, (Maitland Club, 1833).

Pitscottie, *Historie*   R. Lindesay of Pitscottie, *The Historie and Cronicles of Scotland*, (Scottish Text Society, 1899–1911).

Pollen, *Papal Negotiations*   *Papal Negotiations with Mary Queen of Scots during her reign in Scotland, 1561–67*, ed. J.H. Pollen, (Scottish History Society, 1901).

Public Records   *Annual Report of the Deputy Keeper of Public Records*, 1885–87, ed. W.D. Macray, (London, 1887).

R.C.A.H.M.   *Reports of the Royal Commission on Ancient and Historical Monuments and Constructions of Scotland.*

R.C.R.B.   *Records of the Convention of the Royal Burghs of Scotland*, ed. J. Marwick, (Edinburgh, 1866–90).

R.M.S.   *Registrum Magni Sigilli Regum Scotorum*, edd. J.M. Thomson and others, (Edinburgh, 1882–1914).

R.P.C.   *The Register of the Privy Council of Scotland*, edd. J.H. Burton and others, (1877–).

R.S.S.   *Registrum Secreti Sigilli Regum Scotorum*, edd. M. Livingstone and others, (Edinburgh, 1948–).

Register of Ministers Exhorters and Readers   *Register of Ministers, Exhorters and Readers and their Stipends (1574)*, (Maitland Club, 1830).

Row, *History*   John Row, *The History of the Kirk of Scotland*, (Wodrow Society, 1842).

Sadler, *Papers*   *The State Papers and Letters of Sir Ralph Sadler*, ed. A. Clifford, (Edinburgh, 1809).

St. Andrews Acta   *Acta Facultatis Artium Universitatis Sancti Andree, 1413–1588*, ed. A.I. Dunlop, (Scottish History Society, 1969).

Scot, *Apologetical Narration*   William Scot, *An Apologetical Narration of the State and Government of the Kirk of Scotland since the Reformation*, (Wodrow Society, 1846).

Scotia Rediviva   *A Collection of Tracts illustrative of the History and Antiquities of Scotland*, ed. R. Buchanan, (Edinburgh, 1836).

Scots Peerage	*The Scots Peerage*, ed. Sir J. Balfour Paul, (Edinburgh, 1904–14).
Scott, *Fasti*	H. Scott, *Fasti Ecclesiae Scoticanae*, (Edinburgh, 1915–28).
Sheriff Court Book of Dumfries	*Sheriff Court Book of Dumfries*, ed. P.J.H. Grierson, *(Transactions Dumfries and Galloway Archaeological Society*, 1924–25).
Somerville, *Memorie of the Somervilles*	James, 11th lord Somerville, *Memorie of the Somervilles*, (Edinburgh, 1815).
Spalding Misc.	*Miscellany of the Spalding Club*, (Spalding Club, 1841–52).
Spottiswoode, *History*	J. Spottiswoode, *History of the Church of Scotland*, Vol. ii, (Spottiswoode Society, 1851).
Spottiswoode Misc.	*The Spottiswoode Miscellany*, (Spottiswoode Society, 1844–45).
T.A.	*Accounts of the Treasurer of Scotland*, Vol. xii, ed. C.T. McInnes, (Edinburgh, 1970); Vol. xiii, ed. A. Murray, (Edinburgh, 1979).
Teulet, *Papiers*	*Papiers d'état pièces et documents inédits ou peu connus relatifs à l'historie de l'Ecosse au XVième siècle*, ed. A. Teulet, (Bannatyne Club, 1852–60).
Vaus, *Correspondence*	*The Correspondence of Sir Patrick Vaus of Barnbarroch, 1540–84*, ed. R.V. Agnew, (Edinburgh, 1887).
Warrender Papers	*The Warrender Papers*, ed. A.I. Cameron, (Scottish History Society, 1931–32).
Wodrow Misc.	*The Miscellany of the Wodrow Society*, (Wodrow Society, 1844).
Works Accts.	*Accounts of the Masters of Works*, edd. H.M. Paton and others, (Edinburgh, 1957–).

B.   *Secondary*

Balfour, *Annales*	Sir James Balfour of Denmilne, *Annales of Scotland in Historical Works*, ed. J. Haig, (London, 1824–25).
Berg & Lagercrantz, *Scots in Sweden*	J. Berg and B. Lagercrantz, *The Scots in Sweden*, (Stockholm, 1962).
Brunton & Haig, *Senators of the College of Justice*	G. Brunton and D. Haig, *Senators of the College of Justice*, (Edinburgh, 1832).
Chambers, *Dom. Ann.*	R. Chambers, *Domestic Annals of Scotland*, (Edinburgh, 1861).

Cross, *Puritan Earl* C. Cross, *Puritan Earl–The Life of Henry Hastings, third Earl of Huntingdon*, (London, 1966).

Davidson & Gray, *Scottish Staple* J. Davidson & A. Gray, *The Scottish Staple at Veere*, (London, 1909).

D.N.B. *Dictionary of National Biography*, (London, 1900).

Donaldson, *Scottish Reformation* G. Donaldson, *The Scottish Reformation*, (Cambridge, 1960).

Donaldson, *James V to James VII* G. Donaldson, *Scotland–James V to James VII*, (Edinburgh, 1965).

Donaldson, *The First Trial of Mary Queen of Scots* Donaldson, G., *The First Trial of Mary Queen of Scots*, (London, 1969).

Durkan & Kirk, *University of Glasgow* J. Durkan & J. Kirk, *The University of Glasgow, 1451–1577*, (Glasgow, 1977).

Fraser, *Steel Bonnets* G.M. Fraser, *The Steel Bonnets*, (London, 1971).

Gregory, *History of the Western Highlands* D. Gregory, *A History of the Western Highlands and Isles of Scotland*, (Edinburgh, 1836).

Jervise, *Memorials* A. Jervise, *Memorials of Angus and Mearns*, Vol. ii, (Edinburgh, 1885).

Lang, *History, ii* Lang, A., *A History of Scotland*, Vol. ii, (Edinburgh, 1900).

Lee, *Maitland of Thirlstane* M. Lee, *John Maitland of Thirlstane*, (New York, 1959).

Lythe, *Economy of Scotland* S.G.E. Lythe, *The Economy of Scotland, 1550–1625*, (Edinburgh, 1960).

McCrie, Melville T. McCrie, *The Life of Andrew Melville*, Vol. i, (Edinburgh, 1819).

Macgregor, *Scottish Presbyterian Polity* J. Macgregor, *Scottish Presbyterian Polity*, (Edinburgh, 1926).

Rae, *Scottish Frontier* T.I. Rae, *The Administration of the Scottish Frontier, 1513–1603*, (Edinburgh, 1966).

Read, *Walsingham* C. Read, *Mr. Secretary Walsingham*, (Oxford, 1925).

Riddell, *Peerage* J. Riddell, *An Inquiry into the Law and Practice in Scottish peerages*, (Edinburgh, 1842).

Robertson, *History* W. Robertson, *The History of Scotland*, Vol. ii, (London, 1809).

Shaw, *General Assemblies* D. Shaw, *The General Assemblies of the Church of Scotland*, (Edinburgh, 1964).

Smith, *King James VI and I* A.G.R. Smith, ed. *The Reign of King James VI and I*, (London, 1973).

Stewart, *Scottish Coinage* I.H. Stewart, *The Scottish Coinage*, (London, 1955).

Warrack, *Domestic*   J. Warrack, *Domestic Life in Scotland*, (London, 1920).
   Life in Scotland
Williamson, *Scottish*   A. Williamson, *Scottish National Consciousness in the*
National Consciousness *age of James VI*, (Edinburgh, 1979).

C   *Articles and Notes*

Campbell, W.M., 'Robert Boyd of Trochrigg', *Scottish Church History Society*, xii (1958), 220–34.

Devine, T. & Lythe, S.G.E., 'The Economy of Scotland under James VI', *Scottish Historical Review*, 1 (1971), 91–106.

Donaldson, G., 'The Attitude of Whitgift and Bancroft to the Scottish Church', *Transactions of the Royal Historical Society*, 4th Series, xxiv (1942), 95–115.

Donaldson, G., 'Alexander Gordon, Bishop of Galloway', *Transactions of the Dumfries & Galloway Archaeological Society*, 3rd Series, xxiv (1945–46), 111–128.

Donaldson, G., 'Lord Chancellor Glamis and Theodore Beza', *Miscellany of the Scottish History Society*, 3rd Series, Vol. viii (1951), 89–113.

Donaldson, G., 'The New Enterit Benefices', 1573–1586', *Scottish Historical Review*, xli (1953), 93–98.

Donaldson, G., 'The Scottish Episcopate at the Reformation', *English Historical Review*, lx (1945), 349–364.

Kirk, J., 'The Influence of Calvinism on the Scottish Reformation', *Scottish Church History Society*, xviii (1974), 157–180.

Lee, M., 'The Fall of the Regent Morton: a problem in satellite diplomacy', *Journal of Modern History*, xxviii (1956), 111–129.

Murray, A., 'The Procedure of the Scottish Exchequer in the early 16th Century', *Scottish Historical Review*, xl (1961), 89–108.

Murray, A., 'The Customs Accounts of Dumfries and Kirkcudbrightshire, 1560–1660', *Transactions of the Dumfries & Galloway Archaeological Society*, 3rd Series, xlii (1965), 114–132.

'Painters in Scotland, 1301–1700', edd. M. Apted & S. Hannabus, *Scottish Record Society*, New Series, vii (1978).

Sanderson, M.H.B., 'The Feuars of Kirklands', *Scottish Historical Review, lii (1973), 117–136.*

'An Estimate of the Scottish Nobility during the Minority of James VI', ed. C. Rogers, *Transactions of the Royal Historical Society*, First Series, ii (1873), 222–296.

D. Thomson, *Painting in Scotland, 1570–1650,* exhibition catalogue, Edinburgh, 1975.

Trevor-Roper, H.R., 'George Buchanan and the Ancient Scottish Constitution', *English Historical Review*, Supplement 3, (1966).

Index